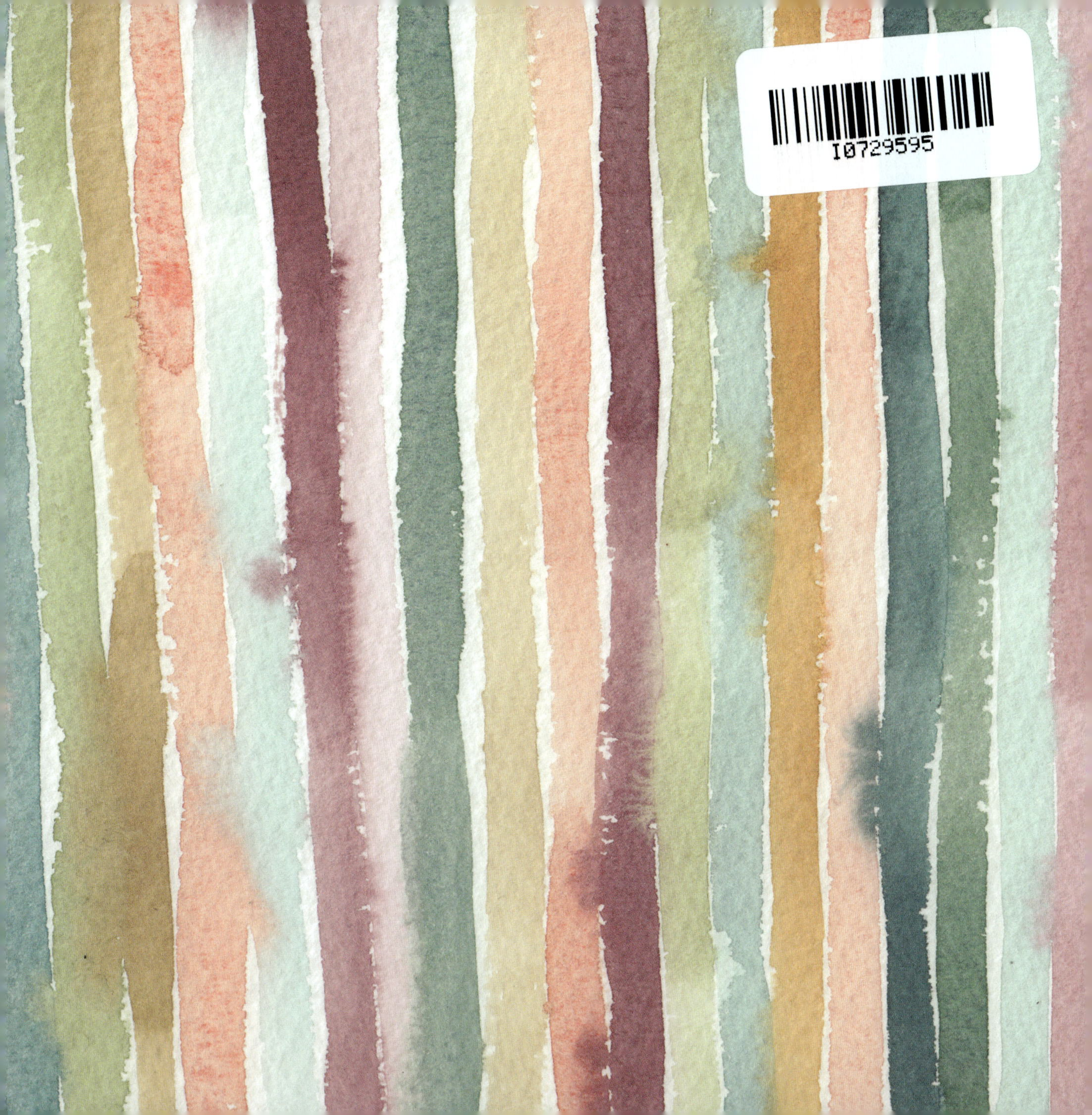

Watercolor Life

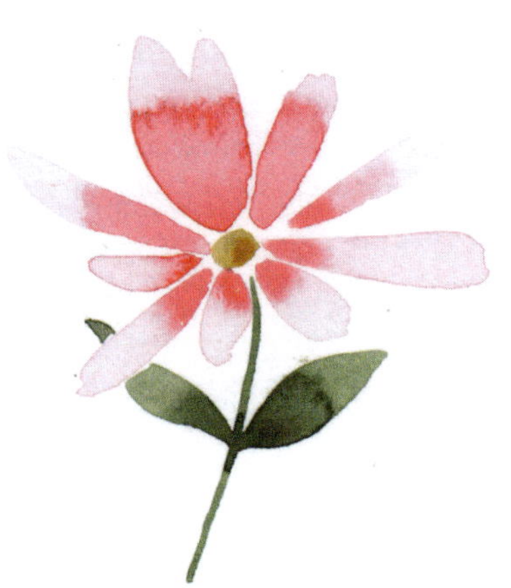

Watercolor Life

40 Joy-Filled Lessons to Spark Your Creativity

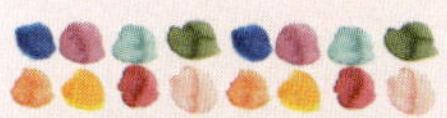

Emma Block

RUNNING PRESS
PHILADELPHIA

Running Press
Hachette Book Group
1290 Avenue of the Americas, New York, NY 10104
www.runningpress.com
@Running_Press

Printed in China

First Edition: April 2022

Published by Running Press, an imprint of Perseus Books, LLC,
a subsidiary of Hachette Book Group, Inc. The Running Press name
and logo is a trademark of the Hachette Book Group.

The Hachette Speakers Bureau provides a wide range of authors for speaking events.
To find out more, go to www.hachettespeakersbureau.com or call (866) 376-6591.

The publisher is not responsible for websites (or their content)
that are not owned by the publisher.

Print book cover and interior design by Amanda Richmond.

Library of Congress Control Number: 2021920006

ISBNs: 978-0-7624-7536-0 (hardcover), 978-0-7624-7535-3 (ebook)

RRD-S

10 9 8 7 6 5 4 3 2 1

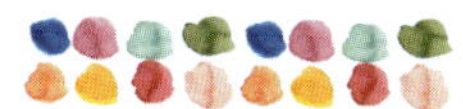

For my two boys,
Alex and Herbie,
my husband
and my son.

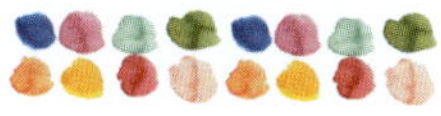

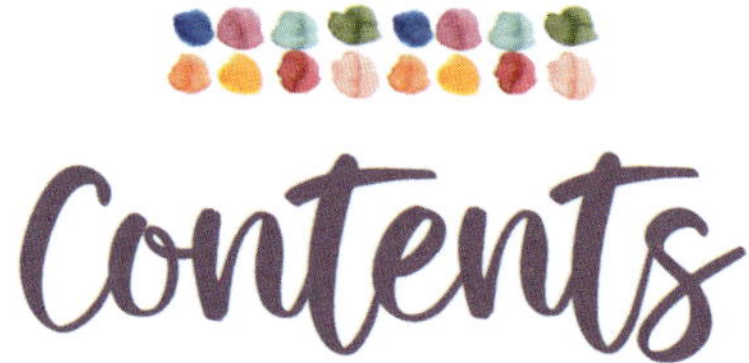

Contents

Techniques and Projects

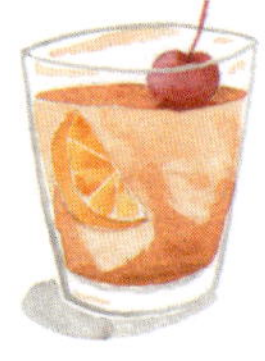

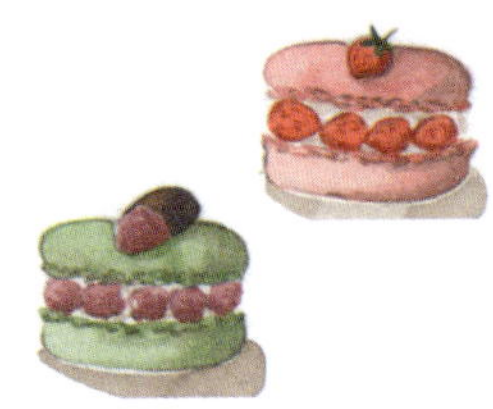

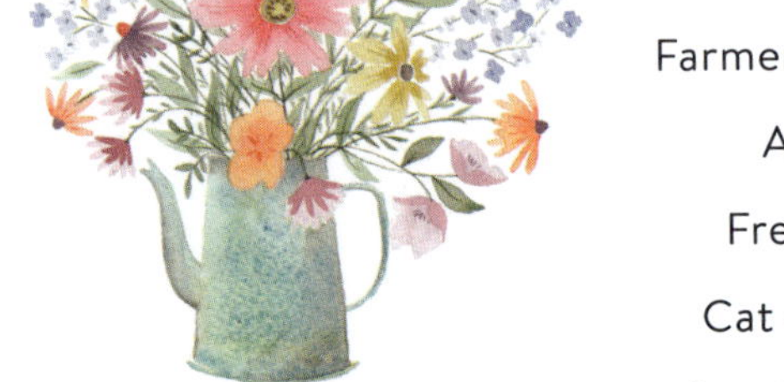

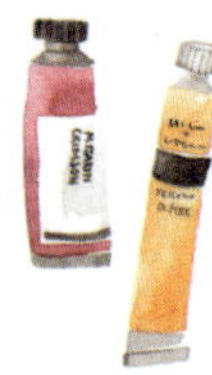

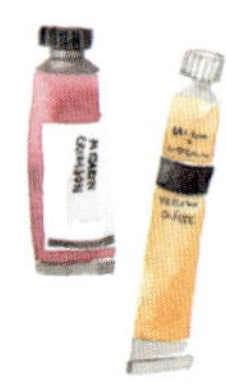

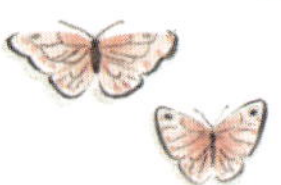

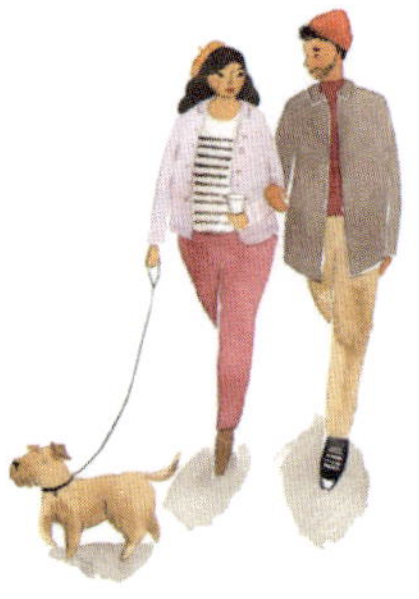

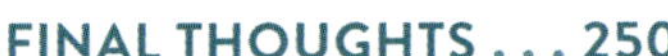

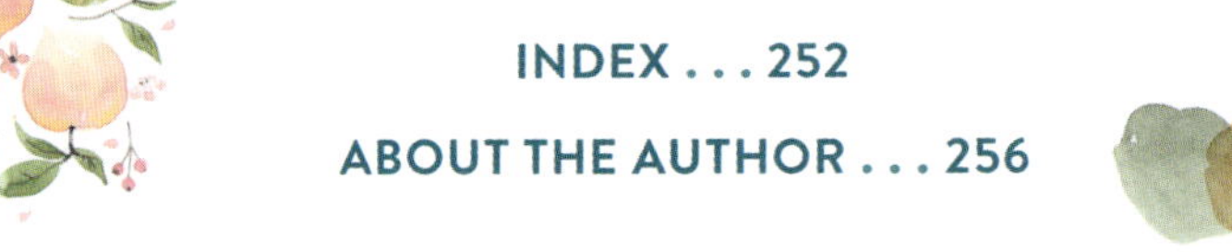

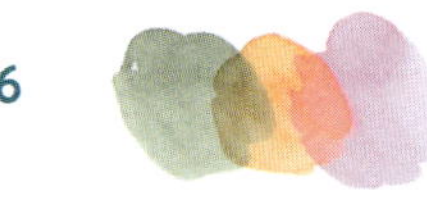

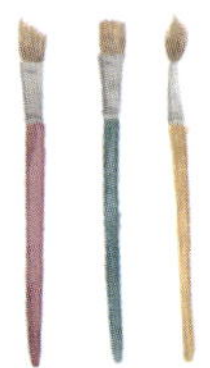

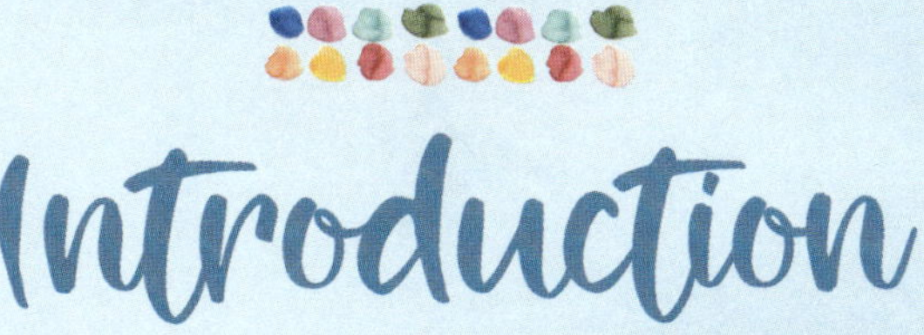

Introduction

I have loved watercolors for a long time. After moving past poster paint and finger paint, watercolors were the first proper paint I used as a child. They are at once so accessible yet contain such depths and complexities that I am still learning. As much as I love to paint with watercolors, I possibly love teaching other people to paint with them even more! Seeing the transformation in a person who thought they weren't creative or artistic suddenly find joy in the application of paint and the swirling of colors is just magical. Seeing people who lack confidence in their creative abilities create paintings they are truly proud of is so special. My painting projects are designed to be accessible to all. No one is too much of a beginner to pick up a brush and start painting with the help of my book. They are perfect for people who haven't painted since they were a child; people who used to paint but have lost confidence; people who want to paint with their friends, their family, their kids. If you want to unwind and enjoy some time painting, this book is for you.

I wrote this book during the 2020 global pandemic. I have always known how soothing and calming painting with watercolors was for me and others, but this year I truly saw the impact it could have. People turned to painting to distract themselves, to occupy themselves, to calm and restore themselves, and to give themselves a mindful moment away from their worries. In this book, I hope to build on my first book, *The Joy of Watercolor*, and focus on technique in more depth, helping you to build confidence and skills and find even more joy in painting with watercolors.

Developing Creative Confidence

I often find that people are waiting for permission to paint. They might say, "I would love to paint if I had the time," or "if I had the space," but usually it's fear holding people back. The fear that the painting might not be good and will be a waste of time and paper, the fear that painting is self-indulgent and there are so many more useful things we could be doing with our time, the fear that we won't be good immediately and will make fools of ourselves. If you are looking for permission to paint, this is it. Whether you are a busy person looking for a creative hobby or perhaps a creative professional looking to learn new skills, give yourself permission to spend time creating. It's never a waste of time or paper. Of course, you'll make mistakes; that's normal. Even I make mistakes. I spend time testing techniques and colors, planning compositions, and painting mini-versions of the projects in this book before creating the final pieces. Painting with watercolors is not about perfection; it's about enjoying the process, learning by doing, and going with the flow.

Finding Your Style

If you've been painting for a little while, you might be thinking about finding your own style. How do you find your style, and how do you know if you found it? I think everybody has an innate style, the way everybody has handwriting unique to them. Your handwriting might change slightly over the years, but there is probably something intrinsically *you* about it that remains. I think painting and drawing are the same; the quality of your line will be unique to you. When I'm teaching students, everybody will be painting the same subject using the same materials, yet every person's painting will be different. The way you put a pencil or paintbrush to paper is inherently unique to you. However, there are things you can do to help that natural style emerge.

I encourage you to make these projects your own. I love seeing how people adapt my projects, trying different background colors or compositions. Learn the techniques and skills from my lessons, but don't be afraid to add your own twist. For some people, the aim is to be able to move onto painting their own subjects and compositions, and adapting the existing projects in this book is a good stepping-stone to start doing that. If you're serious about refining your work and finding your style, the most important thing is lots of practice. As well as spending time completing projects from this book, draw and paint subjects from life, and draw and paint subjects from your imagination. The more painting you do, the better; follow your natural instincts and paint things you are naturally drawn to. Don't worry about needing to find your style instantly; it will develop slowly over time with the more painting you do. Even as an established artist who has been working professionally for 10 years, I still find my style develops and changes as my skills improve, as I try new materials, or as I become influenced by new sources of inspiration. It's a constant evolution, so enjoy the journey.

Finding Inspiration

Finding inspiration goes hand in hand with finding your own style. Finding a broad range of influences that reflect your passions and interests will help inform your style and make it unique to you. Some of my influences include midcentury illustration, vintage textile design, the work of Matisse, and old photos and postcards. The things I find that inspire my work the most are travel, people watching, museums and galleries, antiques and vintage shops, and nature. Of course, the things that interest and inspire you are likely to be completely different. I try not to be too influenced by contemporary illustrators. If I'm feeling in need of inspiration, I find it's always better to go for a walk in the park, visit an exhibition, or browse my old vacation photos rather than go straight to Instagram and Pinterest. It's good to get in the habit of collecting inspiration when you are out and about so you have it in hand when you're ready to start painting. This could be doing quick sketches, making notes in a notebook, or taking a photo of something.

Finding new sources of inspiration often goes along with a new development in style. I had a big breakthrough in painting landscapes as a result of painting on location while on vacation in Tuscany a few years ago. You never know what is going to inspire you. It could be something big like international travel; it could be something tiny like spotting a pleasing color combination when you're out for a walk. The main thing is to always be open to new sources of inspiration. When you look at the world with the eyes of an artist, you will find inspiration everywhere.

Materials

Paint

Watercolor paints come in several forms. The most common are pans of solid paint and tubes of viscous squeezable paint. You can also buy watercolors in bottles of highly pigmented liquid, which are less common. Watercolors normally come in two quality grades—student quality or artist quality. You can also buy children's paints from dollar stores or craft shops, but I really wouldn't recommend using those. You will not get the results you were hoping for, and they will be frustrating to use. A good way to tell if a pan of paint is of good quality is to see if the pan of paint looks darkly pigmented and glossy or if it looks pale and chalky. If the paint has a pale, chalky surface, it likely will be of poor quality. Good-quality watercolors should look dark in the pan because they are packed with pigment and should have a subtle gloss or sheen to them.

If you are picking up watercolors for the first time, it might be a good idea to start with a student set—for example, from Winsor & Newton. The paints will be of good quality and the set will be affordable. If you've already been painting for a little while, why not treat yourself to an artist-quality set. There is an increase in price, but there's also a big increase in quality, and if you've already been painting for some time, you will definitely notice that increase in quality. I personally recommend Winsor & Newton because they have a good-quality student and artist range and are widely available around the world. Another brand that I love using is the German brand Schmincke. Other great watercolor brands include Daniel Smith, Sennelier, or Royal Talens.

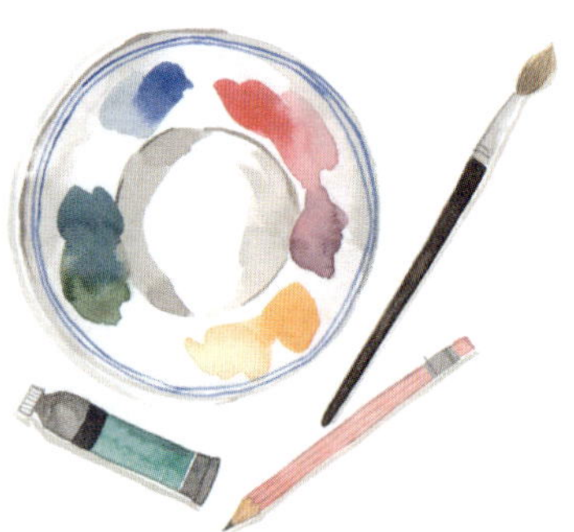

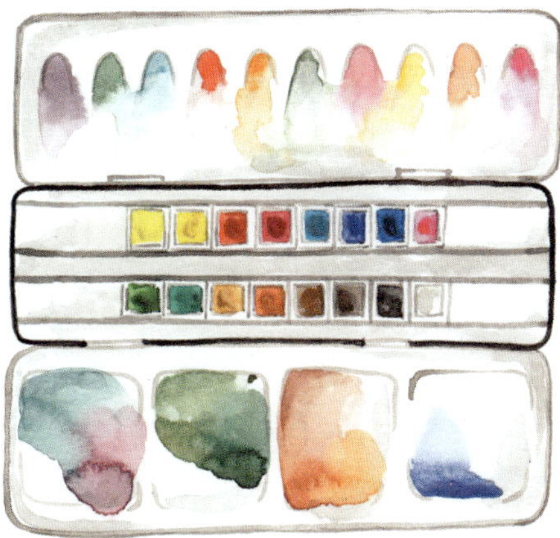

STUDENT-QUALITY VERSUS ARTIST-QUALITY PAINT

I usually advise that when people first start using watercolors they buy a good-quality student set. The Cotman range from Winsor & Newton is very good, and this is the set I teach with in my watercolor classes. However, after you've been painting for a little while, it could be time to invest in an artist-quality set. I say "invest" because there is a significant price increase but also significant improvement in the quality. There are many benefits to using artist-quality watercolors. The colors themselves are more vibrant and more densely pigmented, meaning that a little bit goes a long way, which can help balance the increased cost. With the student-quality

paints, there is more binder and less pigment. Artist-quality paints are often so densely pigmented that it can be difficult to tell the dark colors apart, with Black, Sepia, and Payne's Gray looking very similar in the pan although completely different on paper. With a student set, you'll need to work a wet brush across the pan of paint several times to pick up a significant amount of color, whereas with an artist set, it should be much easier to swipe a damp brush across the pan and pick up plenty of color.

Another advantage of artist-quality paint is the longevity. A painting created with artist-quality watercolors is much more resistant to fading in direct sunlight than one painted with student-quality paints. Artist watercolors should also have excellent clarity, which means they are very transparent and dilute very well. They should have a real vibrancy when combined with good-quality watercolor paper.

Artist-quality paints are often made with expensive natural pigments, which is why

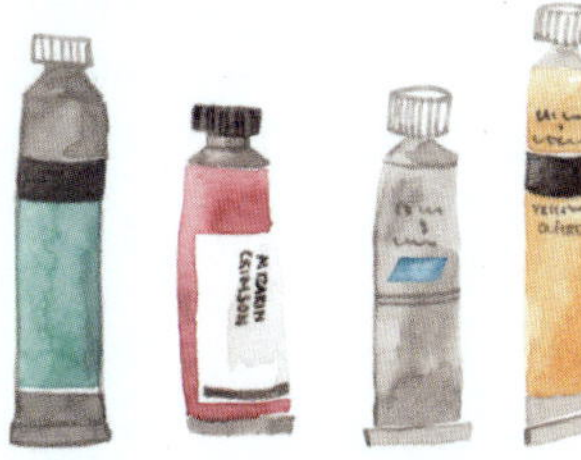

different colors can vary in price across the same brand. With a student range, expensive pigments will often be replaced with a synthetic version, which is why you often find the word *hue* at the end of the paint name. This makes the paints easier to mass-produce, and they can be priced more consistently. The single-pigment artist-quality paints produce dazzling results on their own and mix beautifully. Some people find that mixing student-quality paints produces "muddy" results. Personally, I haven't experienced this, but I only use a small range of primary and earth tones when color mixing, which tends to give good results.

Overall, a set of artist-quality watercolors is an excellent investment and will bring you much joy. My personal favorites are Winsor & Newton artist range, which I use in this book, and Schmincke Horadam.

ADVANTAGES OF TUBES VERSUS PANS

There are pros and cons to using tubes of paint and pans of paint. Pans are solid dried paint in little plastic pans. Most commonly, they come in half pans, but larger full pans are available, too. Tubes of paint come in metal tubes, and the paint has a viscous quality and must be diluted before use. I would personally recommend that a beginner starts with pans of paint, and they are what I use most often. Pans of paint make it very easy to get started. You just open the box, wet your brush, and begin painting. You don't need to unscrew lids and squeeze paint out onto a palette. Pans of paint are convenient for the occasional painter; they can be left unused for years, and the paints will still be perfectly good. If you're not painting regularly, tubes of paint can easily dry out and become unusable. Pans of paint are also more convenient for painting on location because they are dry and are stored neatly in a box. You don't need to worry about losing the lid or not being able to get the lid off.

The main advantage of tubes is being able to squeeze out as much paint as you need, which makes them perfect for painting large areas. If you enjoy working on a large scale or using very large brushes, tubes of paint will be more convenient. In terms of quality, there shouldn't be a difference between a tube of paint and a pan of paint from the same range in the same color.

CHOOSING YOUR COLORS

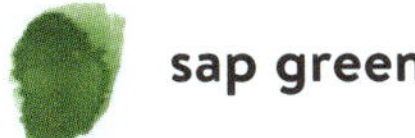 lemon yellow

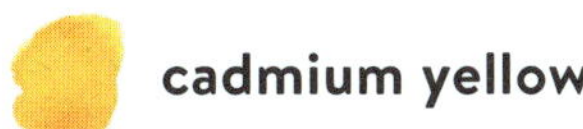 cadmium yellow

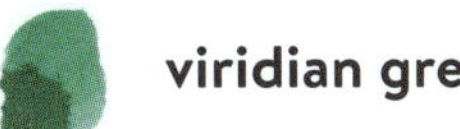 cadmium red

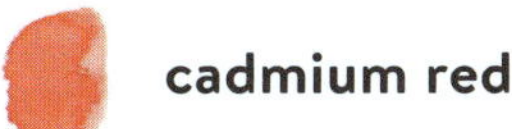 alarazin crimson

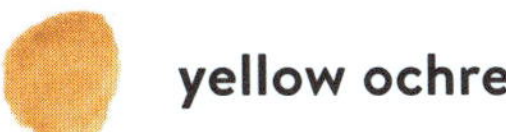 permanent rose

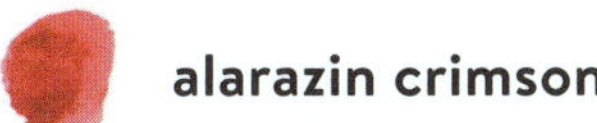 cerulean blue

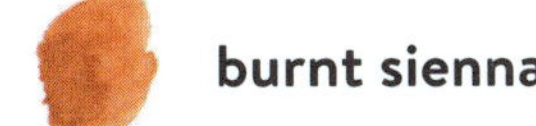 ultramarine

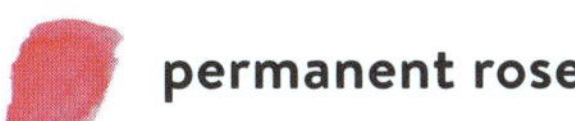 prussian blue

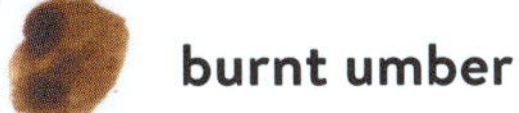 sap green

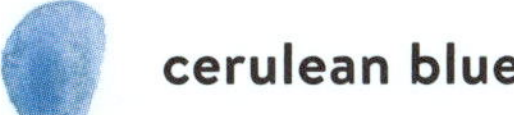 viridian green

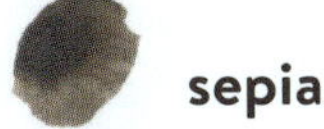 yellow ochre

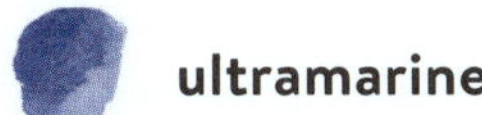 burnt sienna

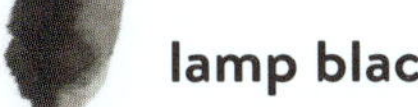 burnt umber

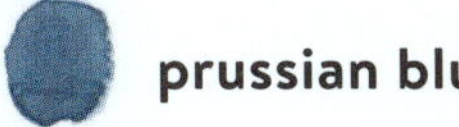 sepia

lamp black

chinese white

The natural place to begin when choosing your colors as a beginner is a preselected set of paints. These can range in size from 10 colors to 30 or even more! I would recommend that a beginner doesn't buy a set of more than 24 colors. Too many colors can be overwhelming, and the tendency is to use colors straight out of the pan rather than learning to mix them. For years I taught students to paint in London with a tiny set of just 10 colors, forcing them to really explore color theory and color mixing and to create lots of different colors from scratch. It is truly amazing how many colors you can mix from a small selection of basic colors.

Something I have realized in years of painting is that you never find a paint set that contains all your perfect colors. It just doesn't exist. My perfect set of colors is different from someone else's. Even if I buy a large set of 24 colors, it will undoubtedly not include some of my favorites and include a few that I would never use. I recommend buying a medium-size set of paints—between 12 and 24 colors—and a few individual pans or tubes to fill the range. As you become more experienced, you will start to know which colors are your favorites and which you use most often. I use a lot of warm earthy colors, so for me it's essential that the set has warm yellows, reds, and browns, and I almost never use premixed purples. For someone who paints a lot of landscapes, a set with lots of greens and browns would make sense, and for someone with a bold, colorful style, maybe a set with pinks, purples, and turquoises would be more useful. Building the perfect set is one of the joys of painting with watercolors, and most good art stores will sell individual colors as well as sets of pans and tubes. Buying a metal tin that makes it easy to remove and replace pans of paint would be wise when building your perfect paint set.

For this book, I've selected my 16 most-used colors, all of which are from Windsor & Newton. They are Lemon Yellow, Cadmium Yellow, Cadmium Red, Alizarin Crimson, Permanent Rose, Cerulean Blue, Ultramarine, Prussian Blue, Sap Green, Viridian Green, Yellow Ochre, Burnt Sienna, Burnt Umber, Sepia, Lamp Black, and Chinese White.

If you want to use these exact colors, I recommend buying a set of paints and then buying a few extra pans if there are any missing. If you can't get your hands on Windsor & Newton, don't worry. I recommend it because it is of good quality, affordable, and usually available worldwide.

There are many other brilliant paint brands, and most brands will have a version of the colors listed above, even if they have a slightly different name. Often, colors are very similar and will perform the same function in your set of paints. Here are some common color substitutions you can make.

CADMIUM RED
Scarlett
Windsor Red

ALIZARIN CRIMSON
Permanent Carmine
Winsor Red Deep

PERMANENT ROSE
Opera Rose
Magenta

PRUSSIAN BLUE
Intense Blue
Indigo

ULTRAMARINE
Cobalt Blue

SAP GREEN
Olive green

VIRIDIAN GREEN
Phthalo Green
Windsor Green
(blue shade)

YELLOW OCHRE
Raw Sienna

BURNT SIENNA
Venetian Red

SEPIA
Vandyke Brown

LAMP BLACK
Ivory Black

Brushes

Watercolor brushes come in a variety of sizes and shapes, and their bristles are made in a variety of materials. There are three parts to the paint brush: the handle, usually made of wood but sometimes plastic; the bristles, either animal hair or synthetic; and the ferule, the metal part that holds the bristles in place. It's a good idea to get a range of sizes. I would suggest getting a selection of round brushes in a variety of sizes from small to large. I tend to work quite small, so my most-used brush sizes are on the small side, sizes 2, 4, and 6. However, brush sizes can vary between brands and countries, which is why I say small, medium, and large throughout the book. Smaller brushes wear out more quickly because they have fewer bristles. You know your brush needs replacing when it no longer keeps a point and stray hairs start to stick out. For most general watercolor painting, you should use a round brush. Large flat brushes are useful for painting large washes of color. An angled brush can help you create fine points and expressive brush strokes.

SYNTHETIC VERSUS NATURAL BRUSHES

Natural brushes are made of animal hair, and synthetic brushes are composed of man-made materials like nylon. Generally, natural brushes are better quality; however, a very good-quality synthetic brush will produce better results than a very cheap natural brush. There are many advantages to using natural brushes when painting with watercolors. One of the most important things with watercolors is that the brush can pick up lots of watery paint. The natural structure of hair means it's ideal for holding lots of watery diluted paint and then releasing that liquid once the brush is pressed against the paper. Large brushes will be able to hold a huge amount of paint when fully saturated, which can help you paint smooth, even washes of watercolor without constantly running out of paint and having brush marks appear.

As well as being perfect for large washes of color due to their liquid-holding capacity, natural brushes can form a very fine point because of the naturally tapered shape of the hair. You can paint fine details with even a large paintbrush, making good-quality natural-hair brushes very versatile and a good investment.

There are several types of natural-hair brushes. Most commonly associated with watercolors are sable brushes, although you can find squirrel, goat, and badger hair brushes as well! The very best watercolor brushes are Kolinsky sable brushes, which are actually made from a different animal from regular sable brushes. A Kolinsky is part of the mink family native to Asia, and their tail hairs are used to produce the finest watercolor brushes. I have a selection of large Windsor & Newton Series 7 Kolinsky sable brushes, which were passed to me by my grandfather. These brushes are certainly an investment, but if well looked after, they can last for many decades, as mine have. The Windsor & Newton Series 7 is named after Queen Victoria; she was a fan of these brushes and favored painting with size 7.

I use a mixture of synthetic and sable brushes in my work. I like small round synthetic brushes for detailed work, and I use synthetic angled and flat brushes, but I also love the expressive quality of large sable brushes. The most important thing is that you find a selection of brushes that works for you and that you enjoy using. Everybody has different priorities when it comes to buying brushes. If you prefer to avoid animal products, there are excellent synthetic brushes available.

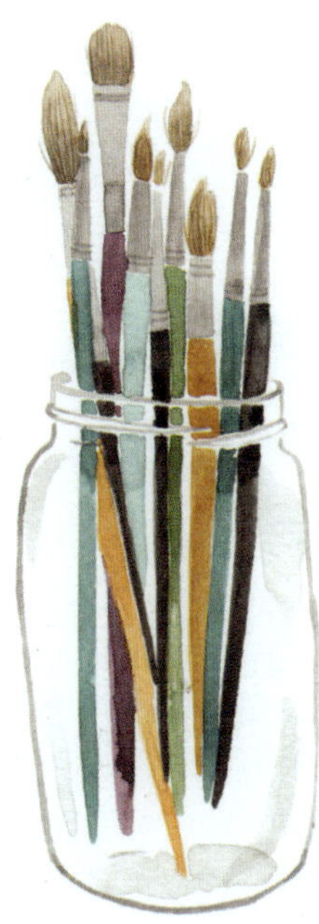

Paper

As with watercolor paints and brushes, watercolor paper comes in many varieties that differ wildly in price and quality. It can feel like a bit of a minefield buying watercolor supplies with so many things to consider, especially when making a leap from student to artist quality, but the main thing is to find material you enjoy using.

TEXTURE

One of the first decisions to make is what texture of paper you are going to use. The three categories are *hot press*, which is very smooth; *cold press*, which has a slightly rougher texture; and *rough*, which has a very rough texture. I used hot press and cold press throughout the book, and I specify which paper I am using at the start of each project.

Cold press, sometimes called "not" because it's not hot pressed, is the most popular watercolor paper and the one I use most often throughout this book. Cold press has a subtle texture, and the exact texture varies among brands, depending on how the paper is made. More expensive papers have more organic random textures, and cheaper papers will have more obviously mechanically made textures. Cold press is the most versatile watercolor paper. The texture is subtle enough to allow fine details and textured enough to help distribute the paint evenly across large areas.

Hot press is very smooth, which is ideal for finely detailed work like botanical illustration and works well with pen and ink. It's the least-absorbent paper, and it can feel like the paint is sliding over the surface, whereas the more-textured paper hugs the brush a little bit and helps evenly distribute the pigment. For a beginner, a smooth paper might seem like a good option to choose, but it actually shows mistakes and brush strokes and is less forgiving than cold press.

Rough watercolor paper has a very rough texture, as the name would suggest. It is used for large, loose, or expressive work like large landscapes or abstract pieces. It's the most absorbent of the three papers and not one that I use personally.

I also use cartridge paper a lot for my commercial illustration work, as it has a very subtle texture that is between hot-press and cold-press texture, and the bright white of the paper makes it very easy to scan and reproduce. The weight is much lower than with a watercolor paper, so it's not suitable for large washes of wet paint but works well for my illustrative style.

WEIGHT

Papers come in a variety of weights. The heavier or thicker the paper, the more water it can hold without buckling or wrinkling. If you're using a thinner paper, it can be stretched; however, this is not a process I use in my work. All the paper in this book is 300 g/140 lb, but you can find paper ranging from 90 lb up to 400 lb in art stores. My favorite way to buy paper is to buy a block that is gummed on several sides. It holds the paper flat while I'm painting so there's no need to stretch it; when the painting is dry, I can peel off the top sheet. Most good watercolor paper brands will sell these blocks in a variety of textures and sizes. You can also buy paper in individual sheets, pads, and spiral-bound pads.

Watercolor paper can be handmade, mould made, or machine made. Handmade watercolor paper is usually sold individually in sheets with a distinctive rough, deckled edge. Mould made is made in a traditional way, produces some beautiful textures, and is less expensive than handmade. Machine made is the most affordable option, although its texture isn't quite so nice to paint with.

COTTON OR WOOD PULP

If you've been painting for a while, you might be thinking about trying cotton rag paper and wondering what the difference is. Much more durable than wood pulp paper, 100% cotton paper is generally considered the best-quality watercolor paper and is made from cotton fibers. This means you can rework the paint, lift away colors, and add many layers of paint without worrying about the surface of the paper being damaged. The 100% cotton papers tend to be of a very good quality and have a great longevity.

Wood pulp paper is more affordable and can still be of a very good quality. The important thing is to check whether the paper you're buying is acid-free and archival.

My two favorite brands of watercolor paper are Bockingford, made by St Cuthberts

Mill, which makes traditional mould-made watercolor paper in England, and Hahnemühle, a German company that makes a range of beautiful wood pulp and cotton rag papers. Choosing a watercolor paper is quite a personal thing, and the most expensive one won't necessarily be the one you like best. I recommend trying a few and finding a texture you like. Buying individual sheets of watercolor paper in an art store is a great way to do this.

Other Materials

PALETTES

You will need somewhere to mix your paints, especially if you're using tubes. You can mix your colors in the lid of your paint box or use a separate palette. You can buy plastic, ceramic, or metal palettes for mixing paint. Ceramic or enameled metal is the best surface for mixing watercolors. A plastic palette can be troublesome because the surface can be too shiny, and the diluted paint can form little droplets that are difficult to pick up with your brush. Also, a plastic palette can easily stain when you're using strong colors. The surface of a ceramic or metal palette allows the paint to stay in one pool of liquid, making it easy to mix and pick up with your brush. Ceramic and metal palettes are also resistant to staining. A white ceramic or metal palette with wells is ideal for mixing watercolors, but a small white plate works very well, too.

SKETCHBOOKS

You can buy sketchbooks with watercolor paper, which are great for painting on location, testing ideas, or recording color palettes. I like the watercolor sketchbooks from Hahnemühle or Moleskine. Some issues with painting in a sketchbook are that you must wait for each page to dry before going on to the next one and it's difficult to get the book to lie flat, which is why I don't often create final pieces in a sketchbook.

PENCILS, PENS, AND ERASERS

Pencils are essential for creating an initial sketch. I would recommend using a medium-softness pencil to sketch with watercolors; this is usually a number 2 pencil in the United States and an HB in other countries. A very soft pencil might smudge and make your colors look gray, and a very hard pencil will leave indentations in the paper. My preferred pencil is the Palomino Blackwing. You will also need some good-quality erasers in your kit to erase pencil sketches. A cheap eraser can smudge the pencil and leave a dirty mark. My favorites are the hexagonal erasers from Koh-I-Noor. Their shape makes them easy to use.

Water-soluble colored pencils are useful to have in your kit. They are great for lightly sketching out a picture because the pencil lines disappear when painted over. They are also great for adding more detail, depth, and interest to an image and highlighting the texture of the paper. I recommend using good-quality water-soluble pencils rather than cheap children's pencils. I also recommend buying individual pencils in a shade you love rather than buying a big set that might contain lots of colors you will never use. My favorite brands are Caran d'Ache and Derwent.

It can also be useful to have some pens in your kit. The most important thing to remember when using pens with watercolors is to make sure they are waterproof. You can do an underdrawing in pen first and then fill in the picture with watercolor, or you can use pens on top of the dry painting (make sure the painting is completely dry, as using pens on a wet surface will ruin them).

MASKING FLUID

In this book, we will be using masking fluid. In fact, there is a whole chapter dedicated to it. Masking fluid is a thick waterproof gel that is applied to the paper to leave an area protected from the watercolor. When it's dry, you paint over the paper as normal then peel off the masking fluid to reveal the white paper underneath. Masking fluid can be applied with a brush, plastic spreading tool, or a special masking fluid pen.

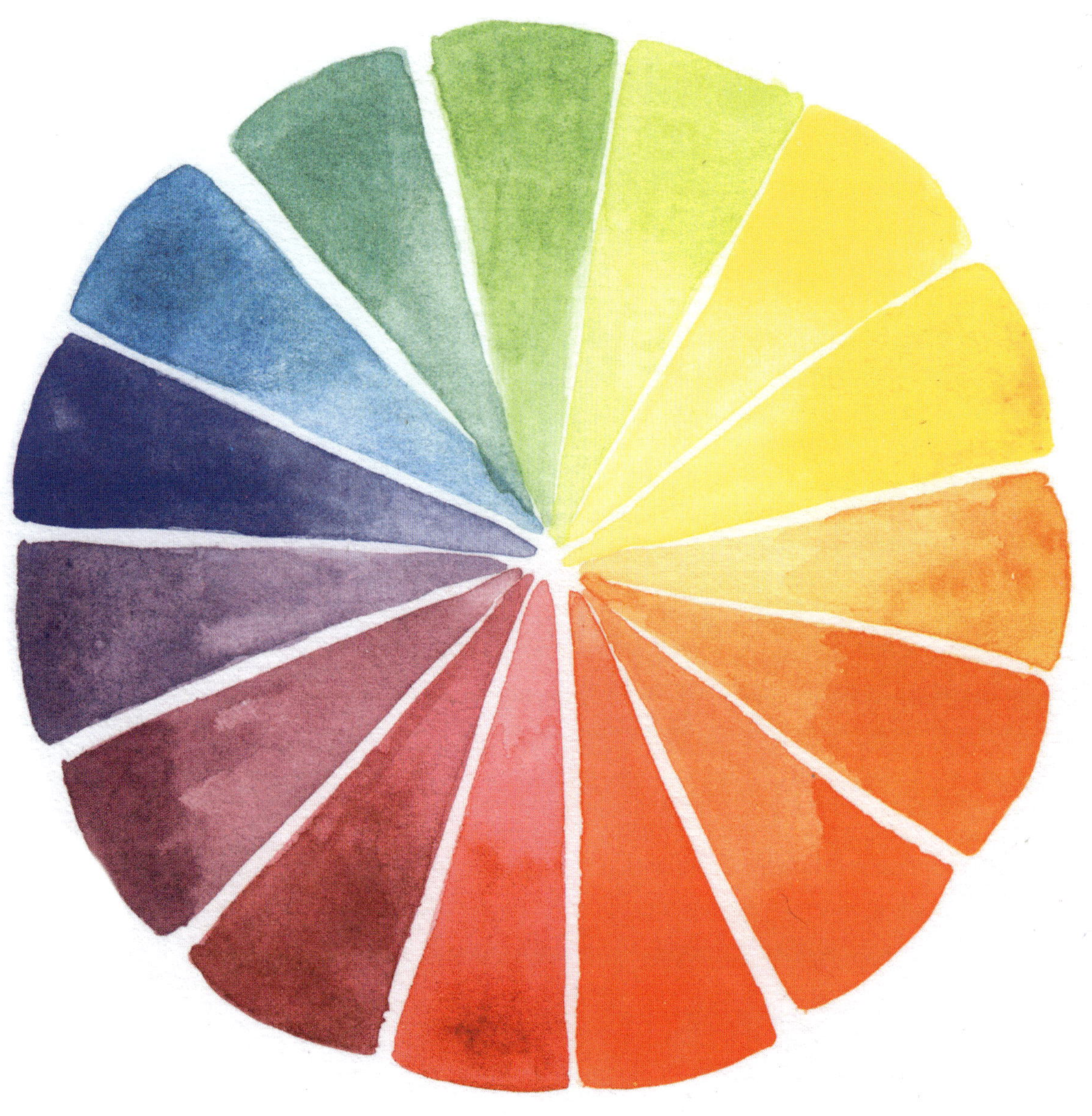

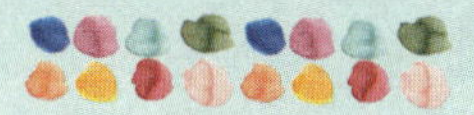

Color Theory

A basic understanding of color theory really enables you to choose and mix colors in a confident and intentional way. Whether you're making up a color or recreating a color you can see in front of you, your choice of tones, shades, and hues will affect the look and feel of your painting. I think color theory is one of those things you simply must learn; however, once you understand the basics and get your head around it, it will open up a whole new world of color to you. It can sound a little bit dry as a subject, but personally I love color theory and find it absolutely fascinating. This section aims to introduce color theory in a simple way that will help you understand how colors interact with each other.

There are three primary colors—red, yellow, and blue. Primary colors cannot be made by mixing any other colors together. By mixing together two primary colors, you create a secondary color. Yellow and blue make green, yellow and red make orange, and red and blue make purple. These three colors—orange, green, and purple—are secondary colors. Tertiary colors come between secondary and primary colors on the color wheel. They are colors that have a high proportion of one primary color, for example, a lime green that has lots of yellow in it or a pinkish purple with lots of red in it.

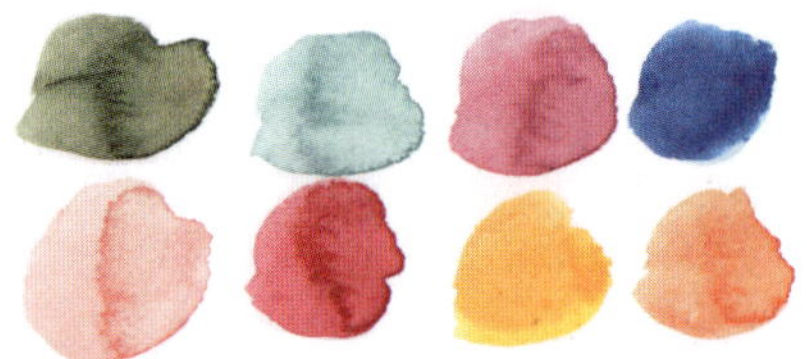

OPPOSITE COLORS

You might have heard the term *opposite* or *complementary colors*. These two terms refer to the same thing: the way a pair of opposite colors complement each other. As you can see on the color wheel, each primary color has an opposite secondary color. Red is opposite to green, blue is opposite to orange, and yellow is opposite to purple. The way to work out the opposite color without looking at the color wheel is to think of which color isn't used when mixing the secondary colors. No red is used to make green, which is why they are opposite colors. Likewise, no yellow is used to mix purple, and no blue is used when mixing orange. Opposite colors create contrast (more on that later) and are naturally eye-catching. Sometimes the effect can be too strong. I'm not a big fan of bright red and green together, but I love pink and green as a color combination. Pink is just a light red and looks great paired with

green. Similarly lemon and lilac, mustard and maroon, peach and navy, or rust and sky blue are all complementary color combinations I enjoy.

WARM AND COOL COLORS

You might have heard people describe half of the color wheel as cool (blue, purple, and green) and half as warm (yellow, orange, and red), but I think this is inaccurate and confusing because every color on the color wheel can be warm or cool. You can get cool green-tinted yellows and warm red-tinted purples. Traditionally, an artist's paint set will consist of a warm and cool set of primary colors. With these colors, you can mix almost any color you need if you have the color-mixing skills. If you had just one of each primary color, you would be much more limited in the range of colors you

could mix. You need both the warm and cool of each primary color to mix a full range of colors. As well as increasing your mixing possibilities, warm and cool colors add mood to your paintings. You can use a warm or cool color palette to create emotion or atmosphere in a picture.

CREATING CONTRAST

The way we see the world and the way a painting works is down to contrast. If there were no contrast between anything, everything would just be a gray blur. We need contrast in hue (different colors), tone (light and dark), temperature (warm and cool), and saturation (bright and muted) to see what's being depicted in a painting. Most paintings will contain several different types of contrast, and many people will create contrast in their painting without consciously thinking about it. Perhaps a painting has contrasting areas of light and dark, creating a tonal contrast, or perhaps a bright saturated area of color pops out against a muted background. I find when people first start painting, the lack of contrast is noticeable. People will use lots of different colors but no variety in tone or saturation, which makes the painting look a bit flat and bland. Think about how you will create contrast in your painting— what things do you want to stand out, and where do you want to draw the viewer's eye? The thing to remember is that how we see colors is always relative to their context; we never see a color in isolation. If you hold a gray piece of paper against a white wall, you would describe it as dark; but if you held the same piece of gray paper against a black wall, you would describe it as light. Whether a color is light or dark, cool or warm, bright or muted really depends on what is next to it.

Temperature

A mixture of warm and cool pinks create contrast in this flower. The contrast is very subtle, but you should be able to see the difference between the warmer peachy pinks and the cooler blue-toned pinks.

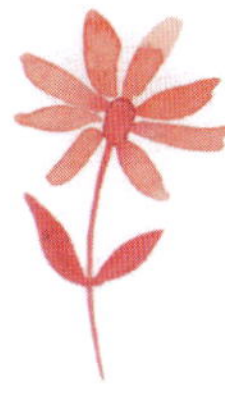

Tone

Different tones of the same shade of pink provide contrast, making the leaf appear much darker than the flower. The main way to create differences of tone is by adding water: The more water, the lighter the color. You could also add white from your set, but this would change the level of transparency of the color and the way it behaves.

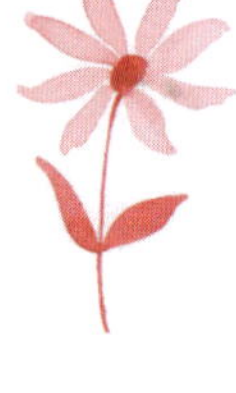

Saturation

Here I've used a mixture of muted and saturated colors to create contrast. Notice how the pink flower stands out against the gray leaf.

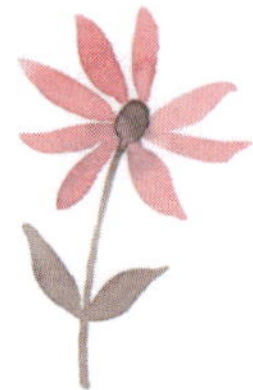

Hue

Here I've used completely different colors for the center of the flower and leaf to create contrast.

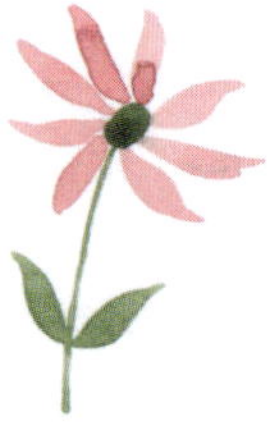

MIXING COLORS

Learning to mix your own colors is really important, which is why I recommend starting with a small set of paints. If you buy a large set of paints with lots of different colors, you will probably just use the colors straight from the pan and not build up the confidence to mix your own. I've taught people who are excellent technical painters but never mix their own colors and have no understanding of color theory, which is such a shame but easy to remedy. If you're nervous about mixing a new color, you can always do a small test swatch on a scrap of paper first so you don't have to worry about making mistakes in your final piece. This way you can learn by experimenting.

Mixing Opposite Colors

Opposite colors are a great place to start when building a color palette. By mixing a little bit of the opposite color into the color you're using, you can make it more subtle and muted. By mixing equal amounts together, you will most likely produce a gray or brown. The exercise that follows will show you the range of colors that can be produced by two opposite colors, red and green. The color palette this produces is a great starting point for painting because it contains a range of colors that are harmonious with each other. By using a green with blue undertones and red with blue undertones, you will produce a cool gray in the middle. If you do the same exercise with Sap Green and Cadmium Red, which both have yellow undertones, you would get a warm brown in the middle.

Materials Medium round brush • Paper
Colors used Viridian Green ● Alizarin Crimson ●

Start by mixing some Viridian Green with water on your palette, and paint a swatch about the size of a fingerprint on your paper.

Add a tiny bit of Alizarin Crimson to the Viridian Green on the palette, mix, then paint another swatch next to the first.

Add a tiny bit more Alizarin Crimson to the Viridian Green on the palette, mix, then paint another swatch next to the second. Continue this process until you've painted a series of swatches going from bright Viridian Green, mute green, cool gray, muted purple through to deep maroon. Finish by painting a swatch of pure Alizarin Crimson at the end.

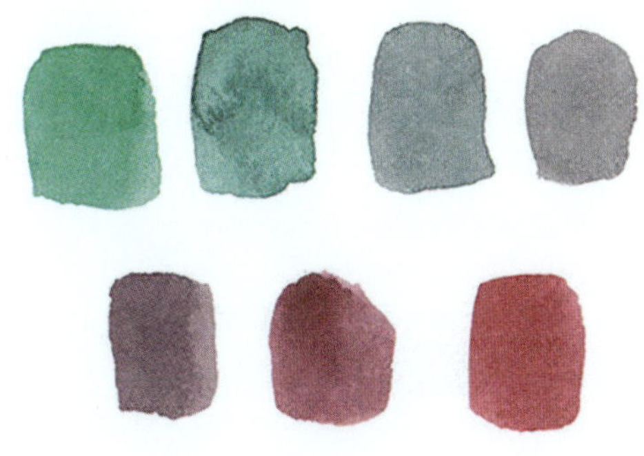

Making a Color Chart

Painting a color chart like the one shown here is a very useful, if time-consuming, initial exercise to introduce you to your set of paints and the range of color-mixing possibilities. The color mixes created in this chart aren't exhaustive. By varying the quantities of each color, adding more water, or adding a third color, you can create an almost endless range of colors!

For the sake of simplicity, I've created this color chart using just 10 of the colors in our set: the primary colors, the earth tones, and black. You can create a color chart using all 16 colors in your set, but obviously it would take longer.

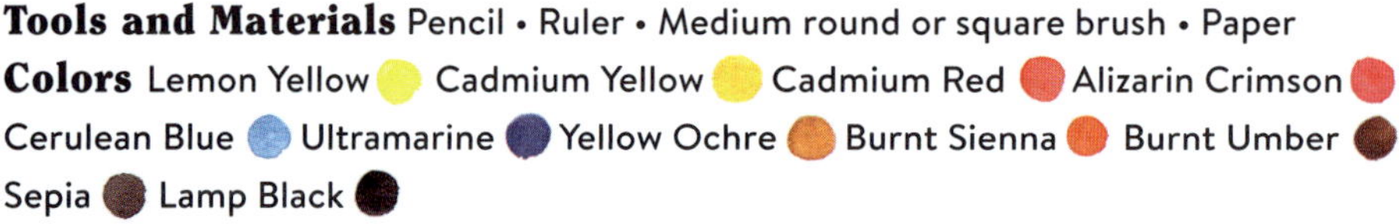

Start by drawing a grid in pencil that is ten 10-inch squares by ten 10-inch squares. Along the top edge, paint a swatch of each color listed above. Do the same thing down the left side. It's important that they are in the same order going across and going down. I've personally used a square brush because it makes it nice and easy to paint neat swatches, but if you don't have one, a round brush is fine.

Where each color on the vertical and horizontal axes intersect, mix the two colors together and paint in the little square swatch. This process can take a while because you need to wash your brush after each color mix to get a true mix between the two colors, and you may need several palettes for this. For all the color mixes on the bottom left side of the chart, I've added slightly more water so you can see how each color mix looks as a lighter and darker version. I would recommend painting the darker version first then adding some more water and painting the second swatch.

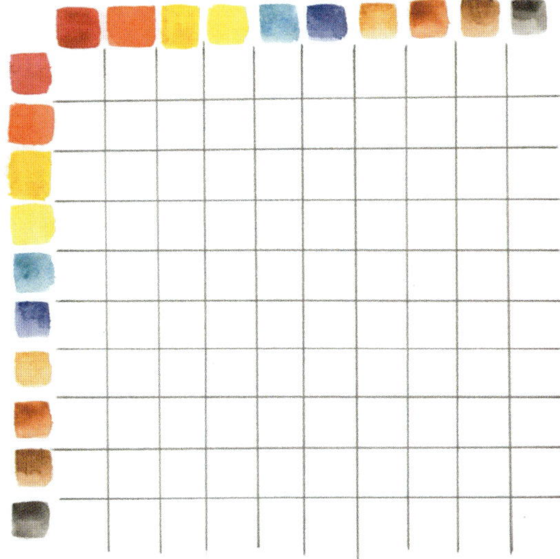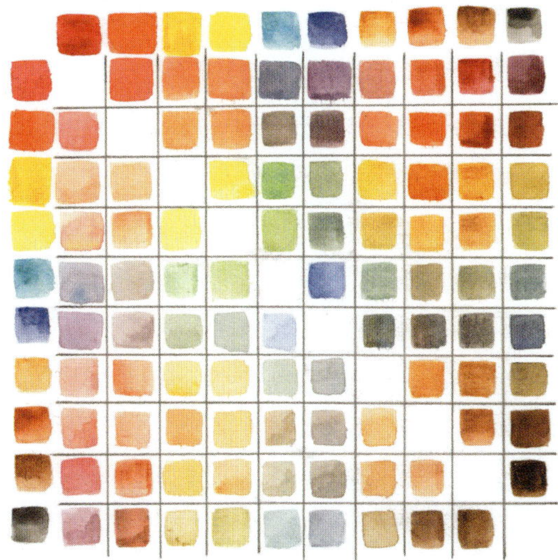

Once you finish the chart, you should have something that looks like mine. I've left the central diagonal line of colors blank because we know what each color on its own looks like.

Spend some time looking at this color chart and the colors that are produced. Some of the color mixes will be obvious—for example, yellow and red create orange. Some unusual color mixes will occur—for example, a deep berry color created by mixing Alizarin Crimson and Lamp Black. Sometimes blue and red create purple and sometimes they don't, depending

TIP Some pigments, particularly dark pigments, are stronger than others. For example, when mixing black with another color—let's say yellow—do not mix half yellow and half black. Use much less black than yellow because black is the stronger pigment. When two pigments are equal in strength—for example, red and blue—you can mix them in equal quantities to create purple. The final color mix on your chart should feel like the color sits between the two colors used to mix it rather than too much like one color or the other.

on which combination of red and blue you use (more on that in the next section). Some of the colors seem to separate slightly as they dry, which is called *granulation*. This happens particularly with a color mix using Cerulean Blue and Ultramarine, and it is a very pretty effect.

UNDERTONES

When doing the color-mixing exercise on page 22, you might have noticed that mixing Lamp Black with Lemon Yellow produces a muted green or that mixing Alizarin Crimson with Lamp Black produces a deep purple. Black has a slightly blue undertone that can be useful for creating very subtle greens and purples. The undertones of the colors in your set can help predict how they will mix. For example, mixing Lemon Yellow and Prussian Blue will create a bright, vivid green, as they both have green undertones. Mixing Cadmium Yellow and Ultramarine, which both have red undertones, will create a much more muted, warmer shade of green.

Ultramarine (red undertones) and Alizarin Crimson (blue undertones) combined will create a bright vibrant purple. On the other hand, mixing Cadmium Red (yellow undertones) and Prussian Blue (green undertones) will create a muted gray. As you can see, the undertones in colors affect the final color produced. If the undertones don't match with the color you're trying to mix— for example, yellow and green undertones in a purple mix—the result will be muted. That is not to say that the resulting colors are in any way wrong; it is incredibly useful to have the ability to mix subtle and muted colors. The undertones of two colors will help you predict what color they will make when mixed. You can refer to this color chart to check the undertone of a color you are using.

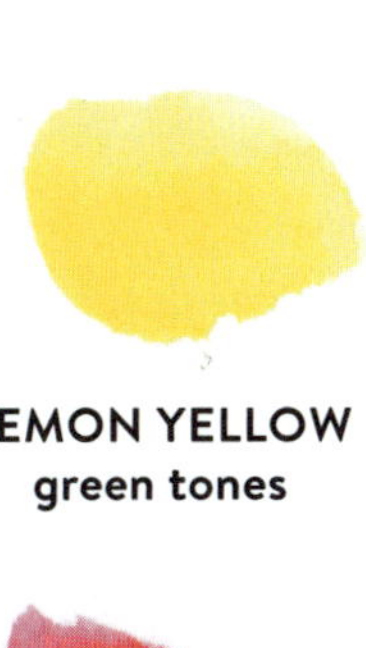

LEMON YELLOW
green tones

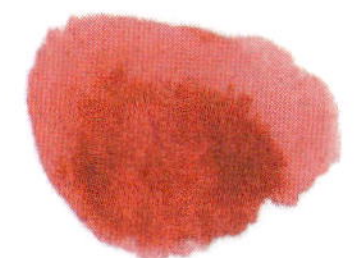

CADMIUM YELLOW
red tones

CADMIUM RED
yellow tones

ALARAZIN CRIMSON
blue tones

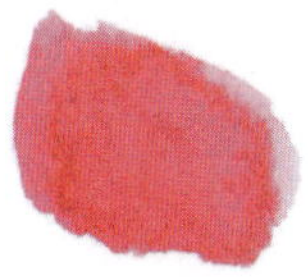

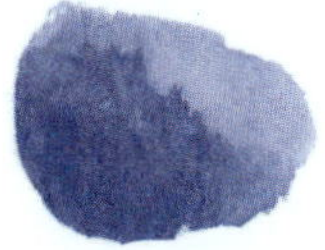
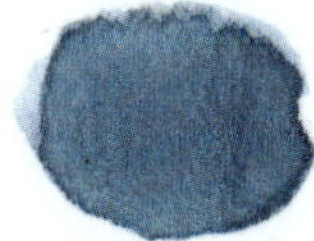

PERMANENT ROSE
blue tones

CERULEAN BLUE
green tones

ULTRAMARINE
red tones

PRUSSIAN BLUE
green tones

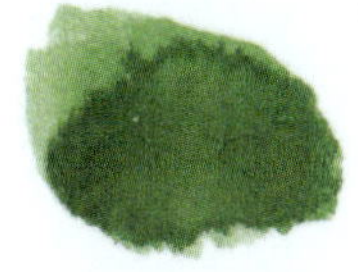

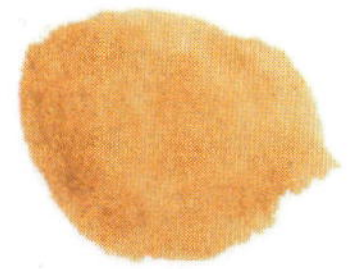
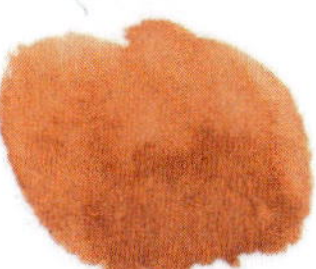

SAP GREEN
yellow tones

VIRIDIAN GREEN
blue tones

YELLOW OCHRE
yellow tones

BURNT SIENNA
red tones

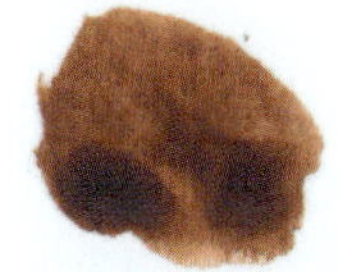

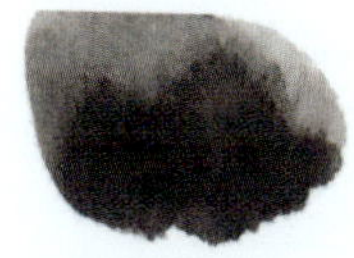

BURNT UMBER
red tones

SEPIA
blue tones

LAMP BLACK
blue tones

Choosing a Color Palette

I've mentioned before that beginners often use lots of different colors in a painting, all straight out of the box, unmixed, with little variation in tone or saturation. It's difficult for even an experienced artist to make a color palette work when there are a lot of different hues. By picking a few key colors, then exploring different shades and tones of those colors, we can create a more sophisticated color palette. Before you start your painting, try mixing some colors and paint some little swatches side by side. How do they look next to each other? How would you describe the colors, and does that match the mood you're trying to convey in the painting? If you're painting a tropical beach scene, maybe you want a clear, dazzling turquoise and bright greens, pinks, and yellows. However, maybe you're depicting a beach walk on a blustery day, and cool muted colors would be more appropriate. By premixing your colors and painting swatches next to each other, you can see how those colors work with each other and what mood they convey.

There are lots of different ways and theories on how to create a color palette. You can go on instinct and base it on what looks good to you, or you can try some of the following approaches.

OPPOSITE/COMPLEMENTARY COLORS

I've mentioned opposite or complementary colors before, and this is a great place to start when putting together a color palette. Using the opposite color mixing exercise we did previously, you can create a whole range of harmonious colors from two opposite colors.

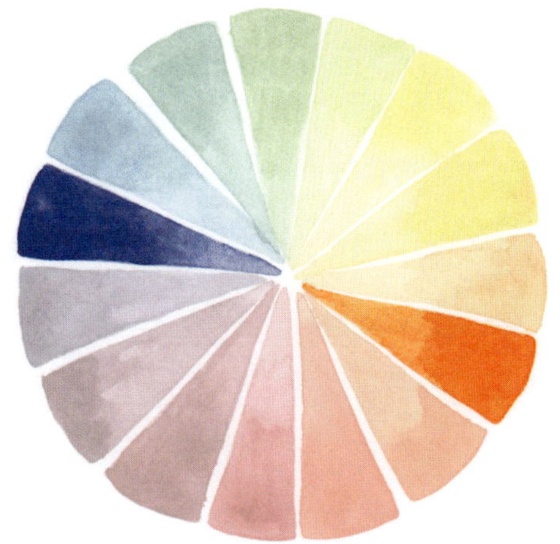

ANALOGOUS COLORS

Analogous colors are next to each other on the color wheel—for example, green and blue or orange and red. Like complementary color themes, if these colors are used in their brightest forms, they can feel overwhelming; however, when used in subtle, muted ways, they can feel harmonious and create a real mood. For example, a piece involving lots of mustard yellow, burnt orange, and maroon will have a warm autumnal feel and will be an analogous color palette.

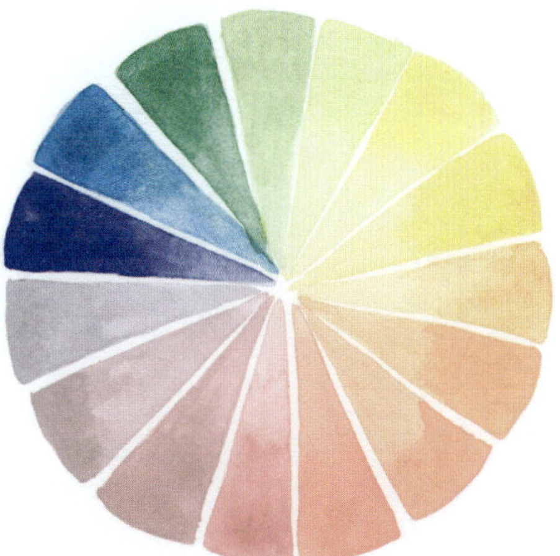

SPLIT COMPLEMENTARIES

This color scheme is similar to a complementary color scheme but uses three colors instead of two. To create a split complementary scheme, start with one color (green), look at the opposite color (red), then select the two tertiary colors on either side (red orange and red purple, in this case).

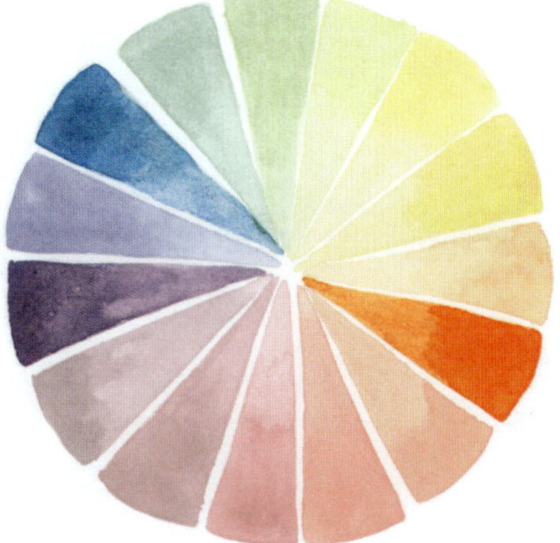

Now that you know about these color schemes, you'll see them everywhere. It can be fun to spot these color palettes in your favorite paintings, films, designs, and so on. For example, think about the striking red and green color palette of the film *Amélie*, a clear complementary color palette!

Color Mixing an Abstract Piece

We previously tried mixing colors in a very organized formal fashion, creating a color chart. Now it's time to mix some colors in a more intuitive, experimental way. This process is incredibly meditative, and the result is a unique piece of abstract art. I love how watercolors create the most beautiful effects with minimal effort. The way the colors blend and flow is just stunning. Now try doing a few of these simple abstract pieces. You can even frame your favorite.

Materials Cold press watercolor paper • Large round brush

You can use any six to eight colors from your palette and mix them in different combinations. The colors I used are: Cadmium Red ● Alizarin Crimson ●
Permanent Rose ● Sap Green ● Viridian Green ● Sepia ● Lamp Black ●

Create a variety of color mixes on your palette. Some of the color mixes I have used include Viridian Green and Alizarin Crimson, Permanent Rose and Lamp Black, Sap Green and Sepia, and Cadmium Red and Permanent Rose.

Use your large brush to paint loose expressive blobs of different colors on your watercolor paper. Make sure the paint is wet so it doesn't dry too quickly; allow the blobs to just touch so the color flows from one to the other. I recommend using a sable brush for this because it will pick up lots of color and give the best expressive brushstrokes.

Gradually work your way down the paper, adding more and more of these colored blobs and varying the amount of water in the mixes, the size of the shapes, and how much they overlap. Notice how the paint flows from one shape to another and how a third color is created as the two colors intermingle. There is no right or wrong in this exercise. The point is just to experiment and enjoy mixing colors both on the palette and on the paper.

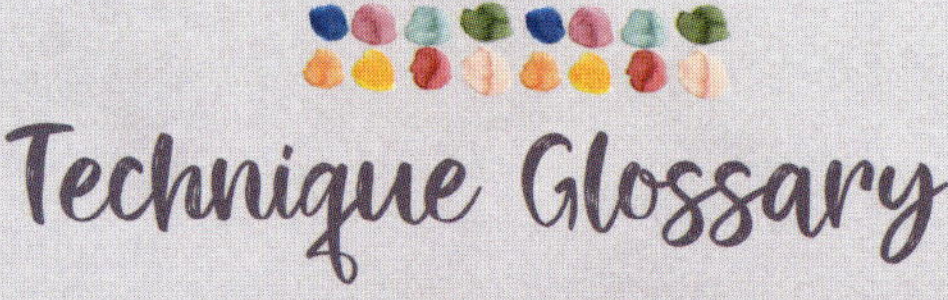

Technique Glossary

This book is organized primarily by technique, not by subject. By focusing on learning a range of beautiful watercolor techniques, you should be able to turn your hand to any subject and any style of watercolor painting. Here are the main techniques we will cover in this book.

Wet-on-Wet

Wet-on-wet technique means adding a wash of paint to paper that is already wet, either with a previous wash of color or just damp with clean water. The colors will blend into each other, and the edges will be soft and blurry.

A wash of paint will remain static on dry paper and only extend as far as you move the paint using your brush. However, if you paint that same wash of paint on paper that's already wet, the color will spread freely, which gives us the wet-on-wet effect. The wetter the surface of the paper, the more the second color will spread. The high water content of the water-color paint mixture allows it to blend and spread in a random organic way. The wetter the paint, the more unpredictable the results.

Wet-on-Dry

Wet-on-dry technique means adding a layer of paint to dry paper. This means letting your first layer of paint dry completely before you add a second layer. By using wet-on-dry technique, you get crisp, defined edges, and you have more control over what the paint is doing. As I mentioned above, wet paint won't spread freely across dry paper; it will only move where your brush moves it. If your brush is overloaded with wet paint and your paper is at an angle, though, it might drip. Wet-on-dry is a more controlled way of working with watercolors than wet-on-wet and gives us precision, fine detail, and layering. I generally like to use a bit of both when I'm painting.

Color Pooling

A variation on wet-on-wet is using white space between the shapes to control the watercolors. The individual shapes will have softly blending colors and tones, but they will have crisp edges and a thin strip of white paper to keep them separate from adjacent shapes. This gives the watercolors a feel of being both controlled and spontaneous, and the white edges between painted shapes keeps everything looking light and fresh. It also means you don't have to wait for one layer to dry before moving on to the next.

Masking Fluid

Masking fluid is more of a material than a technique, but I wanted to spend a bit of time exploring how it can be used in watercolor painting. Masking fluid is a type of liquid rubber that stops the watercolor from adhering to a particular area of the paper. You can paint a section of your watercolor paper with masking fluid first, then paint a wash over the top. Remove the masking fluid once the wash is dry, leaving clean white paper behind. This means you have the contrast of the crisp white edges of the masked-out area and the random organic flowing nature of the watercolor wash around it. If you weren't using masking fluid, you would have to painstakingly paint around the central object, and the background wash of color wouldn't have the same seamless fluidity to it.

Expressive Brushstrokes

To create an expressive brushstroke, you vary the pressure and angle of your brush to create a particular effect. An important thing to understand when mastering watercolors is that the way you apply the brush to the paper will affect the resulting brushstroke. With a small brush, you can paint the outline first, then carefully fill in the shape, but creating a petal or leaf using a single careful brushstroke requires a much more lively, dynamic application of paint. The application and release of pressure varies the shape of the brushstroke and the distribution of pigment. Expressive brushstrokes take practice, but they are well worth mastering for the beautiful effects they create.

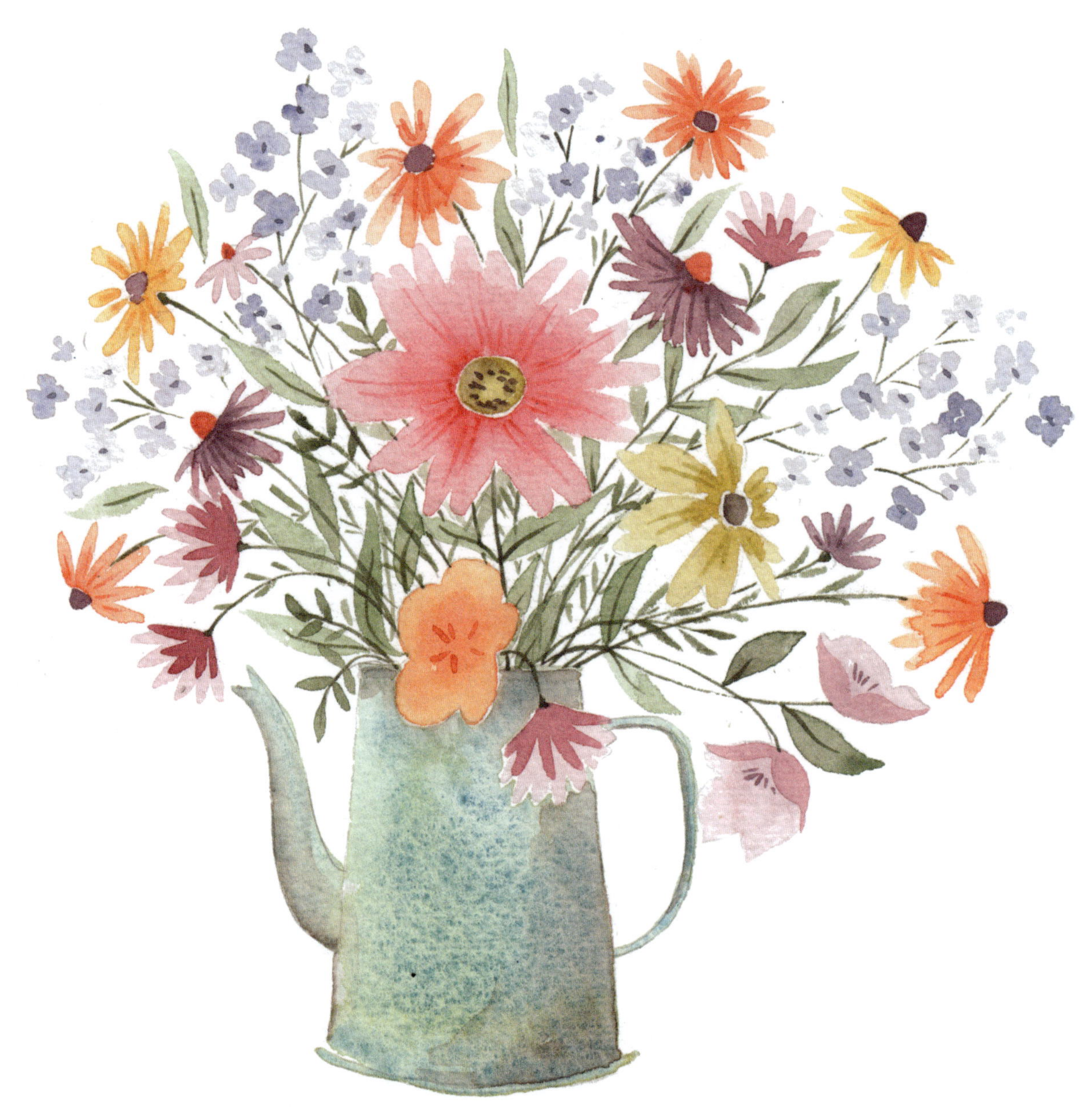

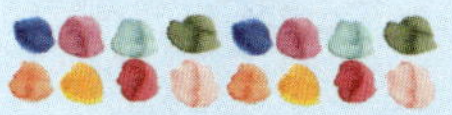

Wet-on-Wet

Wet-on-wet technique allows wet colors to blend into each other. It is a lesson in overcoming our inner perfectionist and giving in to the spontaneity of watercolors. Being bold with this technique can give us some truly stunning watercolor effects with very little effort on the part of the painter.

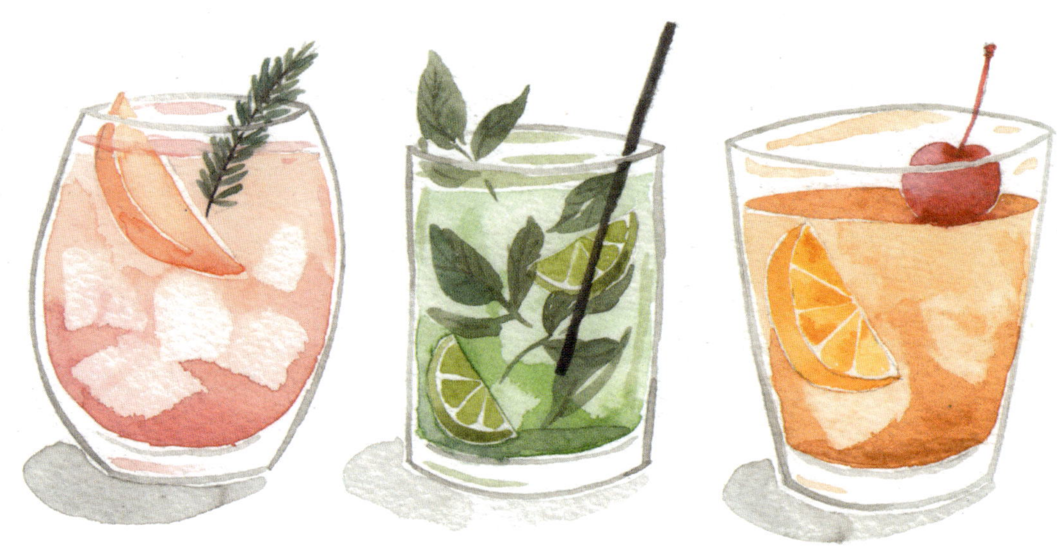

Classic Cocktails

The subtle blending of spirits, mixers, syrups, and fruit is perfectly captured by the beautiful blending of watercolors. This project also contains a very clever technique for creating the effect of ice cubes.

Materials Cold press watercolor paper • Pencil • Eraser • Paper napkin • Large round paintbrush Medium round paintbrush • Small round paintbrush

Colors Used Lamp Black ⬤ Cadmium Red ⬤ Alizarin Crimson ⬤ Sap Green ⬤
Cadmium Yellow ⬤ Ultramarine ⬤ Yellow Ochre ⬤ Burnt Sienna ⬤ Viridian Green ⬤ Sepia ⬤

Very lightly sketch the three cocktails—peach fizz, mojito, and an old fashioned—using my sketch for reference. Mix a light gray using a very watery mixture of Lamp Black, and paint the outlines of the glasses using your small round brush. Try to get these lines as neat and delicate as possible. Practice a couple of brushstrokes on another piece of paper first just to check the consistency of the paint and the pressure needed to get a smooth, even line.

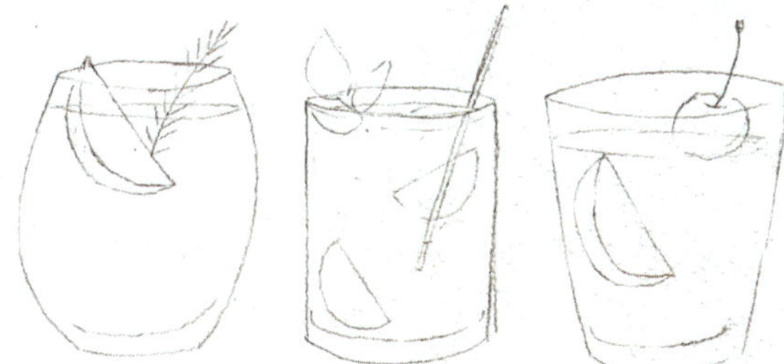

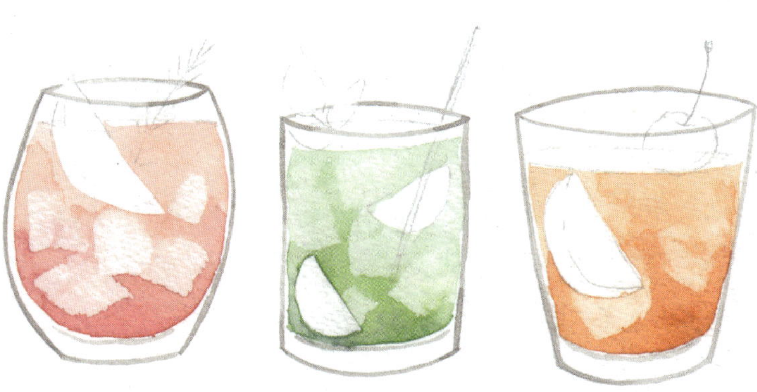

Mix Cadmium Red with a little bit of Alizarin Crimson and lots of water. Paint the peach fizz cocktail using your large round brush and allowing more color to pool at the bottom of the glass. Add a little more Alizarin Crimson to the bottom of the glass, and allow it to bleed into the rest of the paint. While the paint is still wet, fold a paper napkin and carefully use the corner to blot some of the wet paint. Where you have blotted the wet paint with the tissue, it should leave a white space that looks like ice in the glass. Do this randomly four or five times in the glass to give the impression of ice.

Mix Sap Green and Cadmium Yellow with plenty of water. Paint the mojito using your large round brush and allowing more color to pool at the bottom of the glass. Add a drop of Ultramarine to the bottom of the glass. Use your paper napkin to randomly dab areas to create the impression of ice cubes.

Mix Yellow Ochre with Burnt Sienna and plenty of water. Paint the old fashioned using a large brush, allowing more color to pool at the bottom. Add more Burnt Sienna to the bottom of the glass, and allow it to bleed into the rest of the paint. Use the same technique to give the impression of two ice cubes: Blot some of the wet paint from the glass using a piece of folded paper napkin.

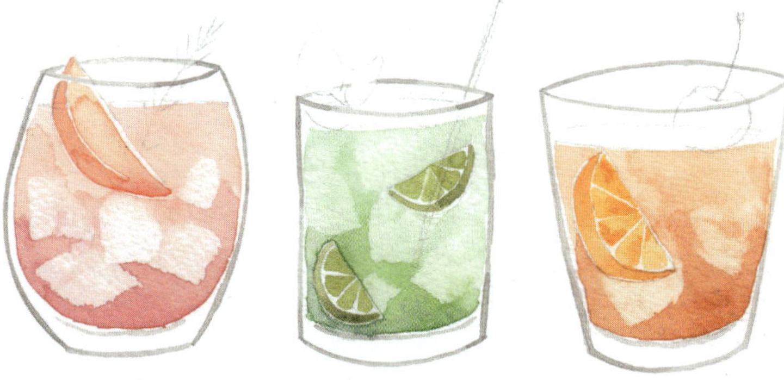

Mix Cadmium Yellow, Cadmium Red, and some water to make a peachy color. Using your small brush, paint the outside skin of the peach in the first cocktail. Add more water to the mixture and a little more Cadmium Yellow, then paint the inside of the peach, allowing the color to pool in different areas.

Mix Cadmium Yellow with Ultramarine to make a green, and paint the outside skin of the lime in the second cocktail with your small brush. Allow the color to pool in different areas. Add more water and more Cadmium Yellow to the mixture, and carefully paint the segments of the lime, leaving white space between each one and allowing the color to pool in different areas.

Mix Cadmium Yellow and Cadmium Red to paint the skin of the orange in the last cocktail. Use your small brush, and allow the paint to pool in different areas. Add more water and more Cadmium Yellow to the mixture, and carefully paint the sections of the orange, leaving white space between each and allowing the color to pool.

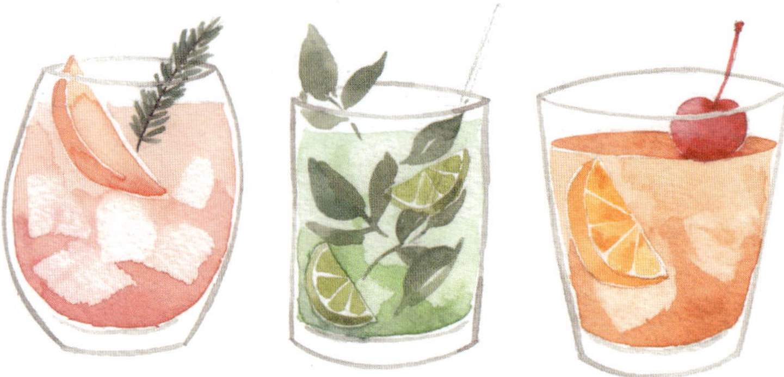

Mix a blue green with Ultramarine and a little Cadmium Yellow, and paint some of the leaves of the rosemary sprig in the first cocktail with your small brush. Mix a green with Viridian Green and Burnt Sienna, and paint some of the other leaves on the sprig of rosemary. Use Sepia and your small brush to draw a stem down the middle of the leaves.

Use the two green mixtures you've just made to paint the mint leaves in the mojito glass using your medium brush. These look better if they're not too perfect.

Paint the maraschino cherry in the last cocktail using Alizarin Crimson, adding more pigment to the top and bottom of the cherry. Paint the top of the cocktail with a watery mixture of Burnt Sienna using a small brush, just allowing the pink of the maraschino cherry to bleed into it slightly.

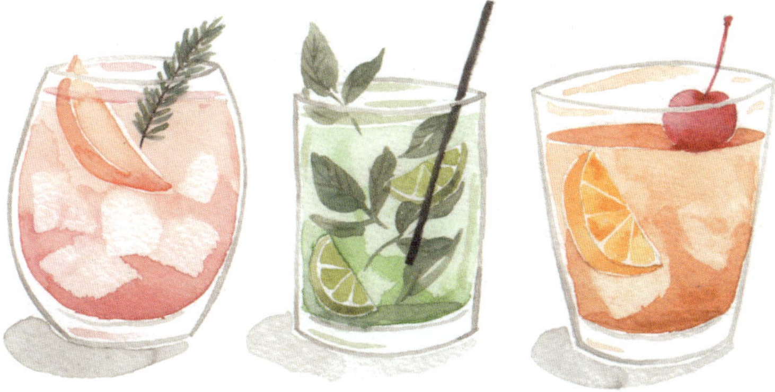

Mix Alizarin Crimson with a little bit of Cadmium Red and lots of water. Using your small brush, paint the top of the first cocktail. Using the same mixture, paint a reflection at the top and bottom of the glass.

Mix Cadmium Yellow and Ultramarine to produce a green. Using your small brush, paint the top of the second cocktail and add a shadow at the bottom of the glass. Add more water to the mixture, and add a slight reflection at the top and bottom of the glass.

Create a watery mixture of Burnt Sienna, and add a shadow at the bottom of the last glass using your small brush. Add more water to the mixture, and add a slight reflection at the top and bottom of the glass.

Use a very watery mixture of Lamp Black to paint shadows under each of the glasses using your medium brush. When the painting is completely dry, erase any pencil marks.

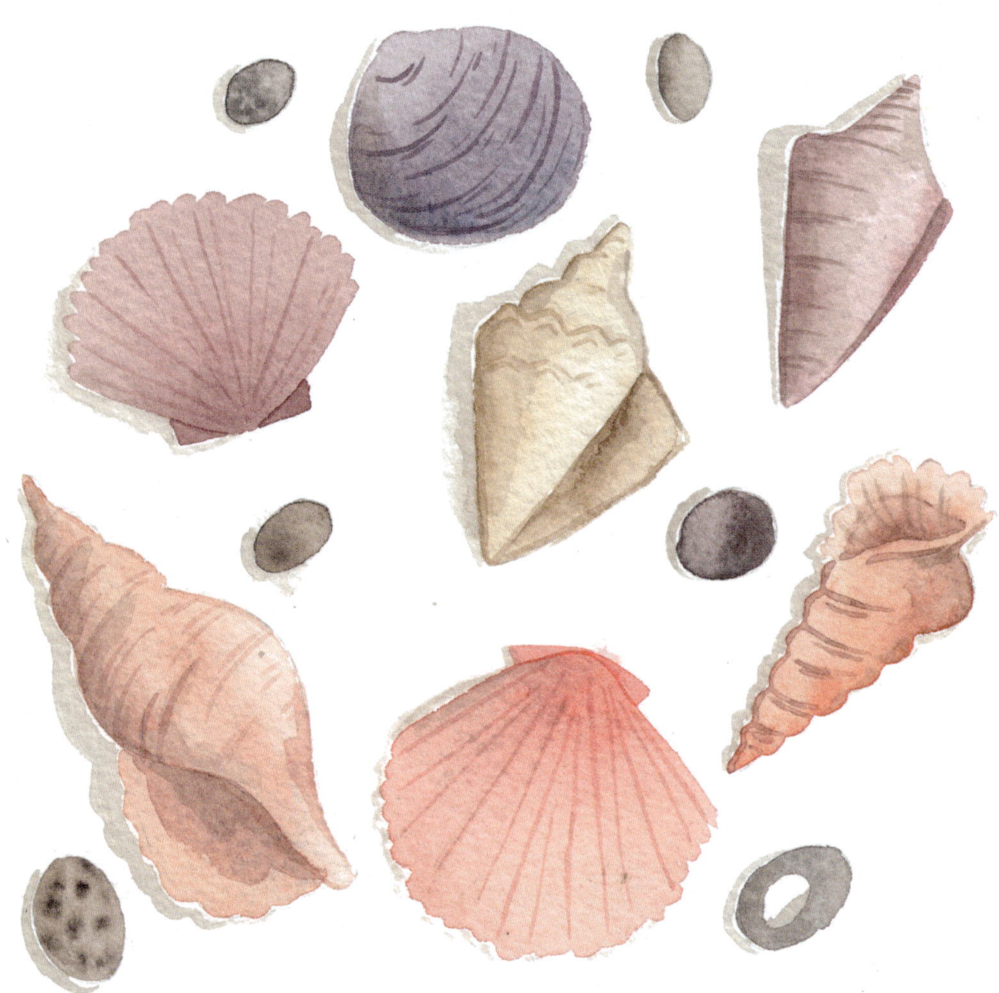

Simple Seashells

This simple project really makes use of the beautiful blending and flowing qualities of watercolors. This painting shows us how we can find beauty in the simplest of things, even pebbles and stones.

Materials Cold press watercolor paper • Pencil • Eraser • Medium round paintbrush
Small round paintbrush
Colors Used Cadmium Red ● Alizarin Crimson ● Sepia ● Permanent Rose ● Ultramarine ●
Lamp Black ● Yellow Ochre ●

Very lightly sketch the shells and pebbles using my sketch as a reference.

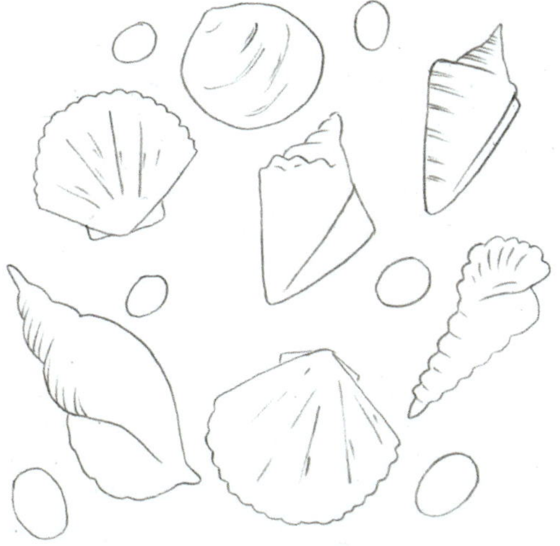

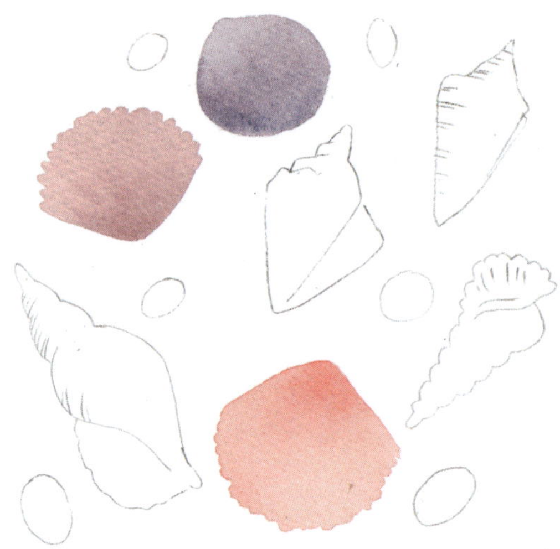

Create a pale pink mix with Cadmium Red, Alizarin Crimson, and lots of water. In another part of your palette, create the same mix of colors with slightly less water. Using your medium round brush, paint the large scallop shell with the paler mixture. While it's still wet, add the darker color to the base of the shell.

Mix a warm muted purple with Alizarin Crimson, a little Sepia, and lots of water. Recreate the same color mix with less water in another part of your palette. Using your medium round brush, paint the second scallop shell with the paler color mix. While it's still wet, add the darker color mix to the base of the shell.

Mix a muted purple with Permanent Rose, Ultramarine, a bit of Lamp Black, and lots of water. Paint the round shell with your medium round brush. While the paint is still wet, add more paint to the edge of the shell.

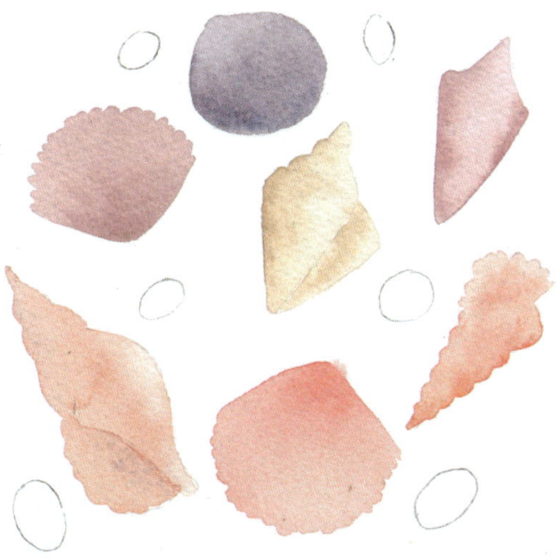

Mix a muted peach with Cadmium Red, a tiny bit of Ultramarine, and lots of water. Paint the large shell on the bottom left with your medium brush, adding more pigment to certain areas and allowing it to pool. Make a cream color with Yellow Ochre, a tiny bit of Sepia, and lots of water. Using your medium brush, paint the middle shell, allowing the color to pool in certain areas.

Mix a warm muted purple with Alizarin Crimson, a bit of Sepia, and lots of water. Paint the top right shell using the same technique as before. Create a soft pink with Permanent Rose, a bit of Yellow Ochre, and lots of water. Paint the bottom right shell using the same technique as before.

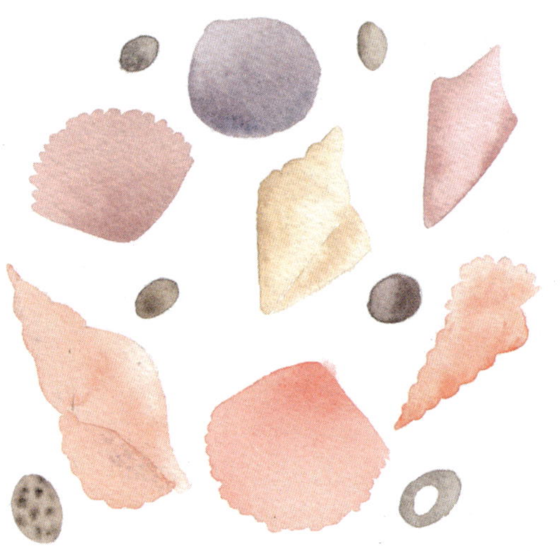 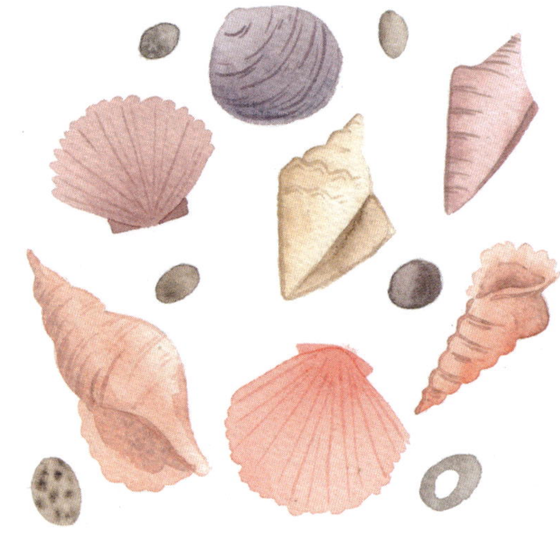

Paint the pebble on the bottom left with a watery mixture of Sepia using your small brush. When it's almost dry, add a few dots of darker Sepia paint. Paint the bottom right pebble using a watery mixture of Lamp Black and your small brush, leaving a circle unpainted in the center. Paint the middle right pebble with a watery mixture of Lamp Black and Alizarin Crimson and your small brush. Paint the top right and middle left pebbles with a watery mixture of Sepia. Paint the top left pebble with a watery mixture of Lamp Black.

Add more Ultramarine to the Cadmium Red and Ultramarine mixture, or mix some more if you've run out, to create a darker, more muted pink. With your small brush, carefully add details to the bottom left shell. Add shadow to the inside, outline the shell, and paint thin lines gently curving around the surface of the shell.

Mix Cadmium Red and Alizarin Crimson with some water, and paint the thin triangles on either side of the base of the pink scallop shell with your small brush. Add a tiny bit of Sepia to this pink mixture, and carefully paint thin lines on the scallop shell. Mix Alizarin Crimson with a bit of Sepia to make a muted purple, and paint thin triangles on either side of the base of the purple scallop shell using your small brush. Use the same mixture to carefully paint in lines on the scallop shell.

Make a muted purple with Permanent Rose, Ultramarine, and Lamp Black, and carefully paint thin curved lines on the round purple shell using your small brush.

Mix Sepia with a little bit of Yellow Ochre and lots of water to outline the cream shell in the center using your small brush. Add shadows to the inside of the shell, and carefully paint lines on the outside.

Mix Alizarin Crimson and Sepia. With your small brush, add horizontal lines to the top right shell, carefully outline the left side of the shell, and add shadows to the inside.

Mix Permanent Rose and a bit of Sepia, and use your small brush to add a shadow to the inside of the bottom right shell. Using your small brush, outline the left side of the shell, and paint thin lines across the shell.

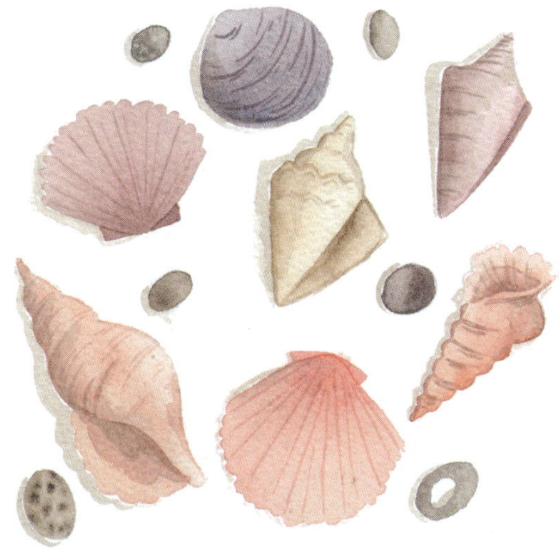

Using a very watery mix of Sepia and your small brush, carefully add shadows to the lower left side of all the pebbles and shells. Less is more when it comes to shadows. Don't make them too dark or too large. Use this watery mixture to add additional shadows or details to any of the shells you feel need slightly more definition. I've added extra shadows inside the bottom left shell, shadows to the bottom right pebble, and a line inside the bottom right shell. When completely dry, erase any remaining pencil marks.

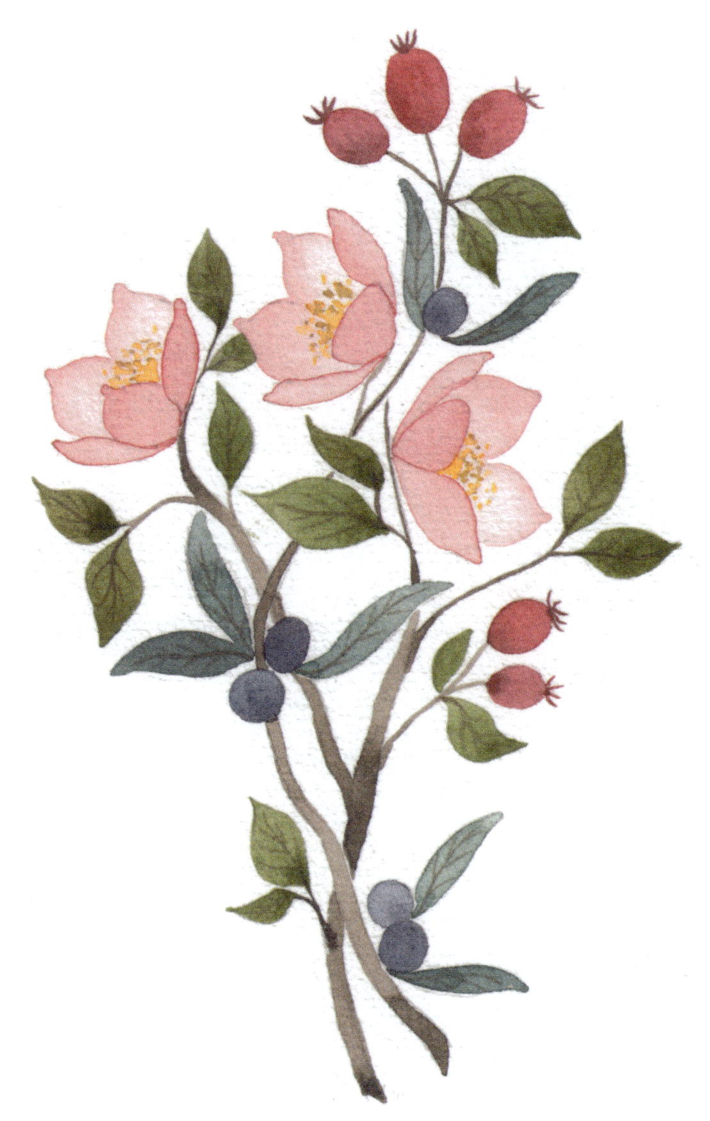

Winter Berries

This piece is inspired by traditional botanical illustration and shows two plants that grow wild in the UK in the winter: sloes and rosehips. This piece does require patience, as it takes a while for the individual petals and leaves to slowly dry, but it's such a pretty effect that it's worth it.

Materials Cold press watercolor paper • Pencil • Eraser • Medium round paintbrush • Small round paintbrush

Colors Used Sepia ● Prussian Blue ● Alizarin Crimson ● Viridian Green ● Sap Green ● Burnt Umber ● Cadmium Yellow ● Yellow Ochre ●

Very lightly sketch the illustration using my sketch as a reference.

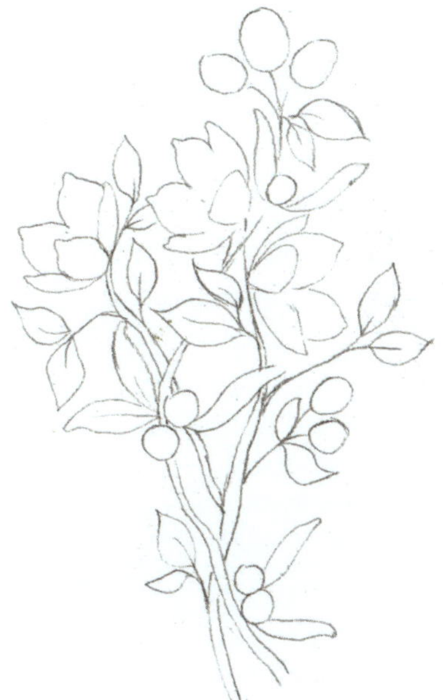

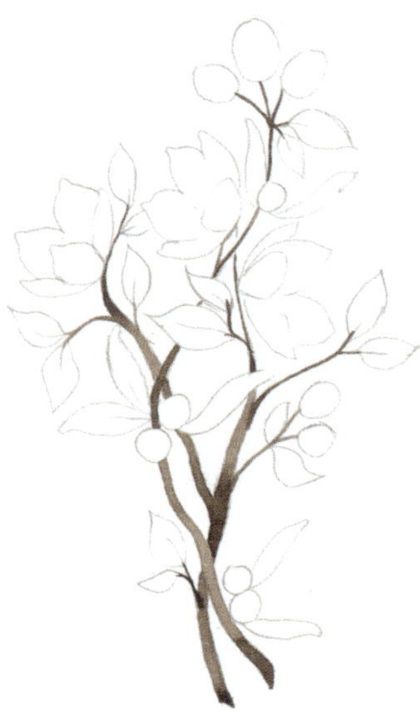

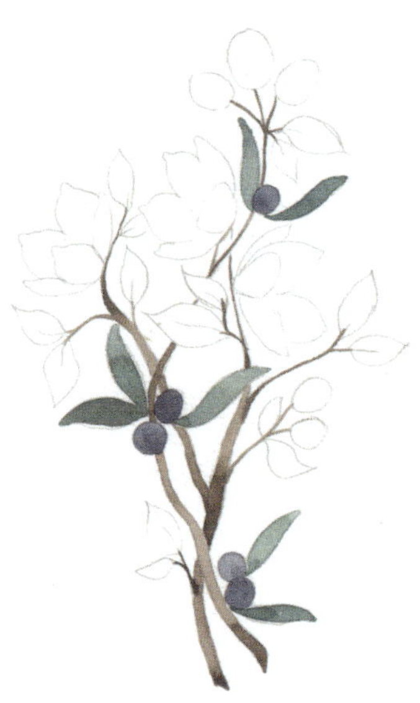

Using your small brush, paint the branches using a watery mixture of Sepia. Allow the color to pool in different areas so that some areas of the branch are lighter or darker than others. When the branches cross over, make sure there is a contrast between the branches, darker branches crossing over lighter branches, or vice versa.

Make a deep blue purple with Prussian Blue and a bit of Alizarin Crimson. Using your medium brush, paint the sloe berries with various amounts of water in each one to create interest. Mix a blue green with Viridian Green, a bit of Alizarin Crimson, and a bit of Sepia. Paint the long, thin leaves of the sloe plant with your medium brush, varying the water content and allowing color to pool in different areas.

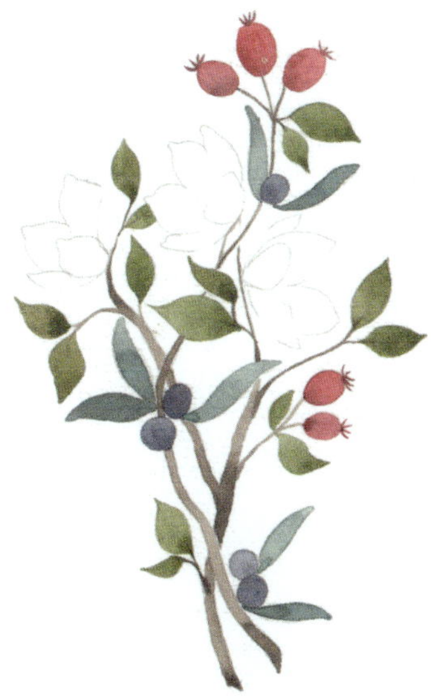

Mix a green using Sap Green, Burnt Umber, and lots of water. Using your medium brush, paint the leaves of the rosehip plant, allowing color to pool in different areas to create contrast. Paint the rosehips with Alizarin Crimson and your medium brush. Mix Alizarin Crimson with a bit of Sepia. Using your small brush, paint small points at the top of the rosehip, and add a drop of this color to the base of the rosehip while it is still wet.

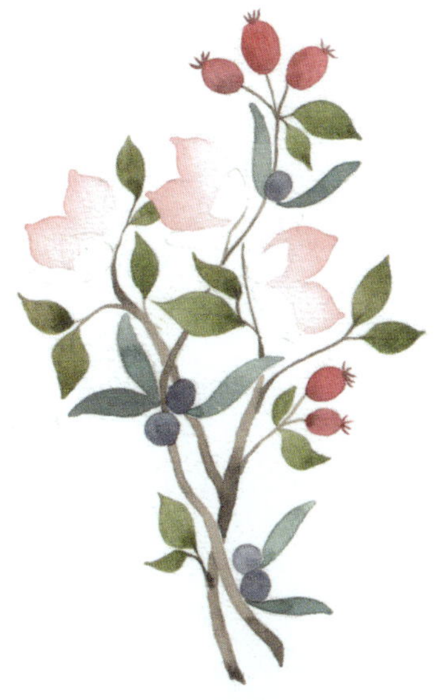

Mix a very pale pink using Alizarin Crimson and lots of water. Using your medium brush, paint the petals at the back of the flower, adding more water as the petals reach the center so that they fade out. This mixture should be very watery and will take a long time to dry.

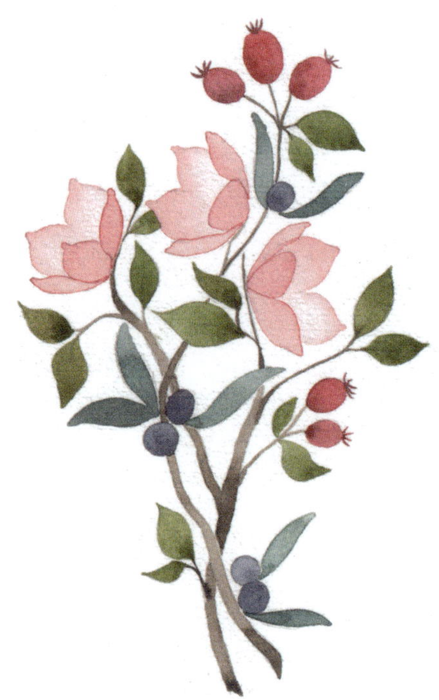

When these background petals are dry, paint the petals in the foreground one at a time in the same watery mixture. If the mixture is very watery on the surface, it should dry very slowly and leave a tiny outline around the petal, which helps define the petals in the foreground. Remember to be patient with these.

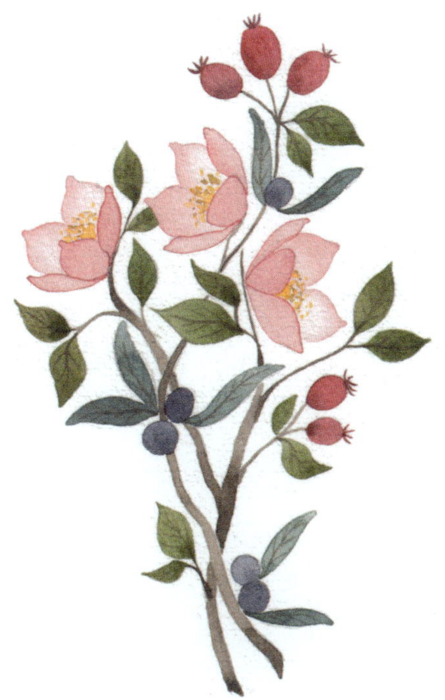

Use a watery mixture of Sepia and your small brush to very carefully add veins to the leaves. Practice drawing a few lines first to check the consistency of the paint and the thickness of your line. You want these lines to be nice and delicate. Create a mixture of Cadmium Yellow and Yellow Ochre, and use your small brush to paint the little dots in the centers of the flowers. Using the watery mixture of Sepia, add more little dots to the center of the flower.

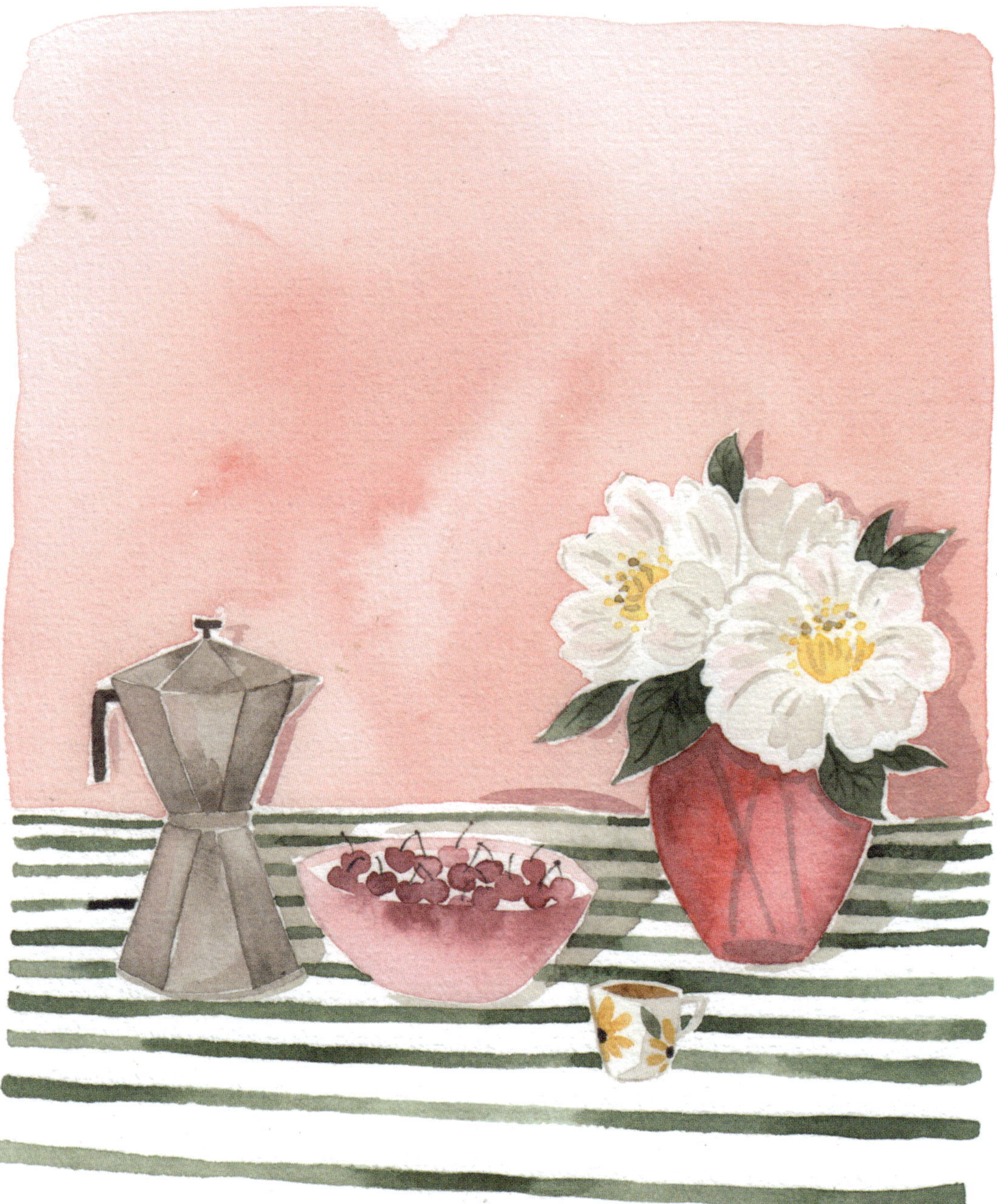

Cherries and Peonies

This piece is inspired by simple pleasures: freshly brewed coffee, ripe cherries, and a bunch of beautiful peonies. It embraces the perfectly imperfect nature of watercolors, with the random spreading and pooling of colors giving a fresh feel to this still life. I love the way the cherries spread into the bowl.

Materials Cold press watercolor paper • Pencil • Eraser • Large round paintbrush • Medium round paintbrush • Small round paintbrush

Colors Used Alizarin Crimson ● Lamp Black ● Sepia ● Sap Green ● Ultramarine ● Cadmium Red ● Cadmium Yellow ● Yellow Ochre ● Burnt Umber ●

Very lightly sketch the piece using my sketch as reference.

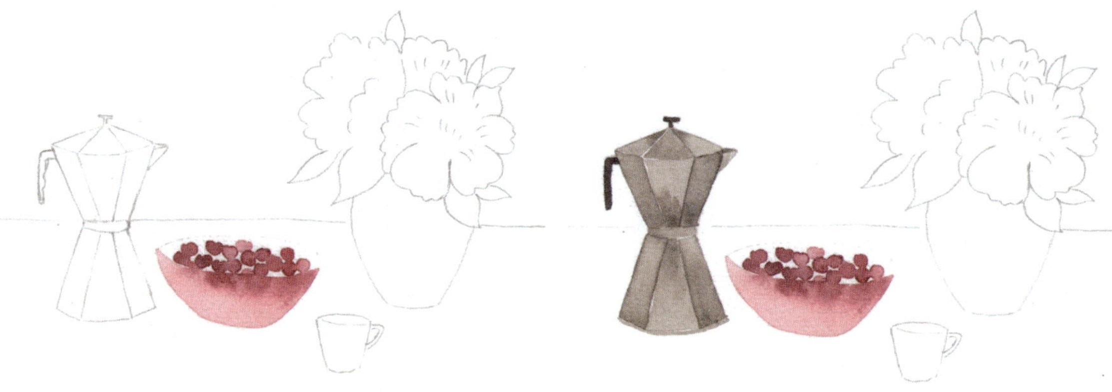

Mix Alizarin Crimson with a bit of Lamp Black to create a deep cherry color. Paint the cherries inside the bowl using your small brush. Vary the amount of water used to paint the cherries, and allow the color to flow from one cherry to another. Create a very light mix of Alizarin Crimson, and with your medium brush, paint the outside of the bowl. The edge of the bowl should just touch the cherries, allowing the color to bleed in.

Create a watery mixture of Sepia and Lamp Black. Using your small brush, paint each individual section of the coffee pot. Paint them one at a time so they don't merge together. Allow the color to pool in different areas. Use Lamp Black and your small brush to carefully paint the top of the coffee pot and the handle.

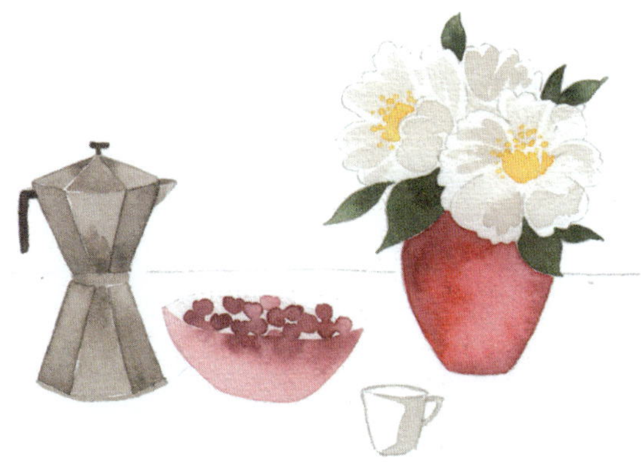

Use a very watery mixture of Sepia and your small brush to paint very light shadows inside the petals of the peonies. Mix a dark green with Sap Green, Ultramarine, and Sepia, and carefully paint the leaves of the peony once the shadows are dry. Create a watery mixture of Cadmium Yellow with a tiny bit of Cadmium Red, and loosely paint centers in the peonies with your small brush. Remember to keep everything very light and loose. It's much easier to add more detail later if things need to be more defined or darker, but once something has become overworked, it's difficult to rectify.

Paint the glass vase using a watery mixture of Alizarin Crimson. Mix some Lamp Black with Alizarin Crimson and, while the vase is still wet, add this darker color to the left-hand edge of the vase. While the vase is still wet, add a drop more water to the center to create a highlight.

Use a watery mixture of Sepia and your small brush to outline and paint shadows on the right side of the coffee cup.

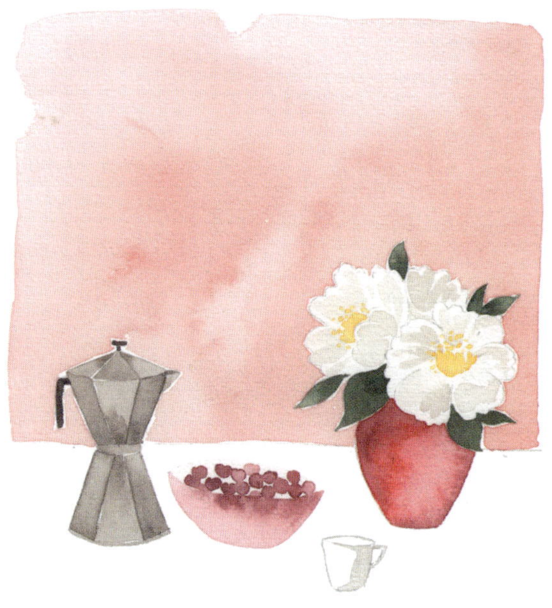

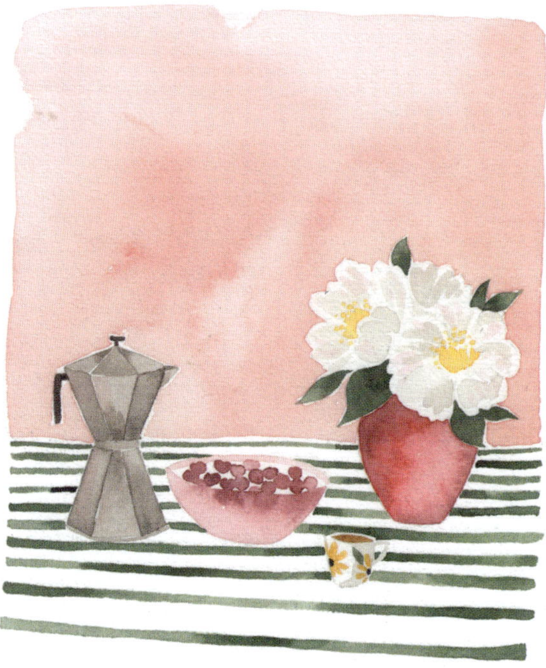

Create a pale watery mixture of Cadmium Red and Alizarin Crimson, and paint the background using your large brush. It's fine to leave white spaces around the edge of the objects; this keeps it looking fresh. Work quickly to cover the whole surface while the paint is still wet.

Using your small brush, paint a flower on the espresso cup using Yellow Ochre for the flower, Sepia for the center, and the green mixture for the leaf. Paint coffee in the center of the cup using Burnt Umber and your small brush.

Use a very watery mixture of Alizarin Crimson to paint the back rim of the bowl and add little pink highlights to the white peonies and the coffee pot. (When you place something shiny or something white in front of a colored wall, you will see that color reflected in the object.)

Create a green mixture with Sap Green, Ultramarine, and Sepia. Paint horizontal stripes of a tablecloth behind the objects. It's fine to leave a slight white space between the object and the stripe. Make the stripes thicker as they come toward you.

Use your small brush to add more of the Sepia shadow mixture to the peony to outline the edges, add detail to the center of the peonies, and paint peony stems just showing through the glass vase. Use this watery mixture of Sepia and your small brush to add shadows to the coffee pot. Once the green stripes are completely dry, use this shadow mixture and your medium brush to loosely paint shadows behind the objects. Use your small brush and a darker mixture of Sepia to paint stems on the cherries. Mix Alizarin Crimson with a bit of

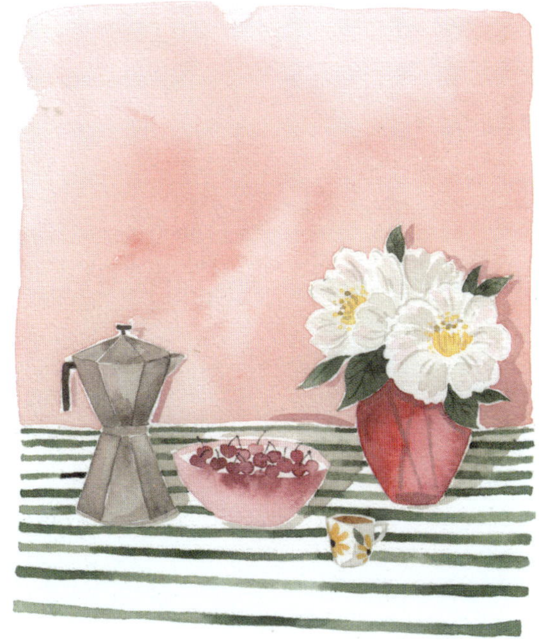

Lamp Black and lots of water. Use your medium brush to loosely paint shadows behind the objects on the wall. Add a little more Sepia to the green mixture, and using a small brush, carefully paint veins on the peony leaves.

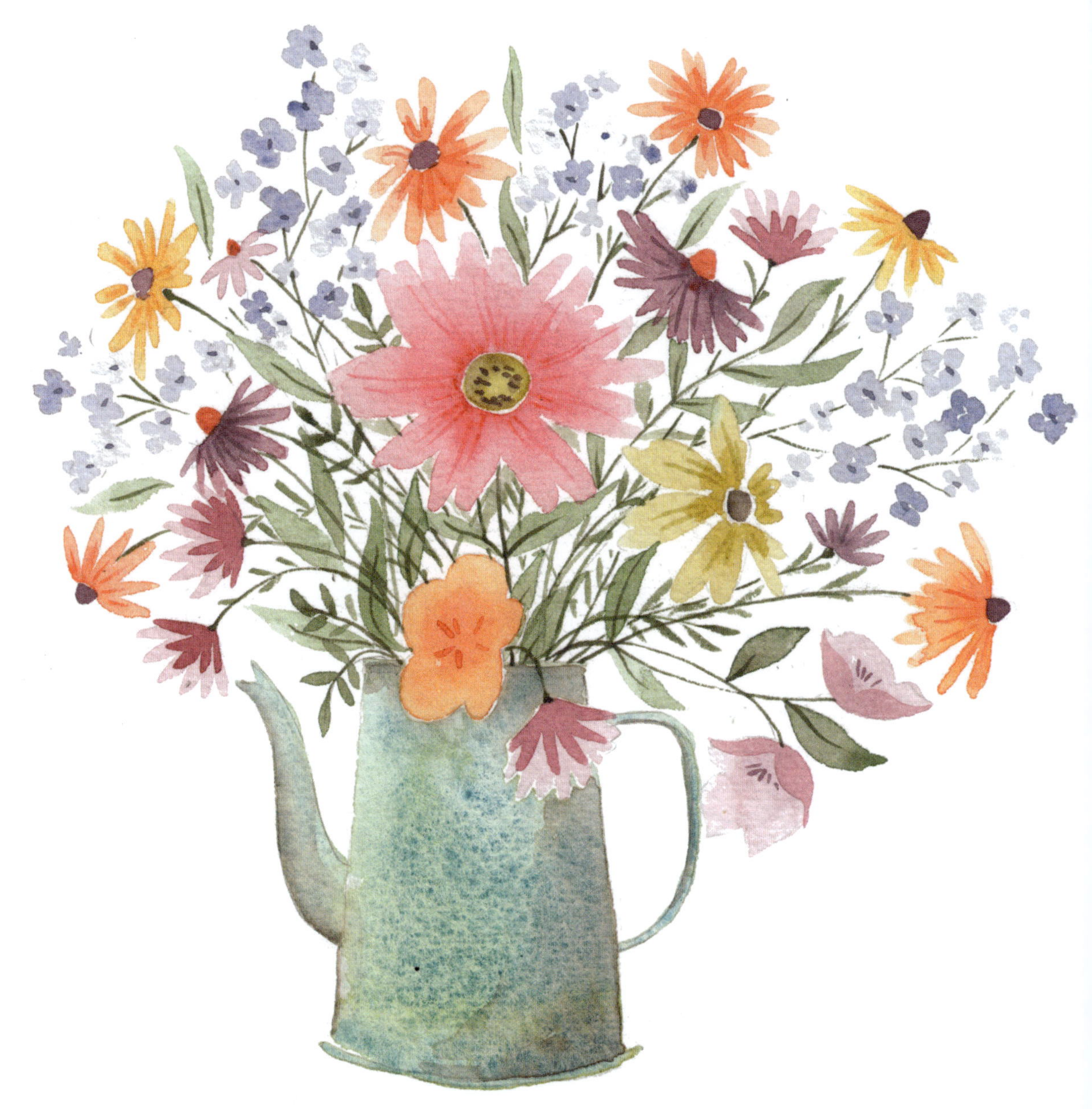

Wildflowers in a Vase

The joy of this piece is that it really embraces the beautiful spontaneous quality of watercolors, which is perfect for a wild, messy bunch of wildflowers. We can encourage the pigment to bleed and flow in certain areas, but there will always be an unpredictable element that is out of our control. This piece uses color pooling to create beautiful delicate effects as well as color layering to create the impression of a messy bouquet.

Materials Cold press watercolor paper • Pencil • Eraser • Large round paintbrush • Medium round paintbrush • Small round paintbrush

Colors Used Alizarin Crimson 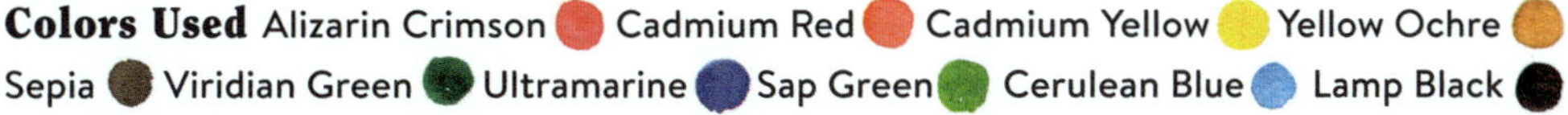 Cadmium Red ● Cadmium Yellow ● Yellow Ochre ● Sepia ● Viridian Green ● Ultramarine ● Sap Green ● Cerulean Blue ● Lamp Black ●

Start by very lightly sketching the vase of wildflowers using my sketch as reference. Don't worry about sketching in every leaf or petal. The sketch is just to give you a rough idea of the composition; you can add more leaves and flowers as you go along.

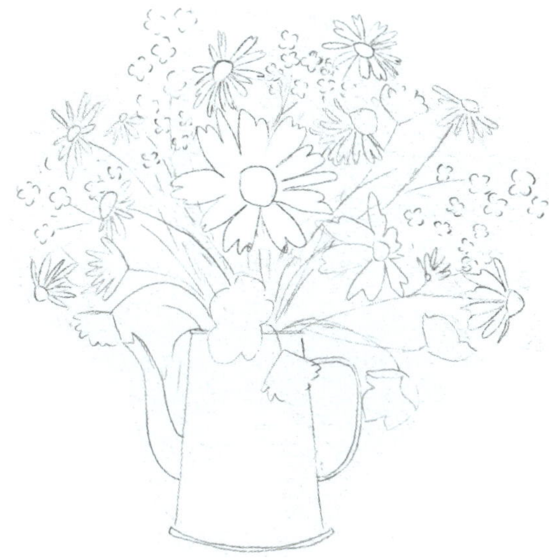

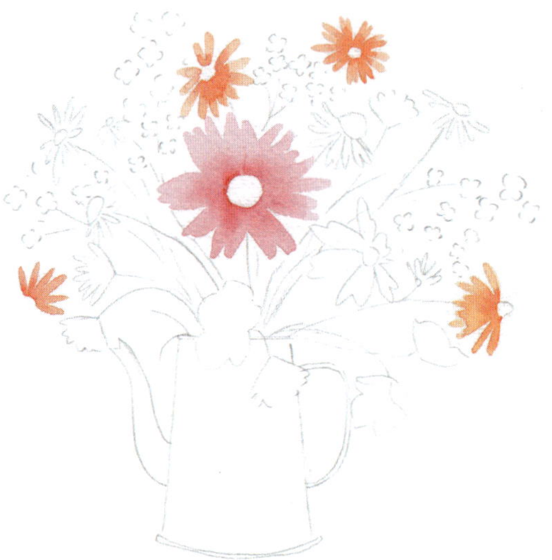 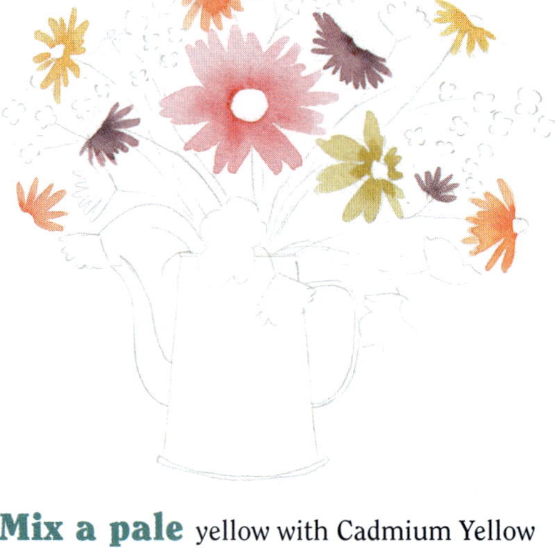

Start by creating a watery mixture of Alizarin Crimson, and paint the large central flower using your medium round brush. While the paint is still wet, use your small brush to add Alizarin Crimson mixture to the center of the flower. It's really important to do this quickly so the paint is wet enough to allow the darker color to spread.

Mix a light orange with Cadmium Red, Cadmium Yellow, and lots of water. Paint one of the smaller flowers using your small brush. While still wet, add more Cadmium Red to the center. Repeat this process for all the orange flowers.

Mix a pale yellow with Cadmium Yellow and a little Yellow Ochre, and paint one of the small yellow flowers with your small round brush. While still wet, add more Yellow Ochre to the center of the flower. Repeat this process for the small yellow flowers. For the large yellow flower, add a tiny bit of Sepia to the mixture and repeat the process as before.

Make a purple mixture with Alizarin Crimson and a bit of Viridian Green. Paint the purple flowers one at a time, adding a more concentrated version of the purple mixture to the flower center as before.

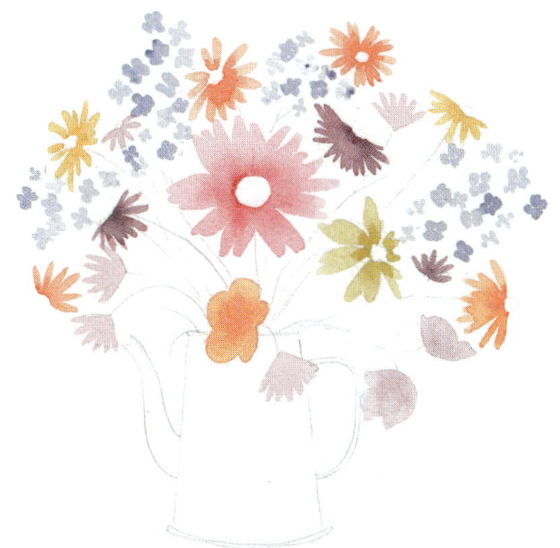

Make a muted purplish blue with Ultramarine, a tiny bit of Cadmium Red, and lots of water. Be very sparing with the red; too much will turn the mixture brown. Using your small round brush, paint the small blue flowers. Each of the four petals should be one dab of your brush. Vary the concentration of the paint mixture as you go so that some flowers are lighter than others.

Mix a pale purple using Alizarin Crimson with a bit of Viridian Green and lots of water to paint the remaining purple flowers using your small brush. With a mixture of Cadmium Red, Cadmium Yellow, and some water, paint the large orange flower with your medium round brush. While still wet, add a drop more orange to the center.

TIP When mixing a color, add a bit more water to one side of the paint mixture on the palette. This is easiest on a flat palette; if you are using a plastic palette with wells, you will need to transfer some of the color into a separate well. This provides you with a lighter and darker version of the same color, which is great for wet-on-wet technique and adding details and shading.

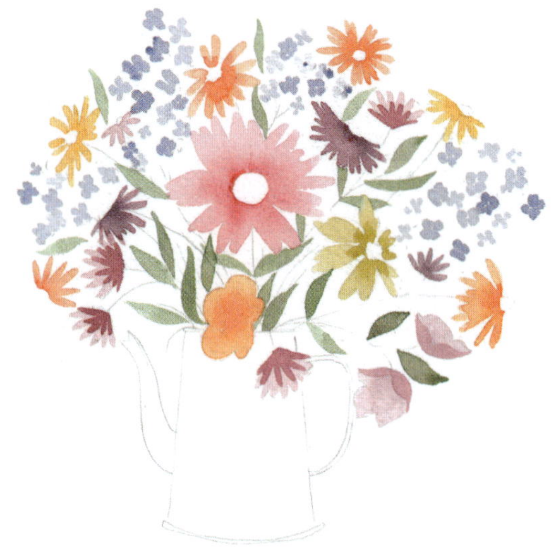

Create a leaf green using Sap Green, a little Sepia, and lots of water. Using your medium brush, paint some leaves coming off the stems in the arrangement. Don't worry if they look too pale at the moment; we will be adding more details over the top.

Add more Alizarin Crimson to the purple mix, and add another layer to the purple flowers with your small brush. For the two hellebores at the bottom right corner, add a bit more water to the mixture and carefully paint the outer petals with your small brush.

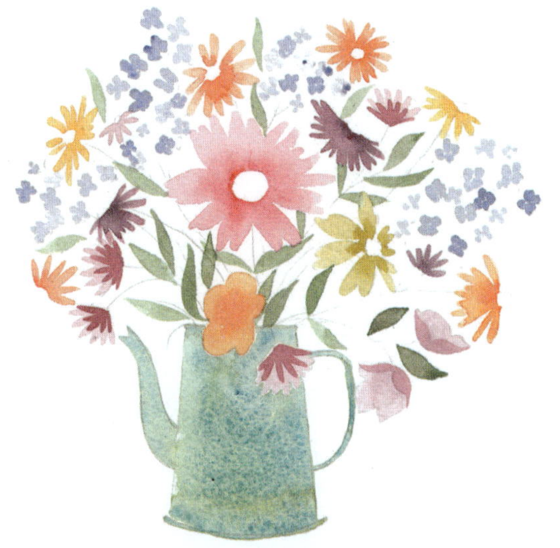

Mix a duck egg blue for the enamel jug using a mixture of Cerulean Blue, Cadmium Yellow, and lots of water. Remember: You are painting a large area with this color, so make sure you mix plenty. It's always better to have too much paint than not enough. Paint the jug using your large brush, swapping to a smaller brush for more fussy areas. Don't worry if you find it difficult to paint neatly around the flowers; you can always leave a small white gap. This combination of colors—Cerulean Blue and Cadmium Yellow—will naturally separate slightly as it dries. Some areas will look greener while others will look bluer, which gives the enamel jug a lovely vintage appearance. It will probably take quite a while for this to dry, but the effect is worth it. Just be patient.

Mix a dark green with Sap Green and
Sepia. Using your small brush, paint the stems
of the flowers and veins on the leaves. Also
using your small brush, paint small leaves on
some of the stems. Don't worry too much about
following your original sketch exactly; use your
instinct for where the leaves and stems should
go. Remember that these are wildflowers, and
it's good for them to look a bit messy.

Mix Cadmium Yellow with a little bit of
Lamp Black to paint the center of the large
pink flower using your medium brush. Use the
same paint mixture and your small brush to
paint thin lines on the large yellow flower. Mix
Alizarin Crimson with Yellow Ochre to create
a burnt orange, and paint the centers of the
smaller purple flowers with your small brush.
Use the same color to paint lines on the petals
of the orange flowers, and add details to the
large orange flower. Create a deep purple with
Alizarin Crimson and Viridian Green, and paint
the centers of the remaining orange and yellow

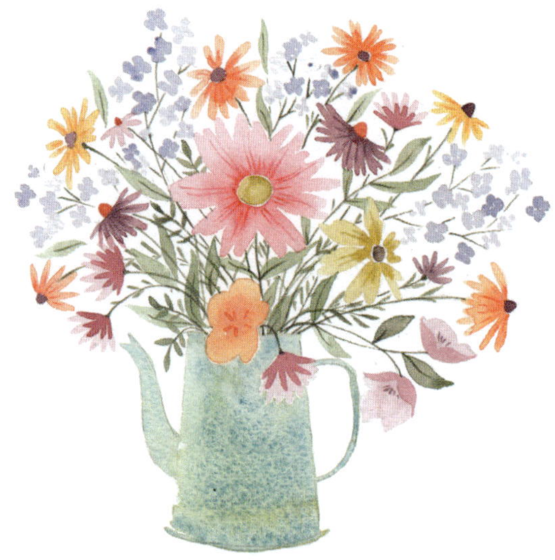

flowers using your small brush. Using your
small brush and the same paint mixture, add
details to the purple flowers. Paint the center of
the large yellow flower with Sepia using a small
brush. Using Alizarin Crimson and your small
brush, paint thin lines on the large pink flower.
Use Yellow Ochre and your small brush to add
thin lines to the remaining yellow flowers.

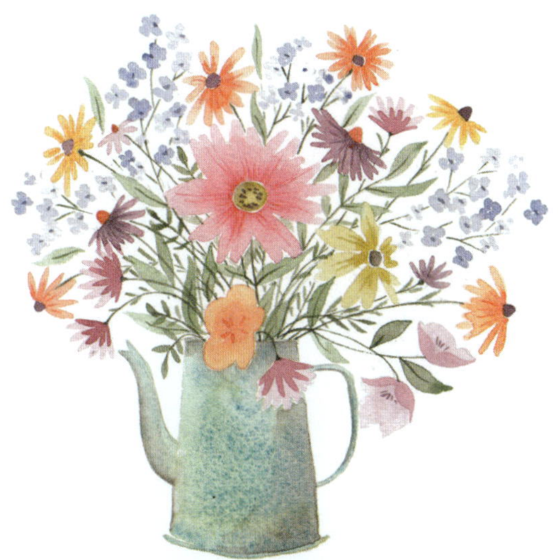

Use Sepia and your small brush to add dots to the center of the large flower. Create a watery mixture of Sepia to paint the shadows on the jug. Add a tiny bit of Cadmium Red to Ultramarine, and add centers to the blue flowers using a small brush. As a finishing touch, add leaves using a mixture of Sap Green and Sepia to fill in any large white spaces. When completely dry, erase any remaining pencil marks.

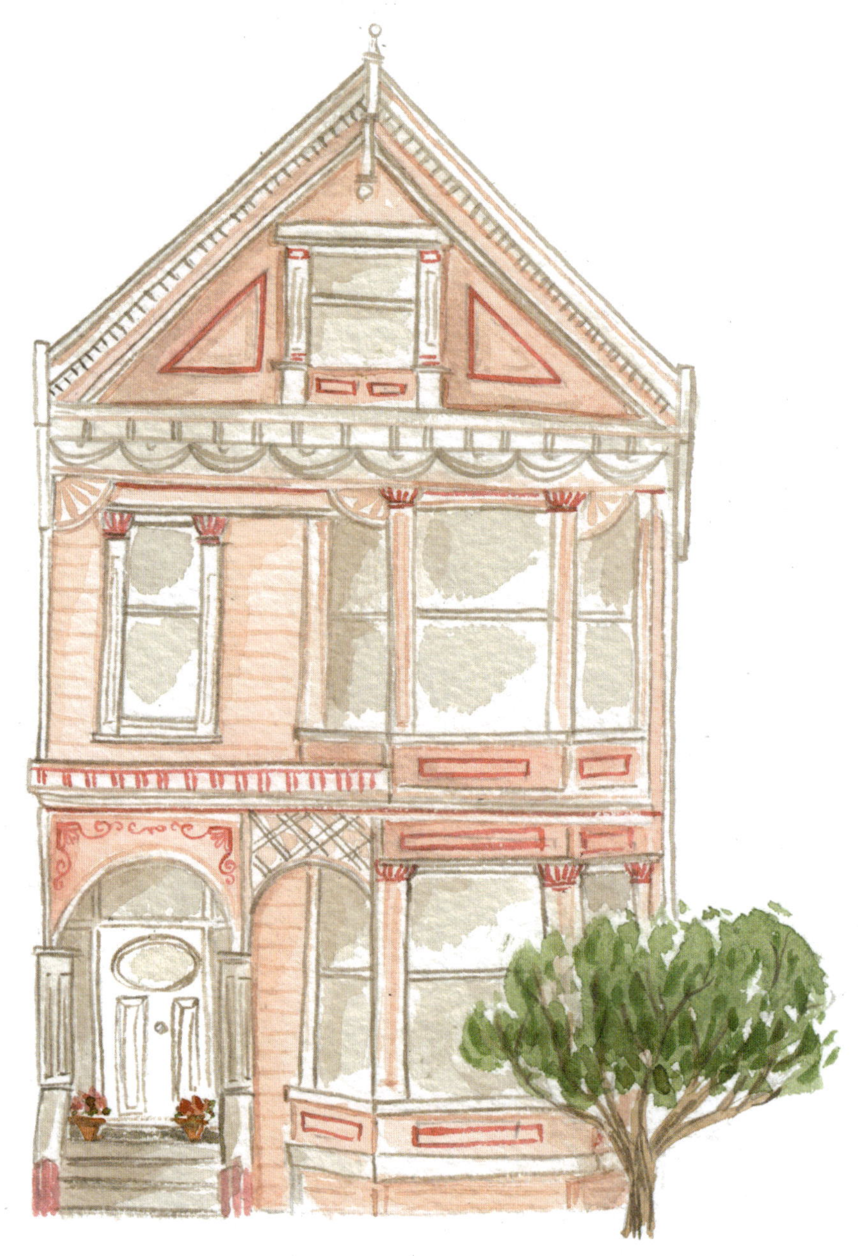

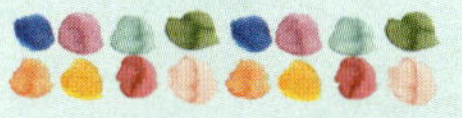

Wet-on-Dry

By waiting for the first layer to dry before adding another, we create two distinct layers; this is called the wet-on-dry technique. This technique is great for building up more complicated pictures and details, although it must be used carefully to avoid the painting becoming overworked or too heavy.

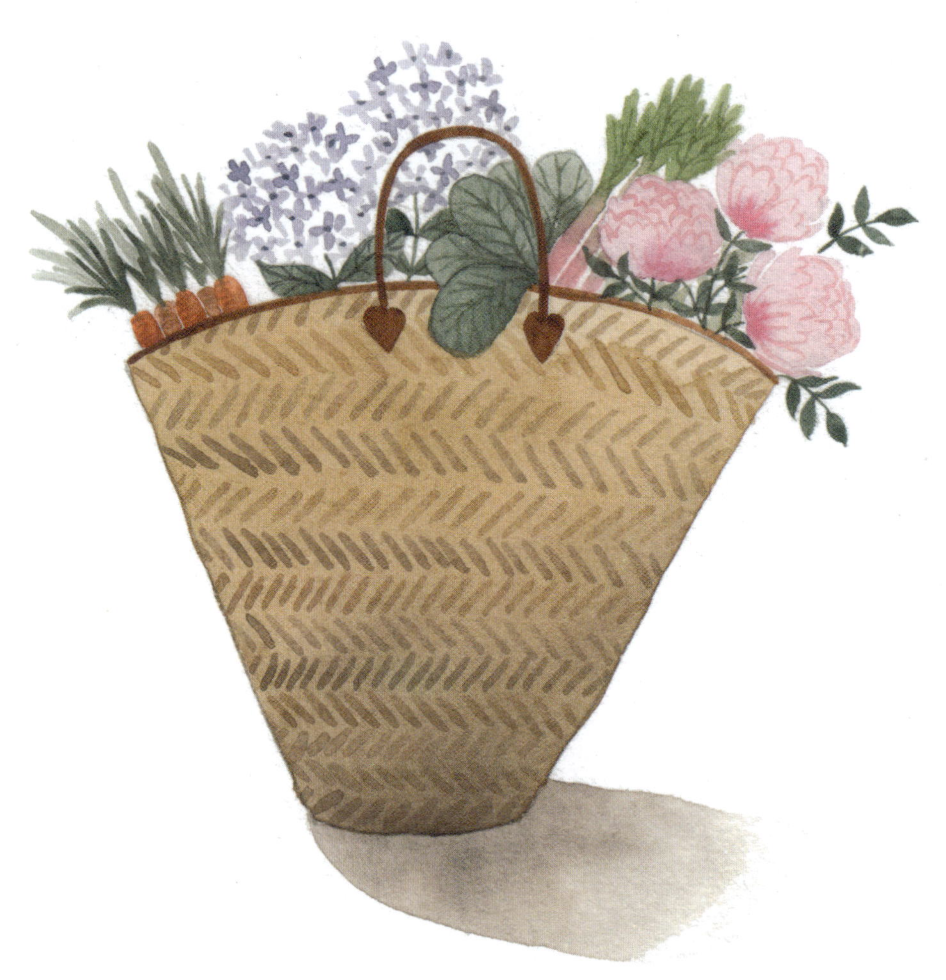

Farmers' Market Basket

This piece features a lovely wicker basket full of seasonal treats from the farmers' market: carrots, hydrangeas, greens, rhubarb, and peonies. This piece makes use of both the wet-on-wet technique and the wet-on-dry technique, adding more details to dried washes of paint to build up texture and interest. Once you've mastered this piece, why not fill the basket with your favorite seasonal items? How about tulips for springtime or dahlias for late summer?

Materials Cold press watercolor paper • Pencil • Eraser • Large round brush • Medium round brush • Small round brush

Colors Used Yellow Ochre ● Sepia ● Burnt Sienna ● Permanent Rose ● Prussian Blue ● Cadmium Red ● Sap Green ● Ultramarine ● Cadmium Yellow ● Alizarin Crimson ●

Lightly sketch the illustration using my sketch as reference.

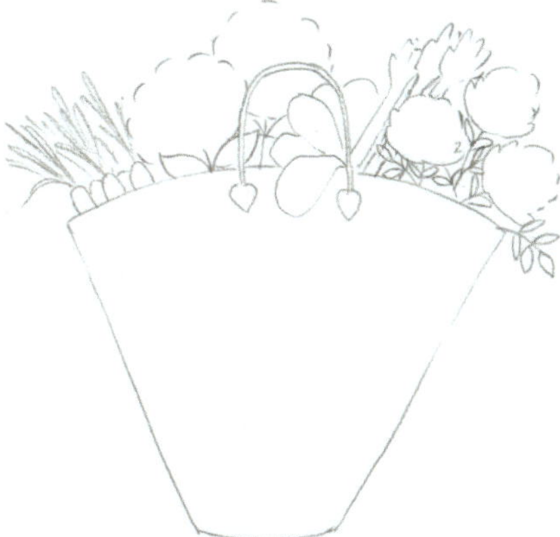

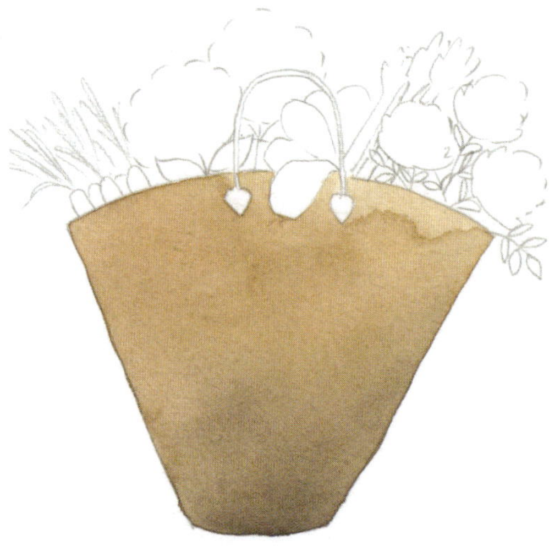

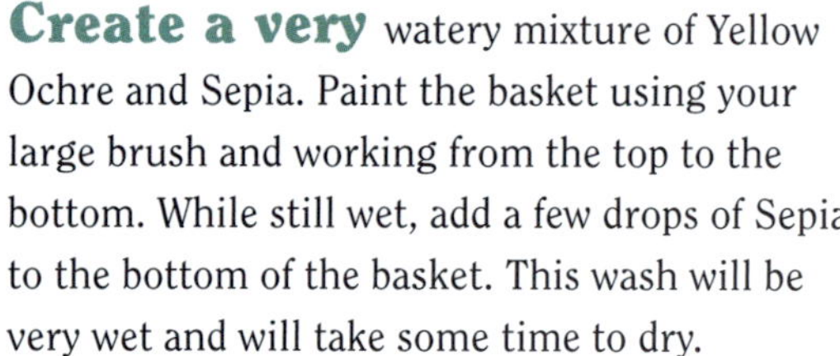

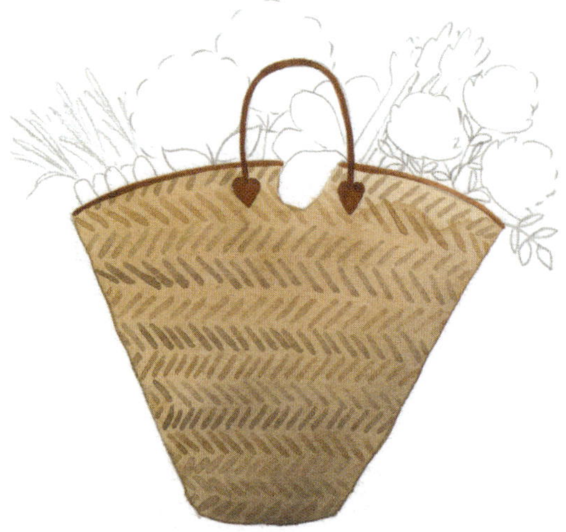

Create a very watery mixture of Yellow Ochre and Sepia. Paint the basket using your large brush and working from the top to the bottom. While still wet, add a few drops of Sepia to the bottom of the basket. This wash will be very wet and will take some time to dry.

Once the basket is completely dry, create a darker mix of Yellow Ochre and Sepia with less water than the original mix. Using your small brush, paint diagonal dashes on the basket to indicate a woven texture, alternating the direction one row at a time. Vary the amount of water used in each row.

Mix Burnt Sienna with Sepia to paint the leather handle and trim with your small brush.

TIP You can speed the drying time by using a hairdryer to remove the last bit of moisture from the paint. Don't use a hairdryer while there is still wet paint/water on the surface; it will move the paint around and disrupt the way it dries. Only use the hairdryer once the painted surface is no longer wet but still feels slightly damp to the touch.

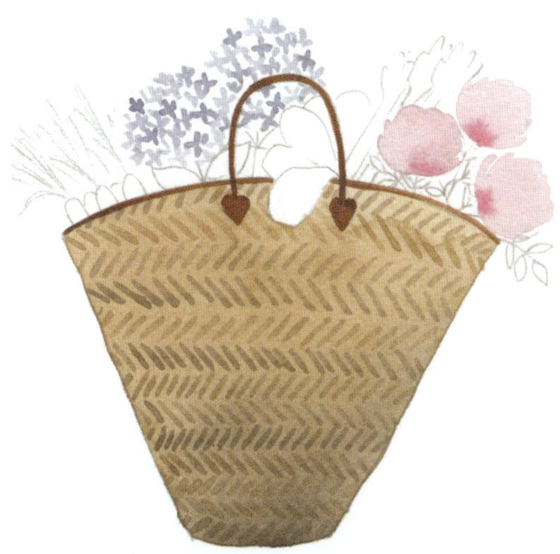

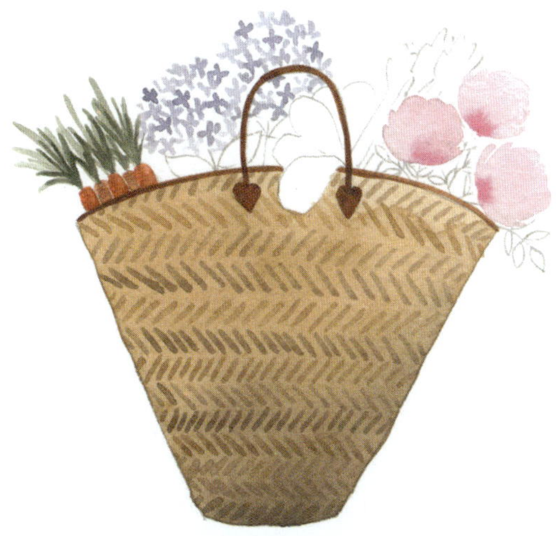

Create a very watery mixture of Permanent Rose, and loosely paint the three peonies using your medium brush. While they are still wet, add a drop more of Permanent Rose at the base of each peony.

Create a purple mixture using Prussian Blue, a bit of Permanent Rose, and lots of water. Using a small brush, paint the hydrangeas. These are made up of lots of little four-petaled flowers. Vary the amount of water in the flowers. Don't worry about making these too perfect; you want them to look natural.

Mix an orange using Cadmium Red and Yellow Ochre. Using a small brush, paint the three carrots in the foreground. Add a little more Sepia and some water to the mixture, and paint the two carrots in the background.

Mix Sap Green with Ultramarine and a little bit of Sepia to make dark green. Add a bit more water to this mixture to create a lighter version in another part of your palette. Using your small brush, paint the leaves of the carrots using the lighter mixture. When that is dry, paint more leaves in the foreground using the darker mixture.

Use the darker carrot mixture to carefully paint little horizontal lines on the carrots in the foreground using your small brush.

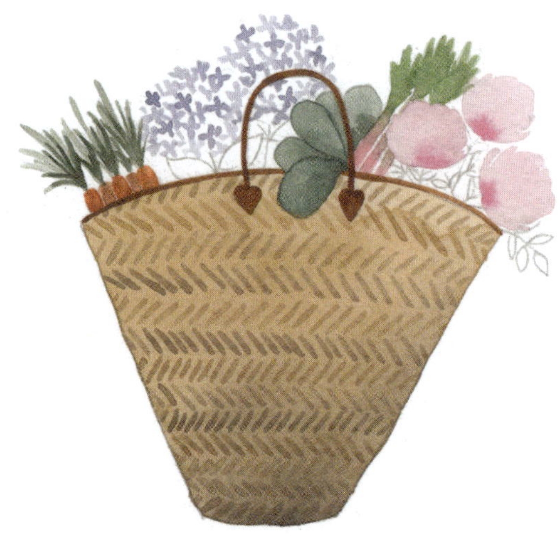

Mix Cadmium Red with a tiny bit of Permanent Rose and lots of water to make a pink for the rhubarb. Mix Sap Green with a bit of Burnt Sienna and lots of water to make a green for the rhubarb. Make a third mix using both the pink and green you've just made. Paint the rhubarb stem with your small brush, starting with the pink, then adding a little bit of the pink/green mixture, then finishing with green tops. The different colors should blend into each other smoothly as they are all wet.

Mix a green with Prussian Blue, Yellow Ochre, and lots of water. Paint the lettuce leaves, starting with a leaf that overlaps the front of the basket. Paint them one at a time, working backward and painting the leaf next to the rhubarb last. By this point the rhubarb stem should be dry.

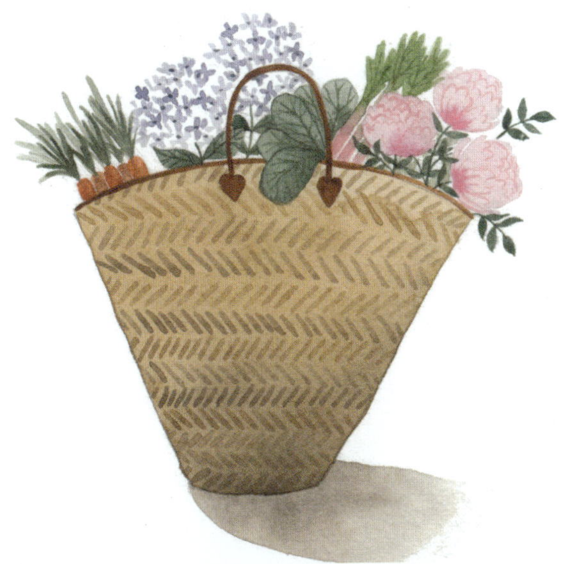

Once the peonies are dry, mix a dark green with Ultramarine and Cadmium Yellow. Using your small brush, carefully paint stems and leaves on the peonies. Once these are dry, add more water to the mixture, and paint a few leaves in the background to fill any gaps and make it look fuller. Create a watery mixture of Alizarin Crimson, and using your small brush, very carefully paint the edges of the peony petals.

Use the same green mixture and your small brush to paint stems and leaves on the hydrangeas. Once that is dry, add a little bit of Sepia to the mixture, and paint veins on the leaves. Mix Alizarin Crimson and Prussian Blue to make a bluish purple, and use your small brush to paint centers in the hydrangeas.

Mix Sap Green with Ultramarine and Sepia. Using your small brush, paint veins on the lettuce. Mix Sap Green with a little Sepia, and with your small brush, paint veins on the tops of the rhubarb.

Create a very watery mixture of Sepia, and using a large brush, paint a loose shadow under the basket. Add more water to the edge of the shadow so that it fades out, and add more Sepia to the wet shadow closest to the basket.

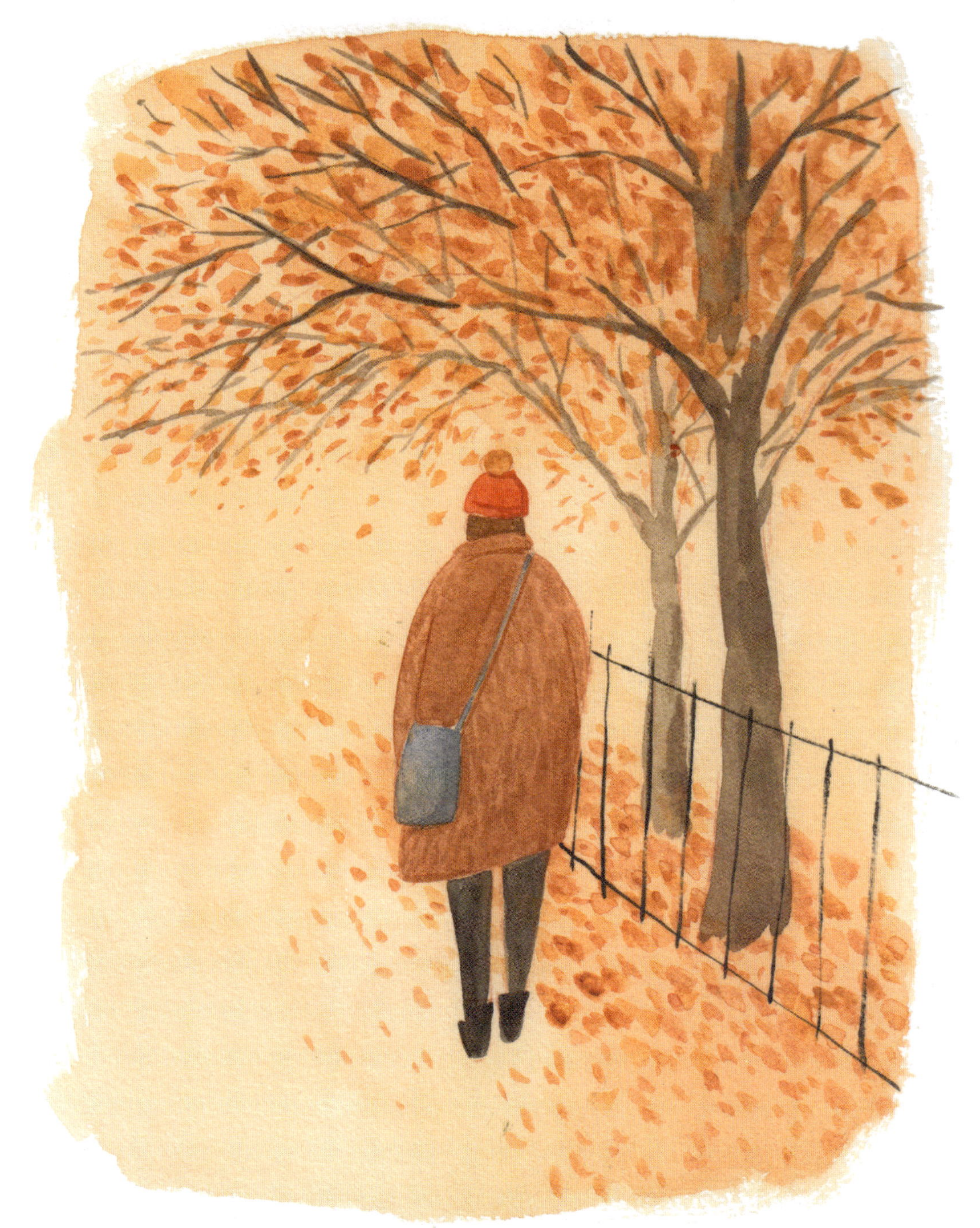

Autumn Walk

This piece is inspired by an afternoon walk in autumn. The use of warm earth tones perfectly captures the soft autumnal light and the golden foliage. By using a large brush to paint small details, we create a loose, expressive effect. This piece uses a very limited color palette and builds up layers to create depth.

Materials Cold press watercolor paper • Brown water-soluble pencil • Large paintbrush (preferably sable) • Medium round brush • Small round brush
Colors Used Yellow Ochre ● Burnt Sienna ● Sepia ● Burnt Umber ● Cadmium Red ●
Ultramarine ● Lamp Black ●

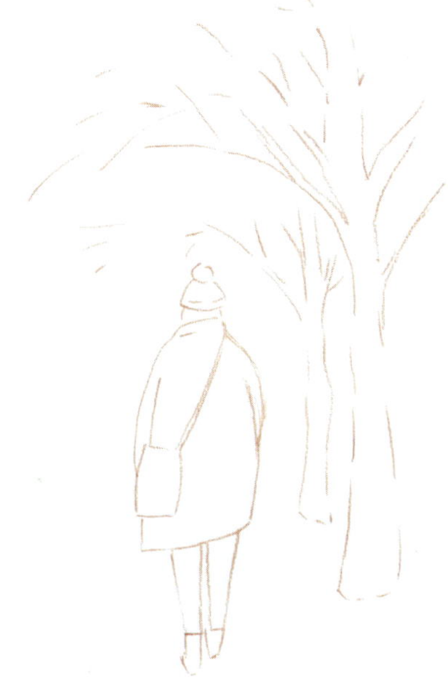

Using a brown water-soluble pencil, very loosely sketch a woman wearing a winter coat and walking with her back to us, and two trees. If you don't have a water-soluble pencil, you could use a regular pencil and just sketch very lightly.

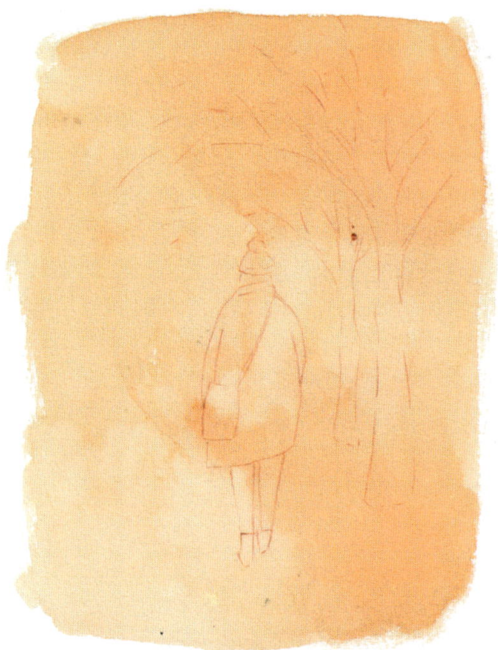 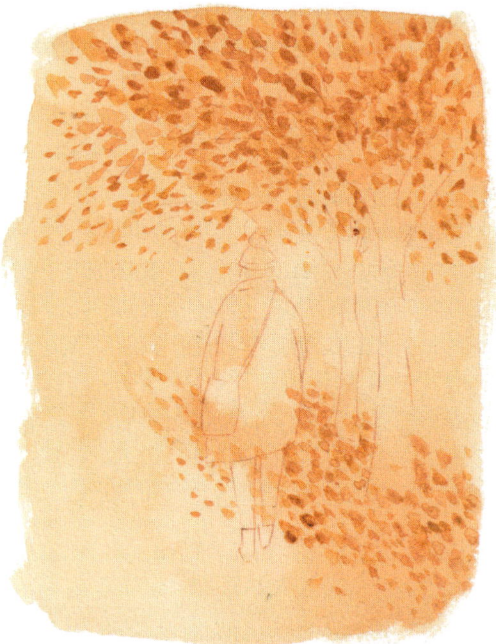

Create a very watery mixture of Yellow Ochre and Burnt Sienna. Make sure you create plenty of this mix. Paint a light watery background using your largest brush, leaving the edges slightly rough. Add more Burnt Sienna to the mixture, and add more paint to the top right-hand corner across the tree branches and the bottom right corner around the tree trunks while the first wash is still wet. The second darker color should fade into the first lighter color. Paint straight over the pencil sketch, which should still be visible underneath.

When that's dry, create another mix of Yellow Ochre and Burnt Sienna but with less water. Use the very tip of your large round brush to paint leaves in the tree branches and fallen around the tree trunks. Vary the size and angle of these leaves; add more Yellow Ochre to some and more Burnt Sienna to others. You could use a small or medium round brush for this, but by using the tip of a large brush, you will get more expressive brushstrokes. Practice this technique on a separate sheet of paper first if you're not confident about painting small details with a large brush. Notice how tiny variations in pressure and angle affect each brushstroke.

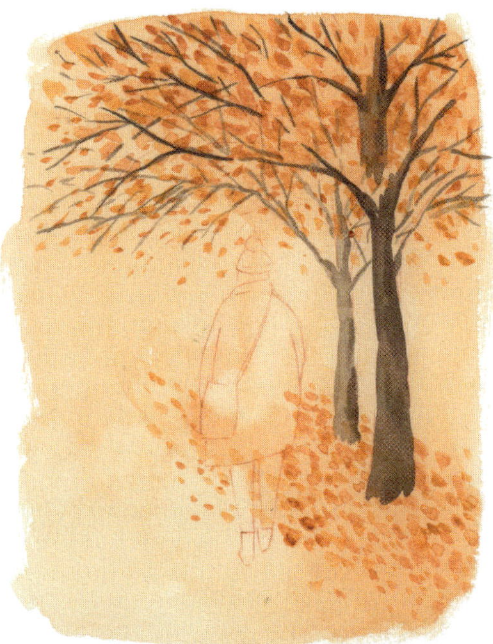

Mix Burnt Umber and Sepia, and paint the tree in the foreground using your large brush. Paint the large branches using the very tip of your brush, and allow broken areas for the leaves to show through. Use a small brush and the same paint mixture to paint the smaller branches. Using Sepia, add shadow to the right side while the paint is still wet. Add more water to the mixture, and paint the tree behind with your round medium brush. Use your small brush to paint the thin branches. Add more Sepia to the right side of the tree trunk. I like to use my large brush as much as I can for the trees because it encourages my brushstrokes to be loose and more expressive.

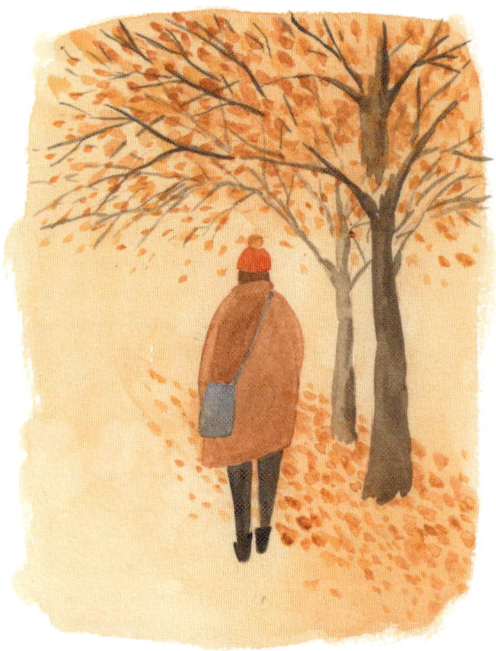

Create a watery mixture of Burnt Sienna and Burnt Umber to paint the woman's coat using your medium brush. Using your small brush, paint the woman's hat with Cadmium Red, paint the bobble of the hat with Yellow Ochre, paint her legs and boots using Lamp Black, paint her hair with Burnt Umber. Create a watery mixture of Ultramarine and Sepia, and paint the woman's bag with your small brush. Paint each item one at a time to allow them time to dry so they don't run into each other.

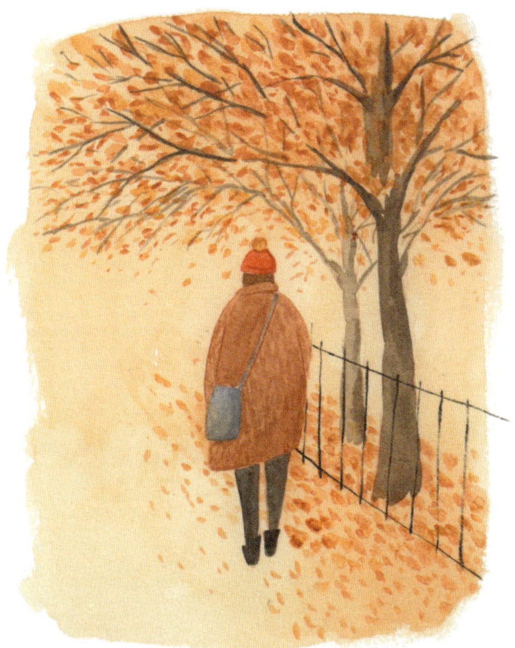

Using your small brush and Lamp Black, paint the iron railings. This paint mixture should be quite dry so the lines are fine and slightly broken. Create a mixture of Burnt Sienna and Burnt Umber. Using a medium brush, add definition to the sleeves and collar of the coat, and paint a shadow under the bag.

Paint little dashes all over the coat to indicate a fluffy texture. Use Cadmium Red and your small brush to add details to the hat.

Use a mixture of Yellow Ochre and Burnt Sienna and your large brush to add a few more leaves coming off branches and scattered on the ground.

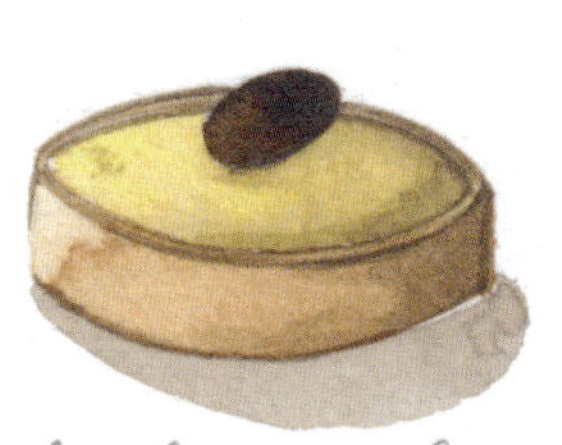

tarte au citron

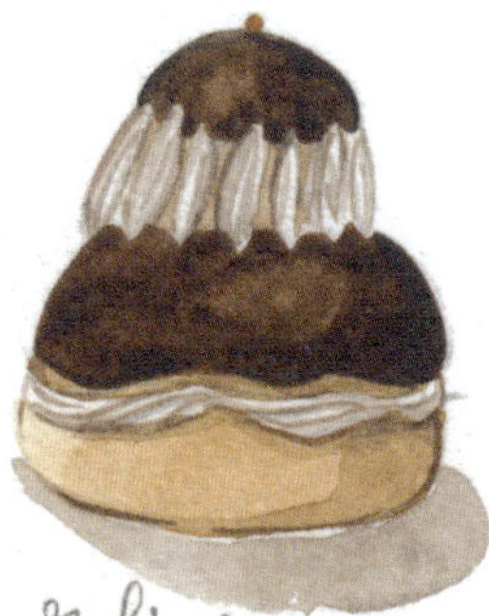

religieuse

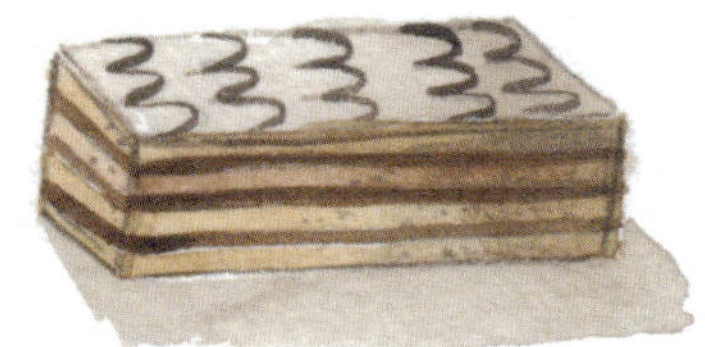

mille fuille

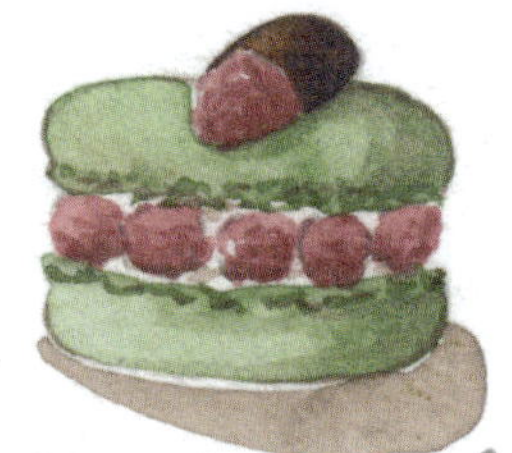

Macaron pistache

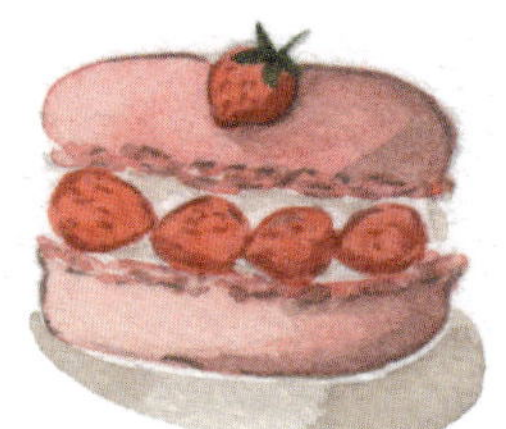

Macaron fraise

Savarin

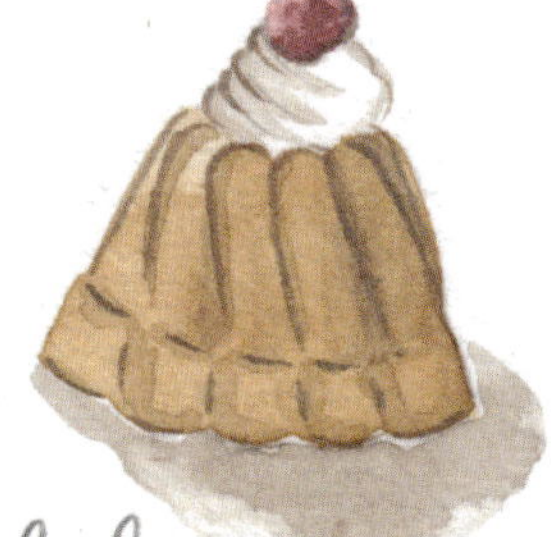

baba au rhum

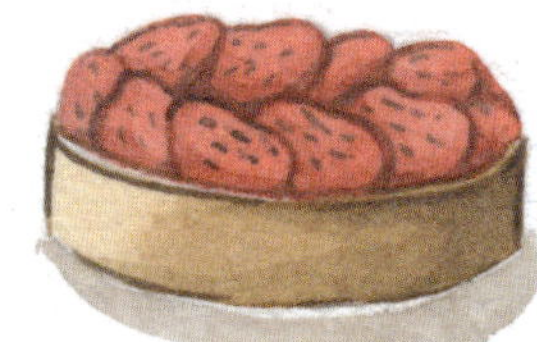

tarte au fraise

French Patisserie

This piece is inspired by beautiful French patisserie counters and vintage illustrated posters. Delicate layering of paint is the perfect way to capture these impossibly pretty pastries.

Materials Cold press watercolor paper • Pencil • Large paintbrush • Medium round brush Small round brush

Colors Used Yellow Ochre ● Sepia ● Lemon Yellow ● Burnt Umber ● Sap Green ● Lamp Black ● Cadmium Red ● Permanent Rose ● Alizarin Crimson ●

Very lightly sketch the pastries using my sketch as reference.

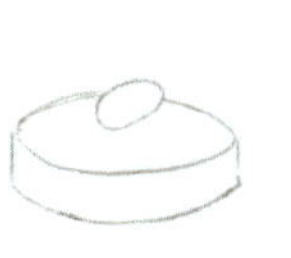
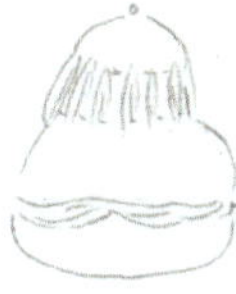
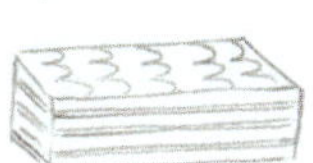
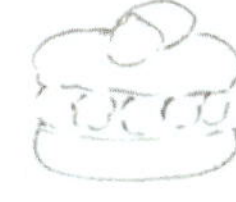
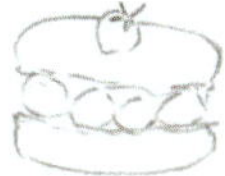
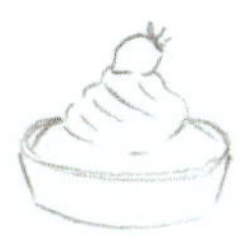
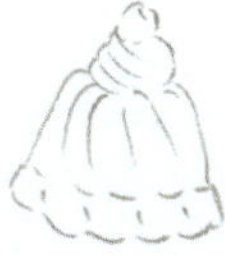
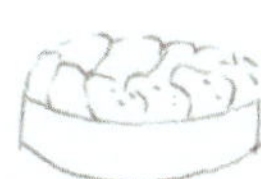

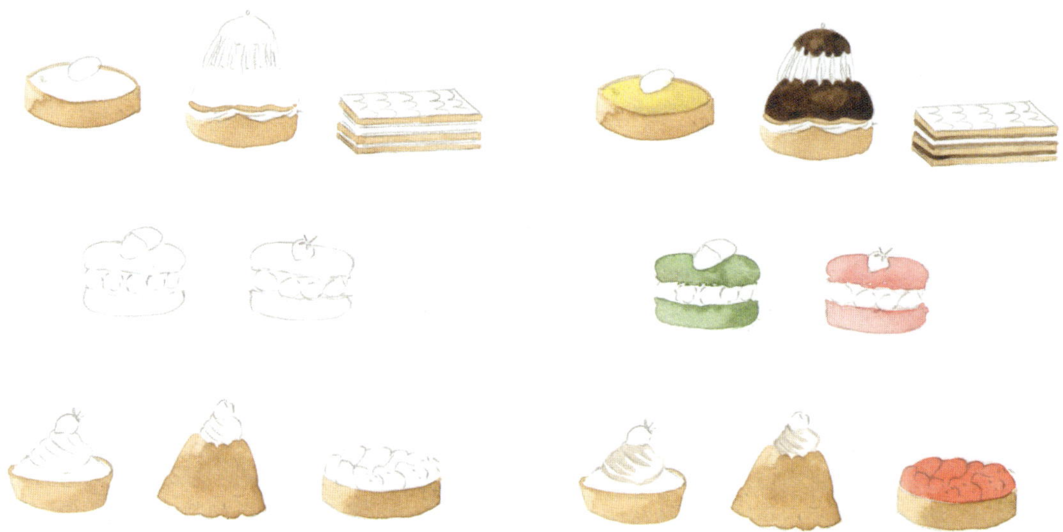

Create a mixture of Yellow Ochre and a bit of Sepia. Add more water to one side of the mix on your palette. Using your large brush and the more watery mixture, paint the sides of the pastry cases of the tarts, the choux bun of the religieuse, and the rum baba. Use your small brush to paint three of the layers of the mille-feuille and the rim of the pastry cases. When the paint is still wet, use your medium brush to drop in some of the darker paint mixture on the right side of the pastries so it blends in.

Mix Lemon Yellow with a bit of Burnt Umber to create a watery yellow mixture. Paint the top of the tarte au citron with your medium brush. Add a tiny bit of Sepia to the yellow mix, and add that color on the right side while it's still wet.

Create a dark brown mixture of Burnt Umber and Sepia, and paint the chocolate topping of the religieuse. Use a clean wet brush to pick up a bit of the pigment from the wet surface of the paper to show light reflecting off the glossy chocolate. Use your small brush and the same dark brown mixture to paint three of the layers in the mille-feuille.

Mix a light green with Sap Green, a tiny bit of Lamp Black, and lots of water. Using your medium brush, paint the pistachio and raspberry macaron, allowing color to pool on the right side around the edges.

Create a watery mixture of Cadmium Red and Permanent Rose, and paint the strawberry macaron with your medium brush, again allowing the color to pool on the right side. Create a mixture of Cadmium Red and Alizarin Crimson, and paint the strawberries on the strawberry tart with your medium brush. Add more mixture to the center and bottom of the strawberries, allowing the color to pool.

Create a very watery mixture of Sepia, and using a small brush, paint shadows on the left side of the whipped cream on the savarin, rum baba, and religieuse. Use the same dark chocolate color you made for the religieuse to paint the chocolate disk on top of the tarte au citron and the pistachio macaron using your small brush.

Use the strawberry color you mixed to paint the strawberries on the macaron and savarin

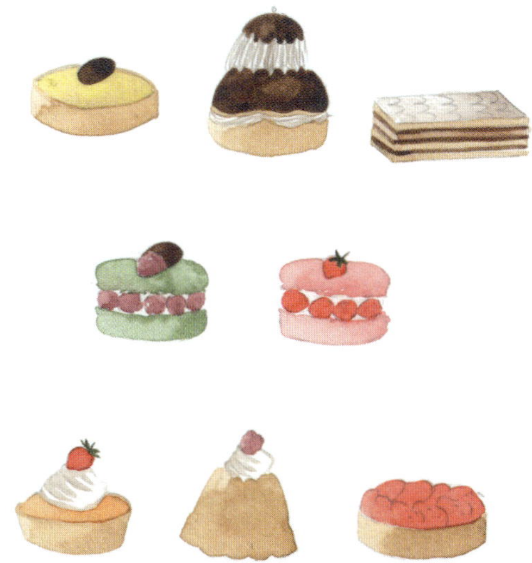

using your small brush. Mix a raspberry color using Alizarin Crimson with a tiny bit of Lamp Black, and paint the raspberry on the run baba and on the pistachio macaron.

Use a very watery mixture of Sepia and your medium brush to paint the top of the mille-feuille. Use a watery mixture of Burnt Umber and your small brush to paint the last layer.

Mix Sap Green with a little bit of Sepia to make a dark green, and paint the tops of the strawberries using your small brush. Mix Yellow Ochre with Burnt Umber to paint the top of the savarin.

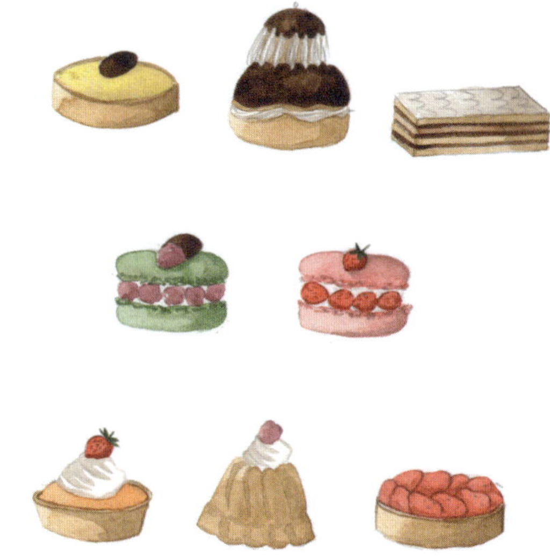

Now that the base layers of colors are painted, we are ready to add more details on the top.

Mix Yellow Ochre with Sepia. Using your small brush, outline the edges and add shadow to the right side of the tarte au citron, savarin, and tarte aux fraises. Use your medium brush and the same mixture to add shadow to the right side and under the whipped cream on the religieuse. Use this color to paint a thin vertical line along the edge of the mille-feuille and add shadow to the right side. Use this mixture and your small brush to add shadows to the rum baba.

Create a mixture of Sap Green with a little bit of Lamp Black, and paint loose dashes around the crinkly edges of the macaron using a small brush. Use the same mixture and your medium brush to paint shadows around the right side of the macaron and under the raspberry and chocolate disk.

Create a mixture of Cadmium Red, Alizarin Crimson, a tiny bit of Sepia, and lots of water. Using a small brush, paint loose dashes around the edges of the strawberry macaron. Use your medium brush and the same mixture to add shadows to the right side and under the strawberry. Add more Alizarin Crimson to this mixture, and using your small brush, outline the strawberries and add little seeds. Outline the strawberry on the savarin and add seeds. Outline the strawberries on the top of the tarte aux fraises, and add shadows to the bottom of the strawberries.

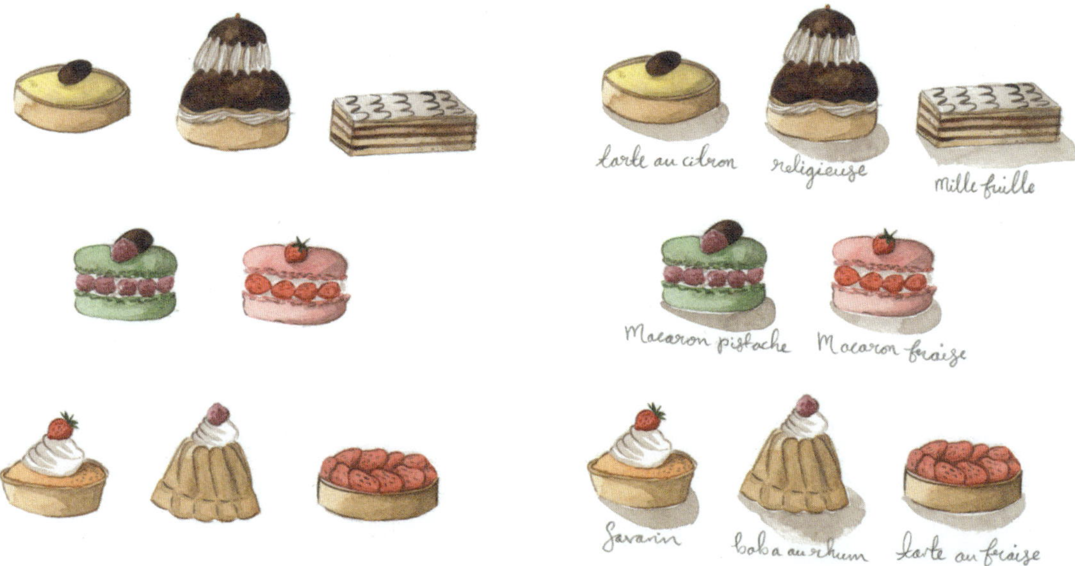

Use Sepia and your small brush to carefully outline all the pastries and add shadows. Make sure to add definition to the swirls of whipped cream, the edges of the pastry cases, and the flutes of the rum baba, and add shadow and definition around the strawberries on the tarte aux fraises. To make sure your brush isn't too wet, blot it on a piece of tissue paper before you start so that you get thin, delicate lines. Use Sepia and your small brush to paint the feathering on top of the mille-feuille. Add more water to this mixture, and using a medium brush, add subtle shadows around the edges of the macaron, the choux pastry bun, and the pastry cases.

Mix Alizarin Crimson and a bit of Lamp Black. Using a small brush, add details to the raspberries.

Use Yellow Ochre and your small brush to add a golden ball at the top of the religieuse.

Use a very watery mixture of Sepia and your large brush to loosely paint shadows under the pastries. Once that is dry, use a sharp pencil to carefully write the name of each pastry underneath as a finishing touch.

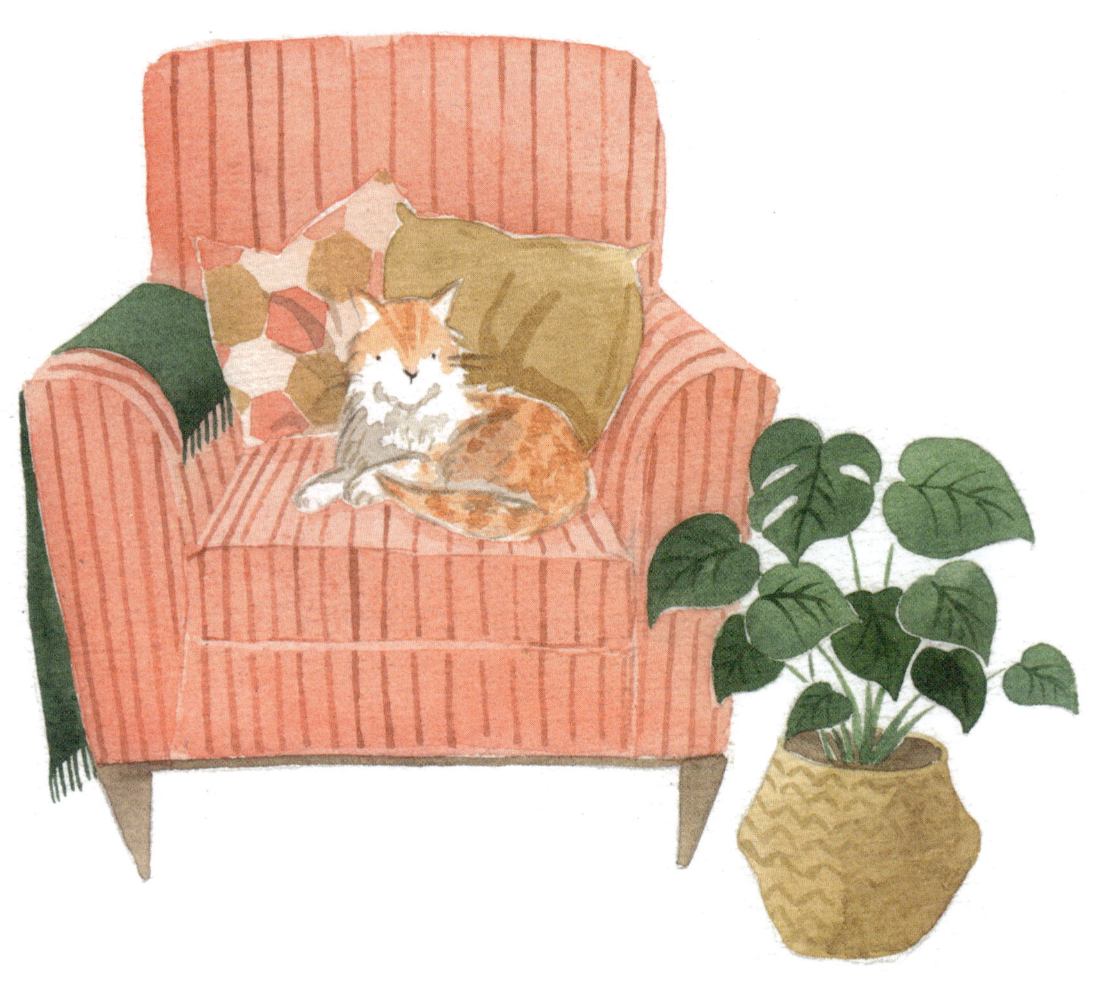

Cat on a Pink Chair

This piece uses layering to add depth and texture to the chair, giving it a three-dimensional look. In this piece we create a warm, cozy scene by using a harmonious limited color palette.

Materials Cold press watercolor paper • Pencil • Large paintbrush • Medium round brush Small round brush

Colors Used Cadmium Red ● Sap Green ● Ultramarine ● Yellow Ochre ● Lamp Black ● Sepia ● Burnt Umber ● Burnt Sienna ●

Lightly sketch in pencil using my sketch as reference. Pay attention to the angles of the chair—the horizontal and vertical lines are all parallel with each other, and the diagonal lines of the arms and seat recede back, giving a sense of perspective.

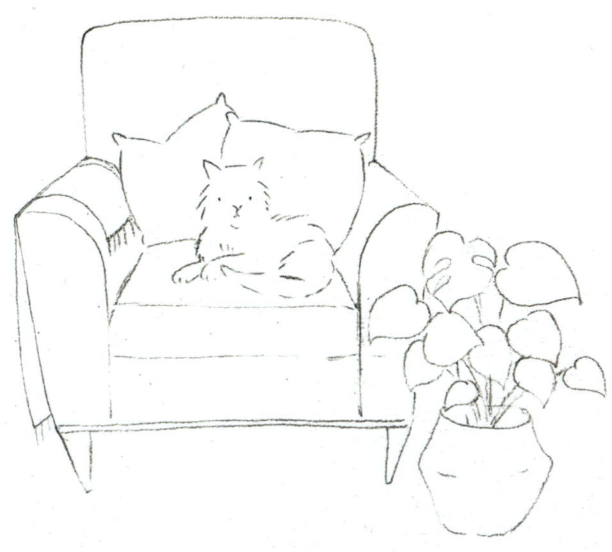

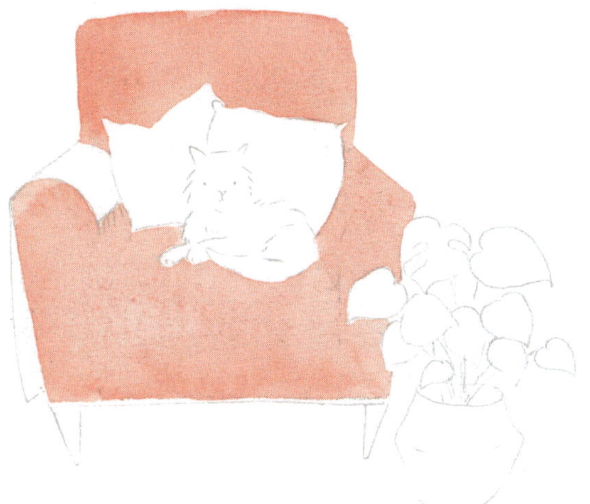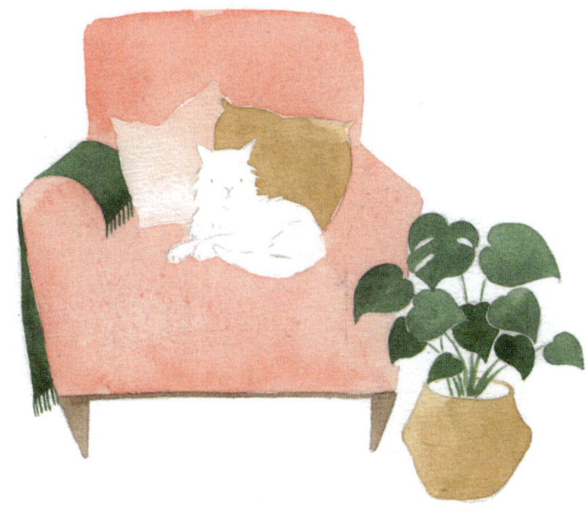

Create a watery mixture of Cadmium Red, and paint the chair pale pink with your large brush.

When that's dry, mix a dark green using Sap Green and Ultramarine, and paint the blanket on the arm of the chair using your medium brush. Add more pigment to the side of the blanket behind the chair so it appears in shadow. Use the same color to paint the plant. Add more water to the green mixture to vary the tone of the leaves, so the leaves at the top of the plant are lighter and those at the bottom are darker.

Mix Yellow Ochre with a tiny bit of Lamp Black and lots of water to make a gold color. Use this color to paint the large cushion behind

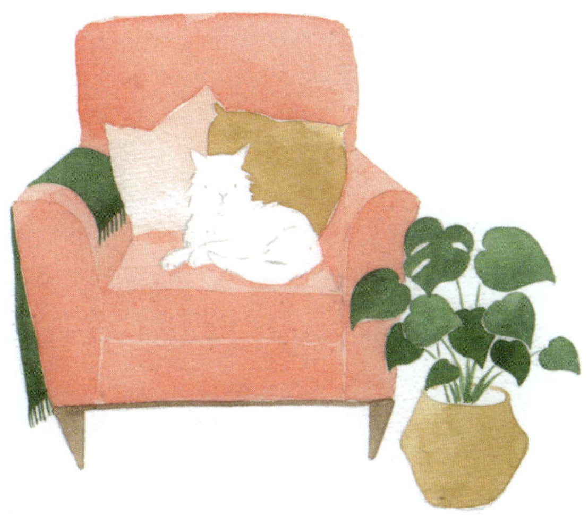

the cat using your medium brush. Use the same color to paint the wicker basket that the plant is in.

Mix Yellow Ochre and Sepia to create a brown. Use this color and your small brush to paint the legs of the chair.

Paint the cushion on the left using a very pale mixture of Cadmium Red with lots of water. This color should be significantly lighter than the pink of the chair.

Mix Cadmium Red with a bit of Sap Green and lots of water to make a muted pink that is slightly darker than the color of the chair. Use this color and your large brush to paint the shadows on the chair using my painting for reference. Paint the front of the arms, the front of the cushion, and the base of the chair. Add shadow underneath the cat and cushions, behind the cushions at the back, and where the arms meet the seat. For the shadow at the back of the chair, use a clean damp brush to blend this shadow so there are no harsh edges.

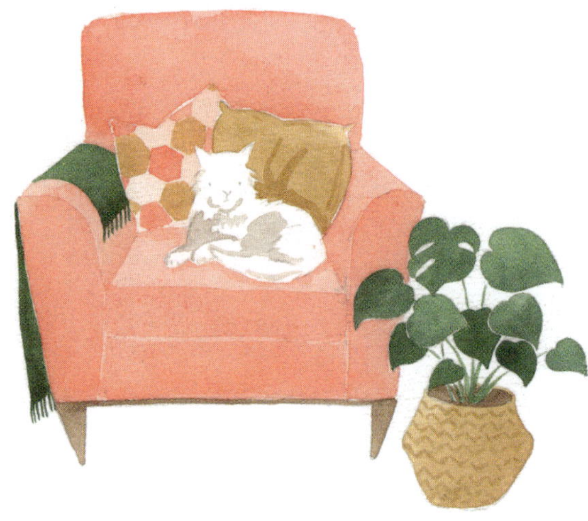

Using Sepia and your small brush, paint soil around the plant. Add more water to the Sepia to paint shadows on the cat using your small brush. Mix a bit of Yellow Ochre with Lamp Black, and paint zigzag lines on the basket using your small brush. Use this color and your medium brush to paint shadows on the cushion behind the cat. Using this color and your small brush, paint patchwork hexagons on the pink cushion. Use Cadmium Red and your small brush to paint more patchwork hexagons on the cushion. The pale pink should show through the unpainted sections to complete the pattern.

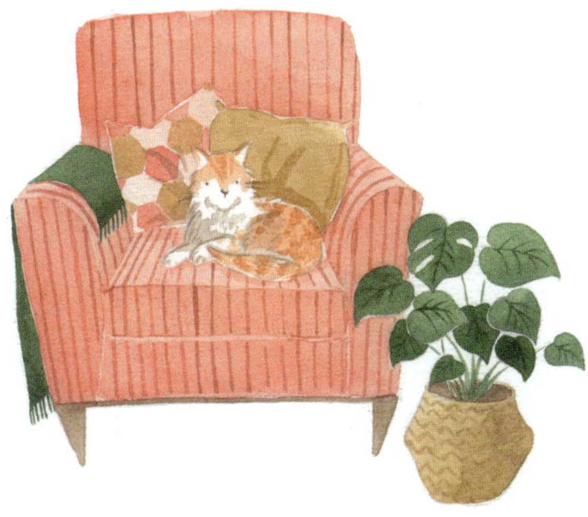

Mix Cadmium Red with a little bit of Sap Green and some water. Using your small brush, paint thin stripes on the chair. Not only will this pattern add interest, but it will help the chair look more three-dimensional. Use this color to outline the chair cushion at the front.

Mix Burnt Sienna with a bit of Yellow Ochre to make a ginger color for the cat. Transfer some of this color to another part of your palette, and add some water to make a lighter version. Paint the top half of the cat's face, tail, and back using your medium brush. When that's dry, use the darker version of the color to loosely paint stripes on the cat's face, back, and tail using your small brush.

Mix Sap Green with Ultramarine to make a dark green, and using your small brush, add veins to the plant.

Create a watery mixture of Sepia, then use your medium brush to add shadow to one side of the basket. Use the same shadow mixture to paint a shadow on the patchwork cushion. Use a darker mixture of Sepia and a small brush to paint the cat's eyes, nose, and whiskers and to add definition around the cat's paws and chest. Add a drop of watery Cadmium Red to its nose.

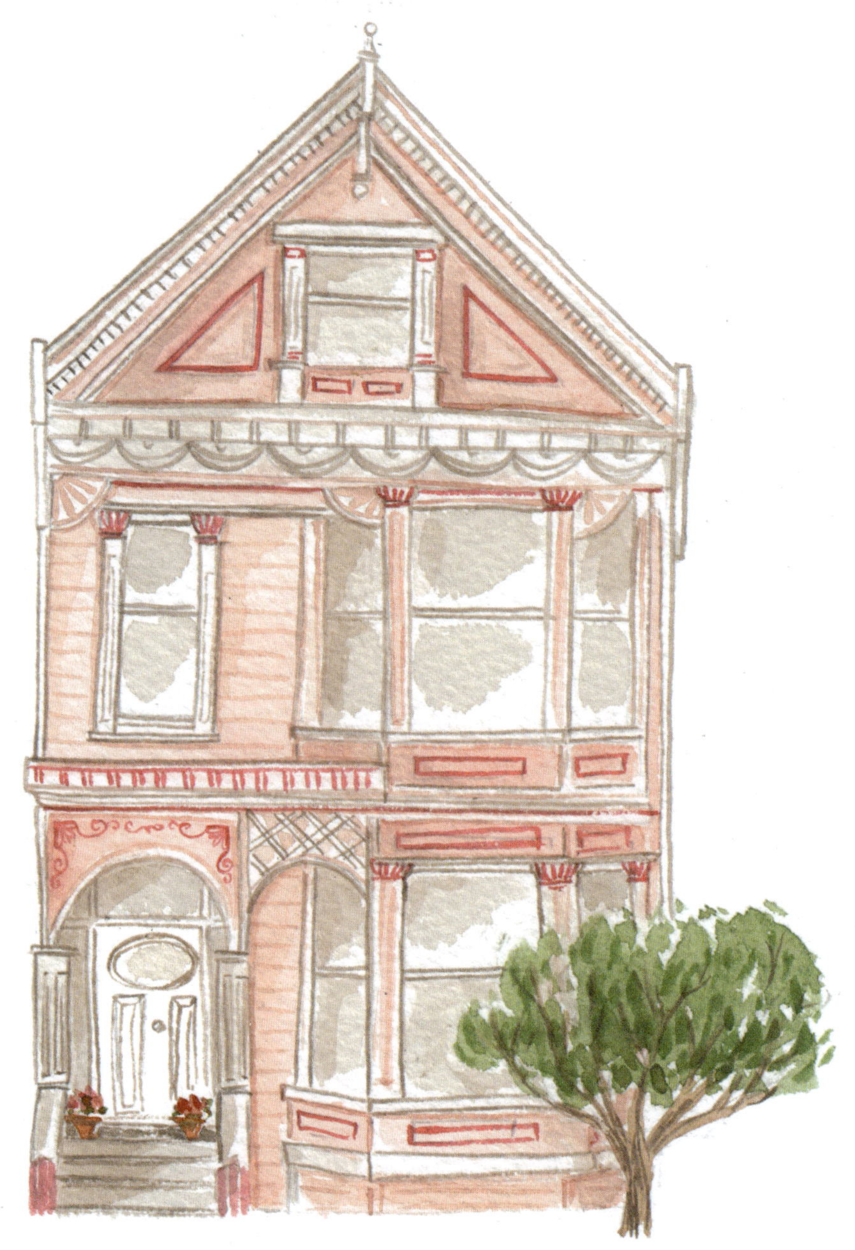

San Francisco House

San Francisco is famous for its colorful Victorian architecture. This piece uses wet-on-dry layering to capture the delicate architectural details of this traditional San Francisco home. By working in layers, we can gradually build up lots of detail and add depth to the image.

Materials Cold press watercolor paper • Pencil • Eraser • Large round brush • Medium round brush • Small round brush

Colors Used Cadmium Red ● Sap Green ● Sepia ● Yellow Ochre ● Burnt Umber ● Alizarin Crimson ● Burnt Sienna ●

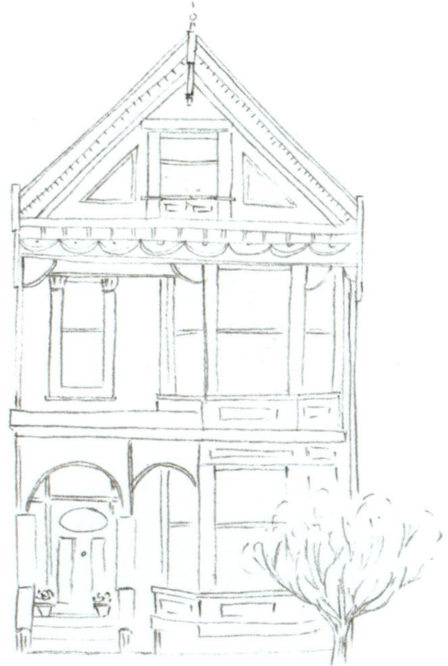

Very lightly sketch out the house using my sketch as reference. You can use a ruler to help you draw the straight lines; however, I prefer to draw my lines freehand.

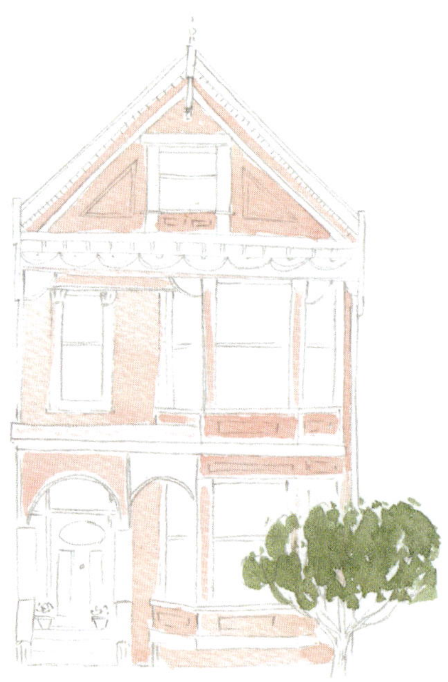

Mix Cadmium Red with lots of water, and paint the peach areas of the house. Use your large brush for the large areas and a medium brush for the smaller areas. I have painted this color quite loosely to keep a freshness to the painting.

When that's dry, create a green mixture of Sap Green with a little Cadmium Red, a little Yellow Ochre, and lots of water. Paint the tree in the foreground using your large brush. Loosely dab the large brush on the paper to create the impression of leaves. You want some of the peach background to show through.

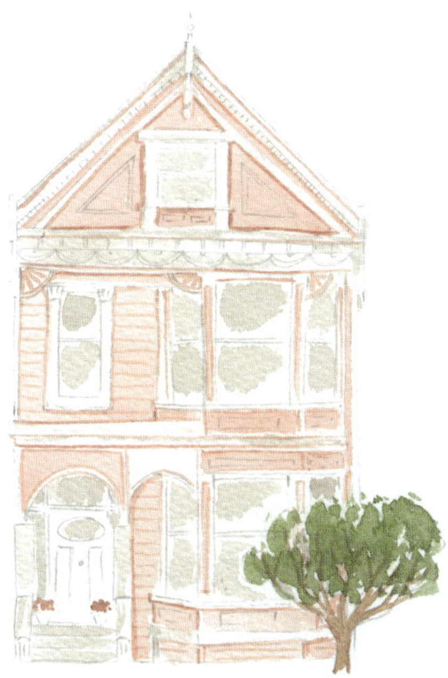

Create a very watery mixture of Sepia, and use your large brush to loosely paint in shadows on the windowpanes and across the white detailing on the house.

Create a watery mixture of Sepia and Burnt Umber, and use your medium brush to paint the trunk of the tree.

When that is completely dry, use your eraser to remove some of the pencil lines from the original sketch. I often remove pencil lines as I go along to keep things looking fresh. Just make sure the paint is 100 percent dry before you do this!

Create a watery mixture of Cadmium Red with a tiny bit of Sap Green, and use your small brush to paint horizontal lines on the house to indicate wood panels. Use this same muted pink color to add shadows and definition to the architectural details using your small brush. Use this color to paint the flowers in the pots.

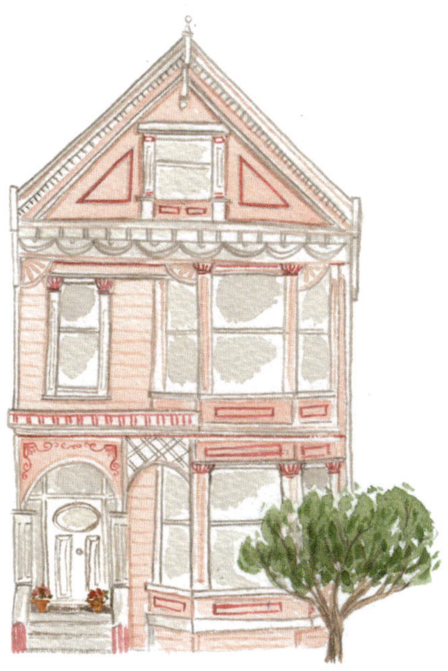

Create a watery mixture of Sepia, and use your small brush to paint the architectural details and outline the windows and the steps. Paint the details on the door, and paint the trellis between the door and window. Add details to the bark of the tree with the same paint mixture and small brush. Use this color to paint the flowers in the pots.

Mix Alizarin Crimson with Cadmium Red. Using your small brush, add the decorative details in red on the window frame, around the door, and on the front of the house. Use a very watery mixture of Cadmium Red and a small brush to fill the gaps of the trellis between the door and window.

Using a mixture of Sap Green with a bit of Sepia and your medium brush, add leaves to the lower half of the tree where it would be in the shadow. Use Burnt Sienna and your small brush to paint the flowerpots on the doorstep.

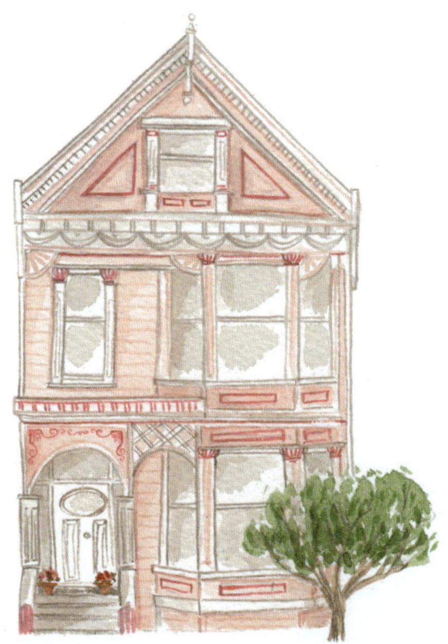

When that's completely dry, use a very watery mixture of Sepia and your large brush to add shadows around the door, across some of the windows, under architectural detailing, and anywhere that would naturally fall in shadow.

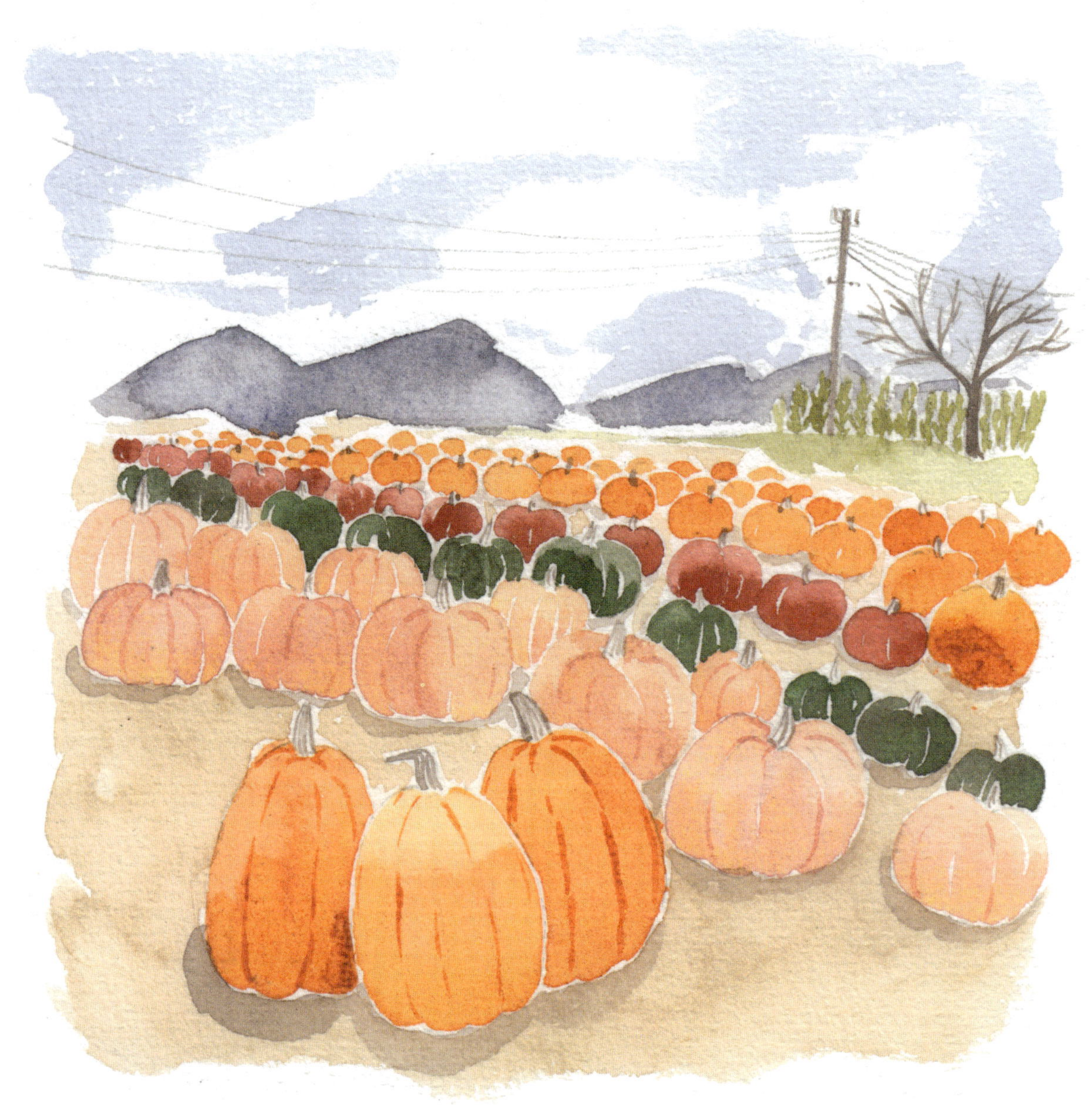

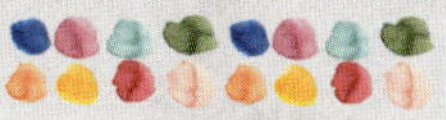

Color Pooling

Color pooling is a technique that allows color to pool in a specific area, leaving white space around it so that it remains a distinct shape. Color pooling is one of my favorite techniques because it balances both the spontaneous and controlled nature of watercolors.

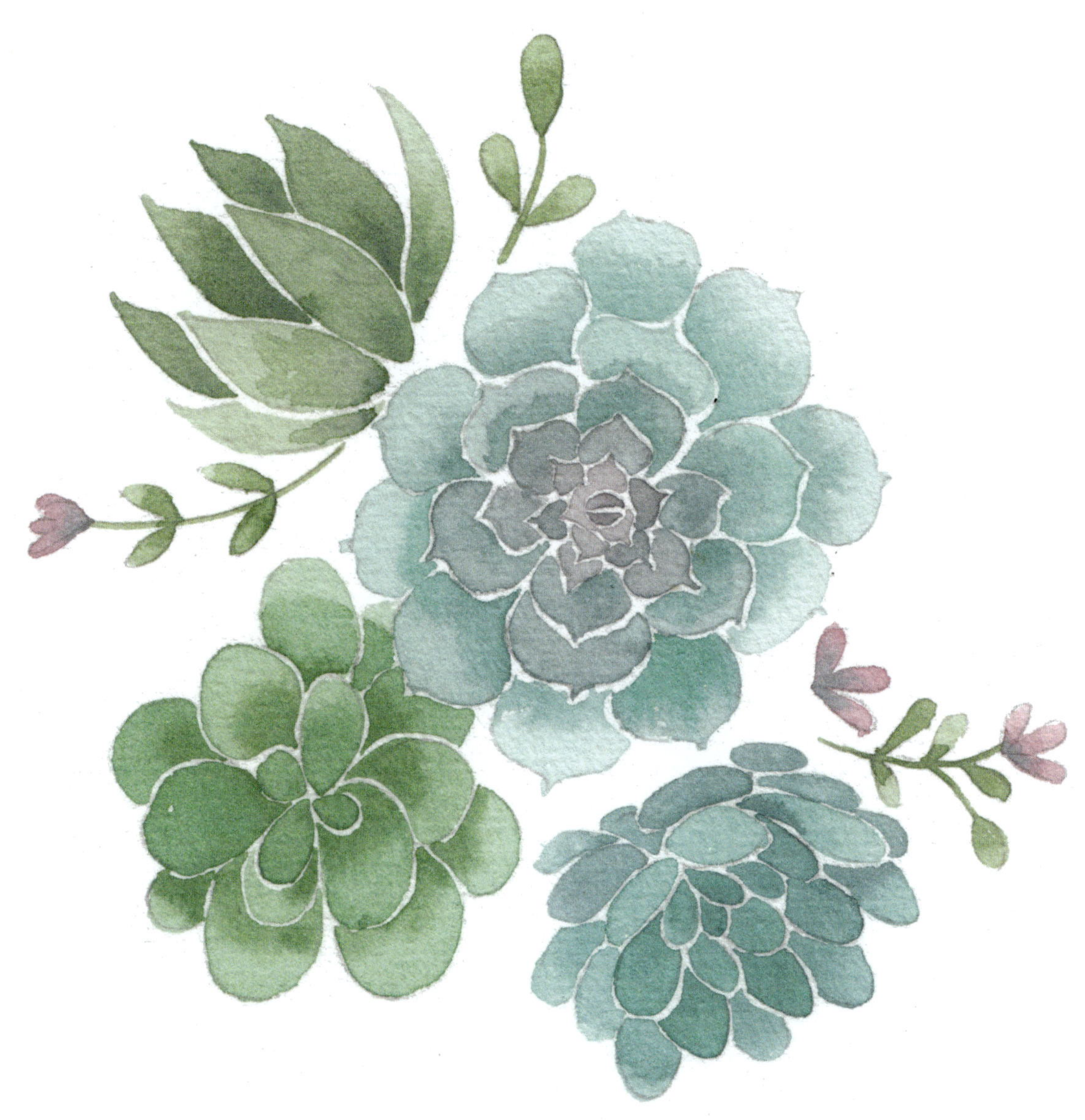

Succulents

Color pooling is the perfect technique for capturing each individual leaf of the succulents and the beautiful shades of green blue and purple they come in.

Materials Cold press watercolor paper • Pencil • Eraser • Medium round brush
Small round brush
Colors Used Viridian Green ● Alizarin Crimson ● Sap Green ● Ultramarine ● Sepia ●
Yellow Ochre ● Cadmium Yellow ●

Sketch the succulents lightly using
a pencil.

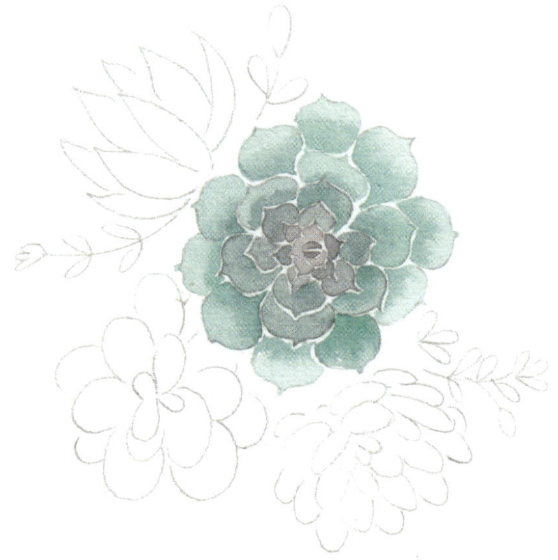

Mix a purple color using the Viridian Green, Alizarin Crimson, and lots of water. Using a small brush, paint the two central leaves on the large succulent. Add a little more water, and paint the next three leaves, allowing white space to show between the leaves. Add a tiny bit more Viridian Green and some water, and paint the next ring of leaves. Repeat the process, adding a tiny bit more green and some more water to the mixture and painting the next ring of leaves. As the leaves start getting bigger, you can play around with varying the tone somewhat. Paint the whole leaf with a light wash of watery paint, then drop a more concentrated version of the same color into the center of the leaf to add depth. Continue in this way, making the paint mixture lighter and greener as the leaves get bigger and closer to the outside, being careful to keep a small white space between all the leaves.

Create a green mixture using Sap Green with a little bit of Ultramarine and a little bit of Sepia. Move half this mixture to another part of your palette and add more water so you have a lighter version of the same color. Use this light color to paint the succulent with pointed leaves. Paint the outside leaves first using your small brush and the lighter mixture.

Add a drop of the darker mixture to the base of the leaves while they are still wet. Paint the next layer of leaves using the same light mixture, and add more of the darker mixture to the center while the leaves are still wet. Make sure there is a thin white space between the leaves so they do not run into each other.

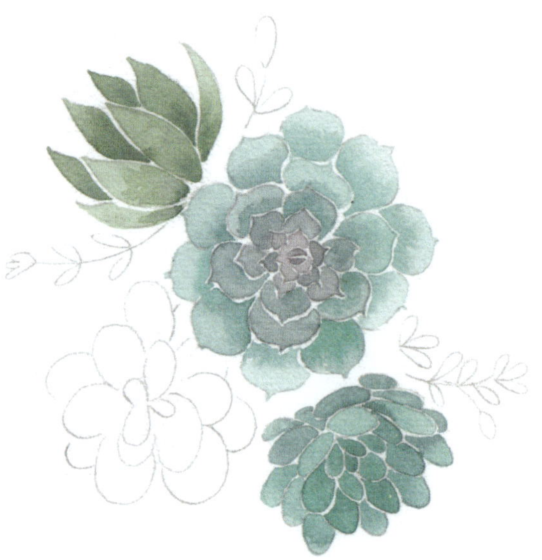 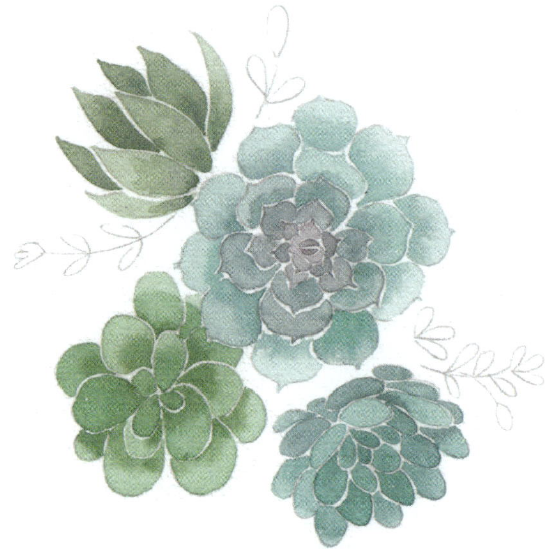

Mix a green with Viridian Green and a bit of Alizarin Crimson. Paint the smallest leaves in the center of the succulent using this mixture and your small brush. Add more water as you paint the leaves getting bigger toward the outside. The leaves in the foreground that appear to be coming toward you should be the lightest. As before, make sure there is a thin white space between leaves, and add a drop more color to the center of some leaves to add depth.

Mix Viridian Green, a bit of Yellow Ochre, and lots of water. Transfer some of this color into another part of your palette, and add more water to make a lighter version of the same color. Paint the small central leaves of the remaining succulent using a small brush. Paint the rest of the leaves moving outward, painting them first with the lighter mixture, then adding a drop of the darker mixture to the center using your small brush.

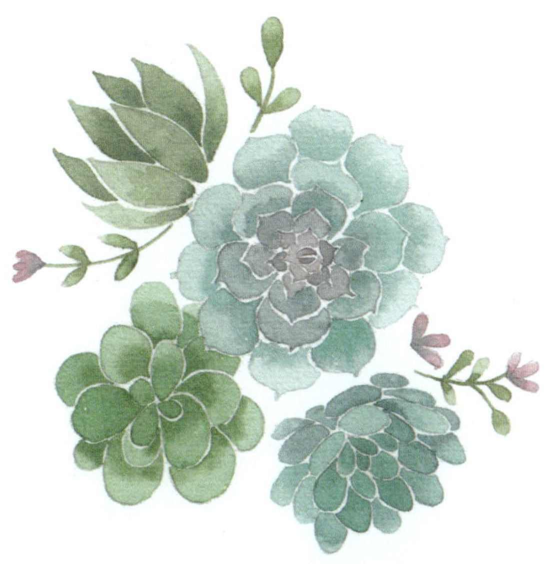

Create another green mix using the Viridian Green, Cadmium Yellow, and lots of water. Using your small brush, paint the leafy tendrils. Add a drop more mixture to the center of each leaf. Create a pinkish purple using Alizarin Crimson with a bit of Viridian Green. Using a small brush, paint the flowers at the end of the tendrils. Add a drop more Viridian Green at the base of each flower.

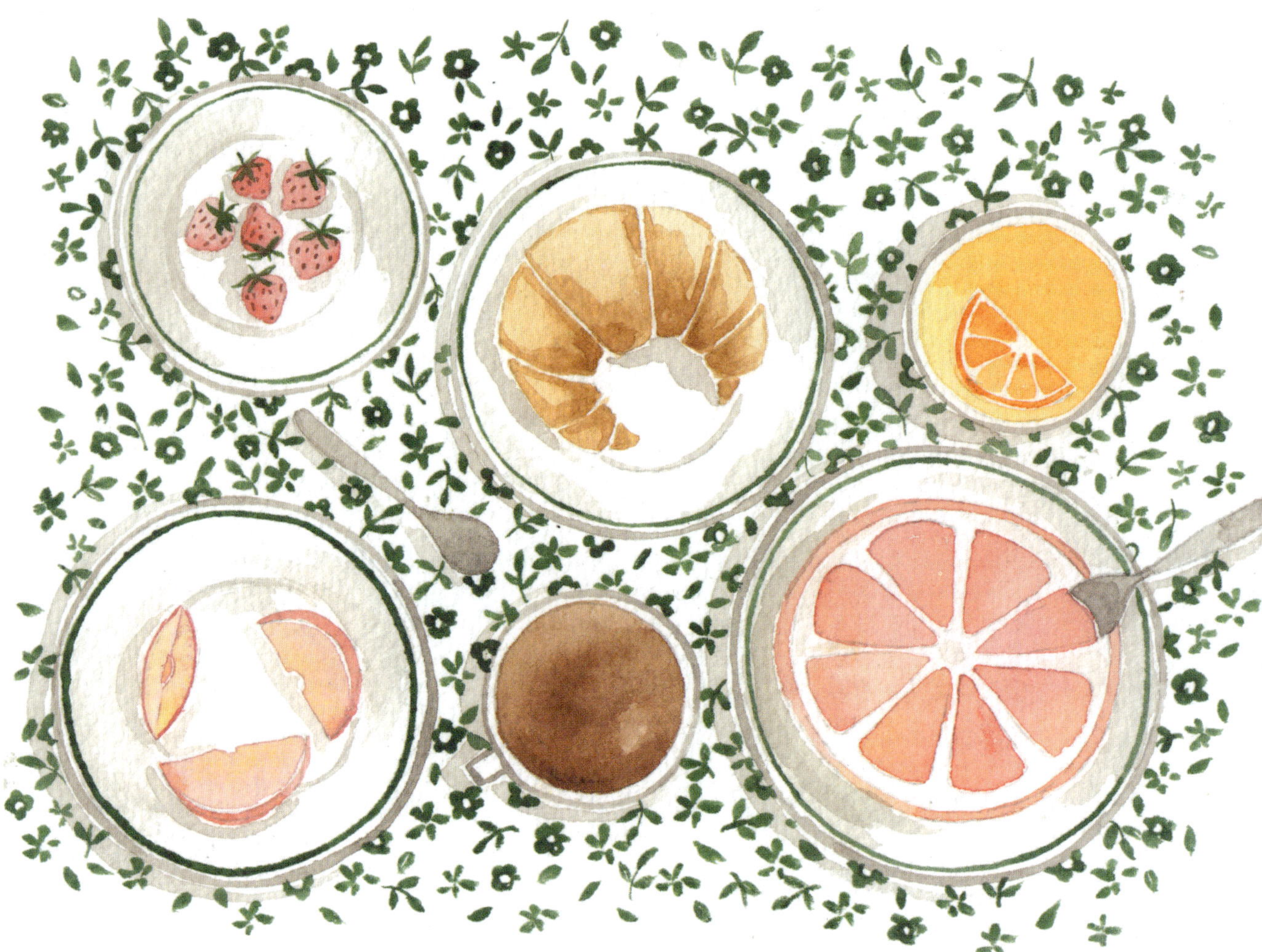

Breakfast Table

This piece shows a pretty breakfast table from an overhead view, which means we see it from directly above. This gives us an interesting perspective and a repeating circle motif. The color pooling technique is perfect for making the coffee and orange juice look liquid and adds a lot of variety to the fruit and croissant.

Materials Cold press watercolor paper • Pencil • Eraser • Medium round brush • Small round brush
Colors Used Yellow Ochre ● Burnt Umber ● Cadmium Yellow ● Cadmium Red ●
Burnt Sienna ● Sepia ● Alizarin Crimson ● Lemon Yellow ● Permanent Rose ● Sap Green ●
Lamp Black ● Ultramarine ●

Very lightly sketch the design using a pencil. If you're struggling with the circles, find small round objects to trace, like a glass, can, or cup.

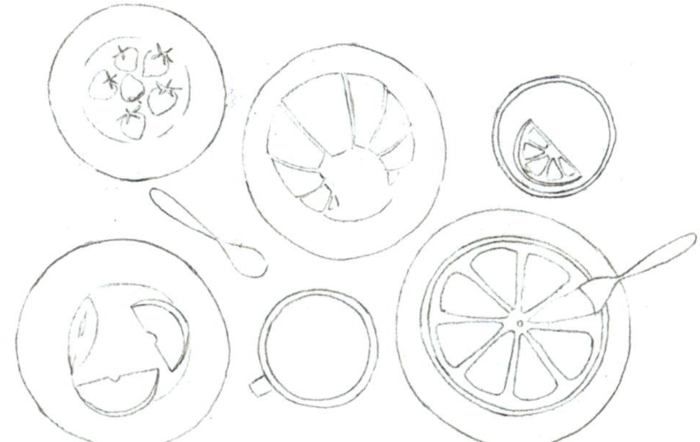

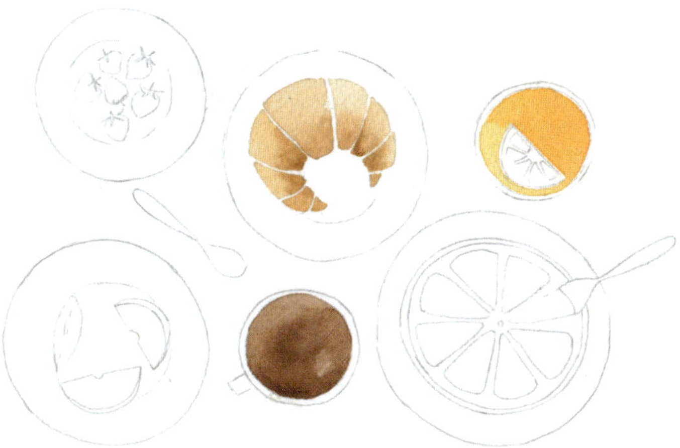

Mix Yellow Ochre with a bit of Burnt Umber to make a light brown for the croissant. Transfer a little of this mixture to another part of your palette, and add more water to create a lighter version of the same color. Paint each individual segment of the croissant using your medium brush and the light mixture. Add a drop of the darker mixture in the center of each segment while it is still wet. Allow a thin white line to remain between each segment.

Mix a light orange using Cadmium Yellow, Cadmium Red, and lots of water to paint the glass of orange juice using your medium brush. Add more pigment to one side of the glass.

Mix Burnt Sienna with a little Sepia and lots of water to make a rich coffee color. Paint the coffee in the cup using your medium brush, and allow the color to pool in the center and around the edge. Add a drop more Sepia to the edge of the cup.

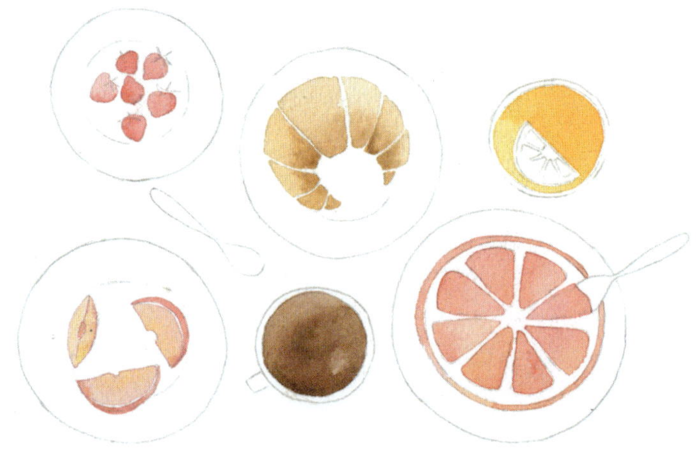

Mix Cadmium Red with Alizarin Crimson and lots of water, and paint your strawberries using your small brush. Allow the color to pool in some strawberries to give a varied look.

Mix Lemon Yellow with a little Permanent Rose and lots of water to make a color for the peach flesh. Mix Lemon Yellow with a bit more Permanent Rose and slightly less water to make a color for the peach skin. Paint the peach flesh using your small brush and the lighter color. Paint the peach skin using the darker color with your small brush, leaving a white space between the skin and the flesh. Just allow the darker color of the skin to touch the peach flesh at the end of the segment so a tiny bit of the darker pink bleeds into the peach. For the upright segment of peach, paint one section at a time using the lighter peach color, and add a drop of the darker color for the center.

Mix Cadmium Yellow with a bit of Permanent Rose and lots of water to make a color for the pink grapefruit. Use your medium brush to paint each individual section of the grapefruit, allowing pigment to pool in different areas. Use your small brush and the same mixture to paint the skin around the outside.

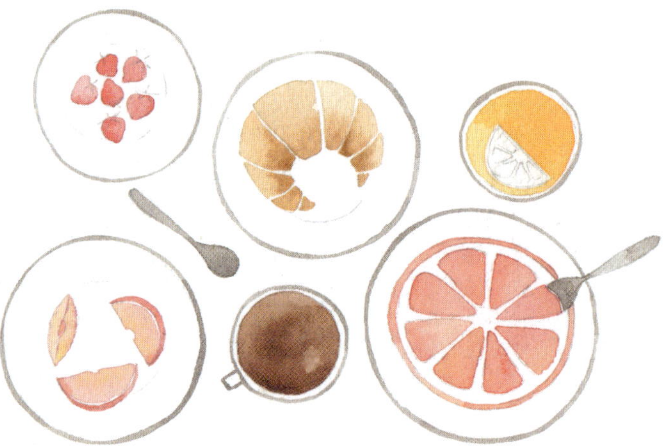

Mix Lamp Black with the Sepia and lots of water to make a warm gray. Use this color and your small brush to outline all the plates and cups. Use the same color on your medium brush to paint the two teaspoons, allowing more pigment to pool in the bowls of the teaspoons.

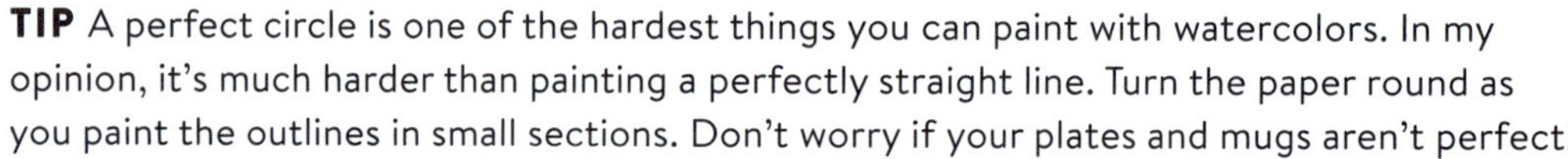

TIP A perfect circle is one of the hardest things you can paint with watercolors. In my opinion, it's much harder than painting a perfectly straight line. Turn the paper round as you paint the outlines in small sections. Don't worry if your plates and mugs aren't perfect!

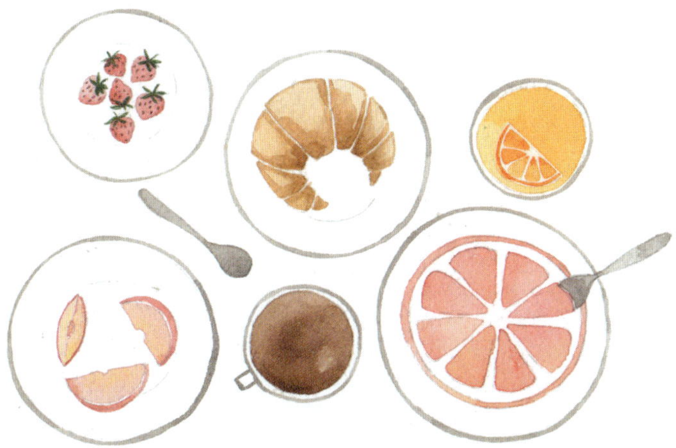

Mix Sap Green with a little Lamp Black, and paint leaves on the strawberries using your small brush. Mix Cadmium Red with a tiny bit of Lamp Black, and use your small brush to paint dots on the strawberries.

Mix Cadmium Red and Cadmium Yellow to make an orange, and paint the slice of orange floating in the glass of orange juice using a small brush. Leave white space between each segment and the skin.

Use your small brush and a bit of the mixture you made for the peach skin to add a tiny strip of skin on each side of the upright peach slice.

Use the Yellow Ochre and Burnt Umber mix you made for the croissant to add more shadows to the sections of the croissant, and roughly outline the segments using your medium brush to give the croissant more depth and a flaky, layered look.

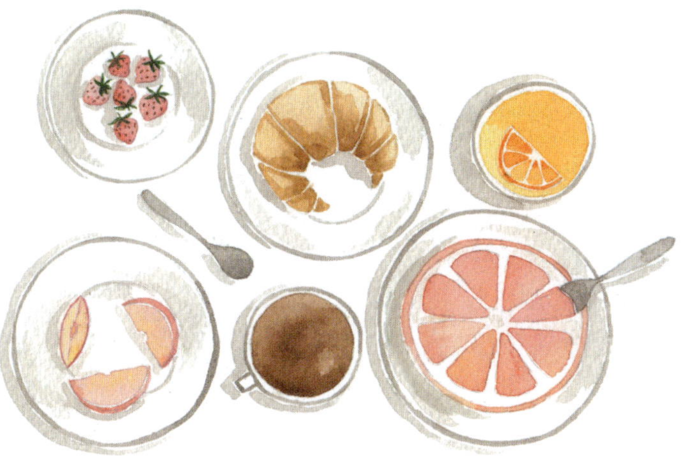

When everything is dry, erase any remaining pencil marks. Add more water to the warm gray mixture you made earlier. We are going to use this color to paint the shadows. Paint pale shadows around the fruit, the croissant, and under the spoons using your medium brush. Add pale shadows on the plate rims. Paint a thin line of shadow under the rim of the plates and a larger shadow under the cup of coffee and the glass of orange juice.

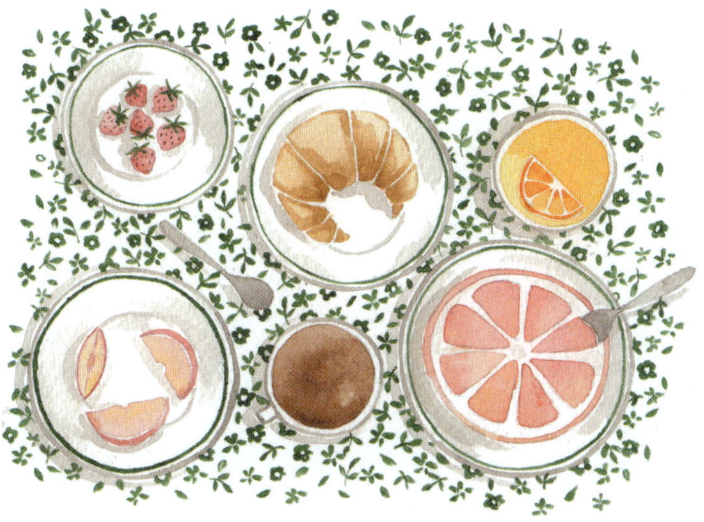

Mix Sap Green with Ultramarine to make a dark green. Use this color and your small brush to carefully add a thin green line around the edges of the plates. Use this mixture and a small brush to paint a scattered floral pattern behind the plates to indicate a tablecloth. For the simple flowers, paint each petal with a single dab of the brush. For the flowers with the white center, paint a small circle first then add four or five petals around the outside. For the little stems, paint a curved line first, then add three leaves. Make sure you paint some half flowers and leaves disappearing under the plates and cutlery so that it looks like they are sitting on a tablecloth. This is obviously a time-consuming process. If you want to speed things up a little bit, you can make the flowers and leaves larger and leave more space between them.

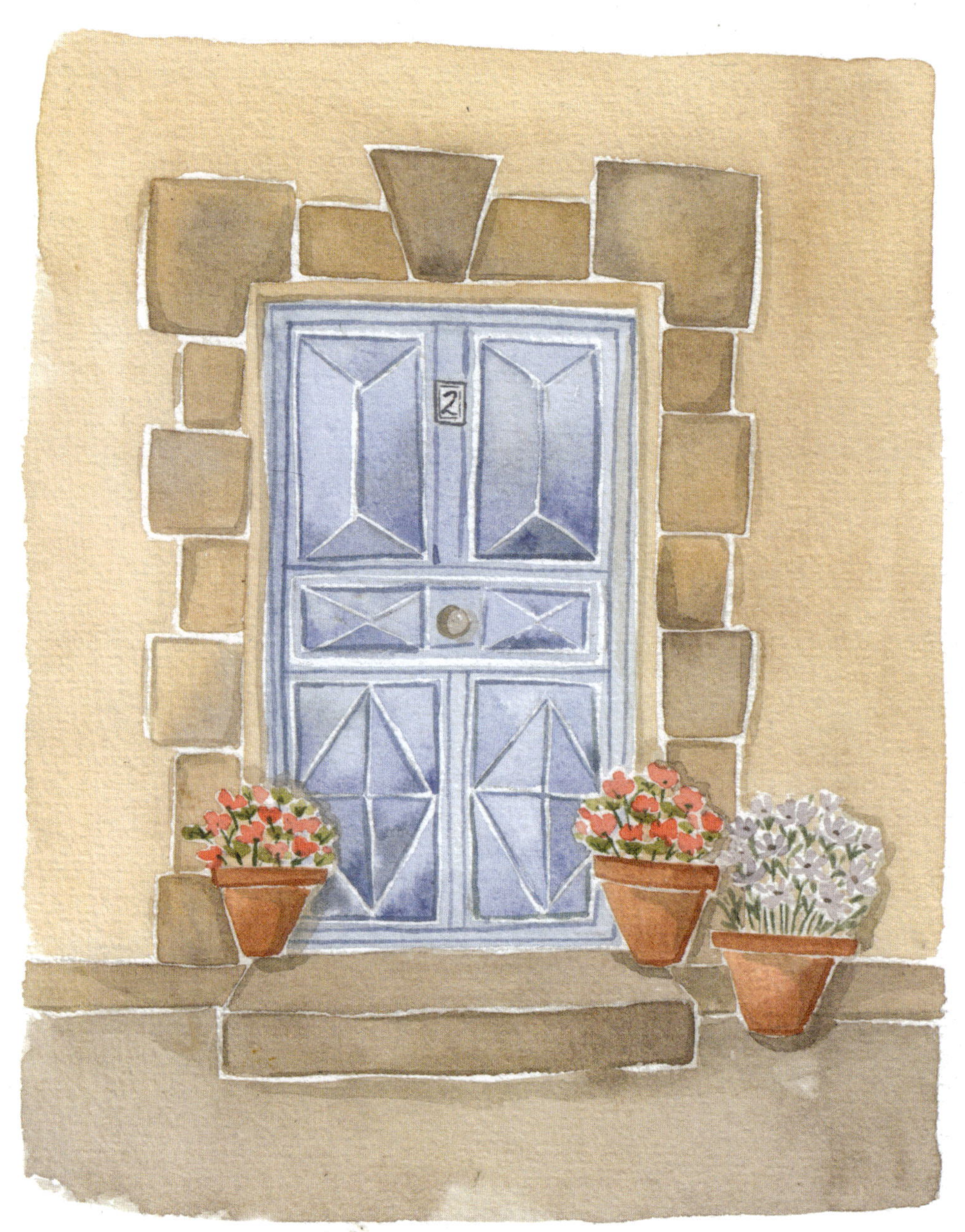

French Door

This piece is inspired by all the beautiful antique doors I saw while visiting Île de Ré in France. The color pooling technique is perfect for capturing all the beautiful variations in tone in the stonework and in the intricately carved wooden door. This piece is very easy to adapt. If you would rather the door be a different color or the pots contain a different type of flower, go for it!

Materials Cold press watercolor paper • Pencil • Eraser • Large round brush • Medium round brush • Small round brush

Colors Used Sepia ● Yellow Ochre ● Cadmium Red ● Cadmium Yellow ● Ultramarine ● Sap Green ● Burnt Sienna ●

Very lightly sketch the design using my sketch as reference. Don't worry about getting the lines perfectly straight; it will add to the charm if they are a little bit wonky.

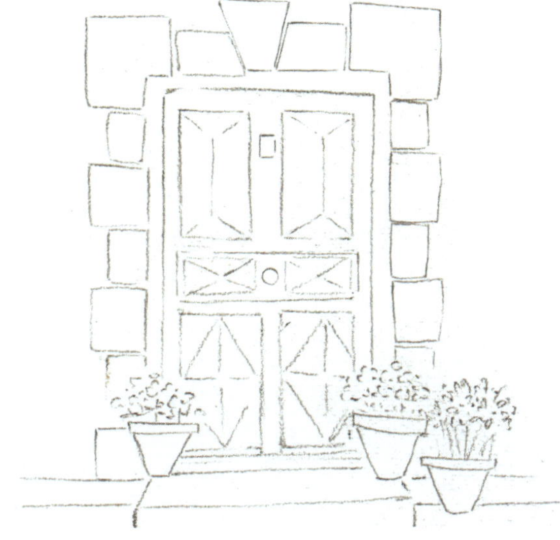

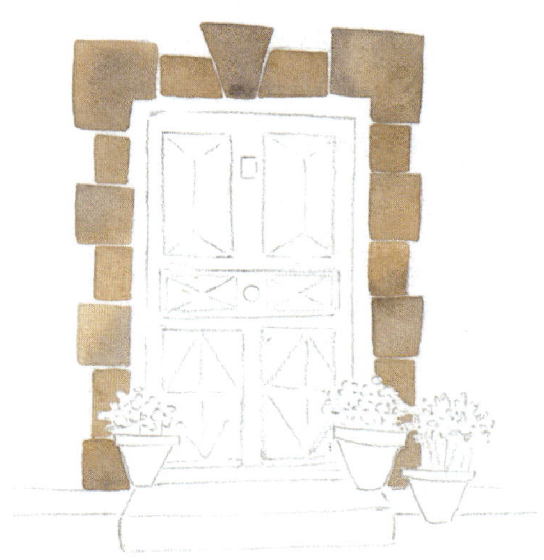

Mix Yellow Ochre, Sepia, and lots of water. Make another color mix of just Sepia and water. Using your medium brush, paint the large stones around the door, leaving a thin white gap between them. Start by painting them with the Sepia and Yellow Ochre mixture, then add a drop of Sepia to some of them. Allow the color to pool randomly.

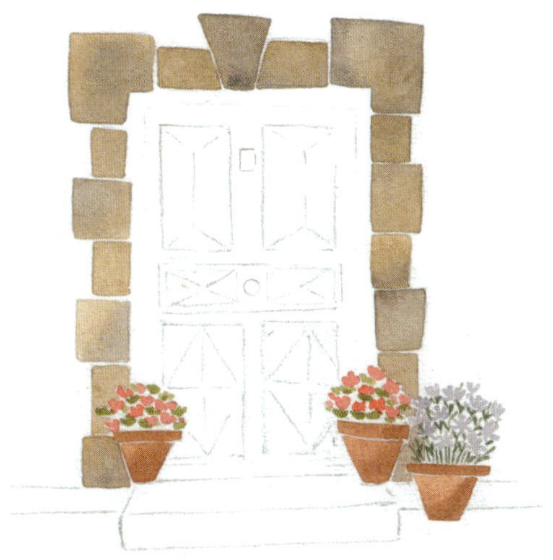

When that is dry, paint the pots of flowers. Paint the geraniums using a watery mix of Cadmium Red and your small brush. Use your brush to make loose dabs of the red mixture to indicate flowers. Create a green with Cadmium Yellow and Ultramarine, and paint the leaves of the geranium. Mix Ultramarine and Cadmium Red to make a muted purple, and use your small brush to paint the purple daisies. Add more Ultramarine to the green mixture, and paint the stems of the daisies using your small brush.

Mix Yellow Ochre with Burnt Sienna and a tiny bit of Sepia to create a terra-cotta color. Using your medium brush, paint the terra-cotta pots. Allow more color to pool in some areas to add a variation. Leave a tiny white line between the rim and the base of the pot.

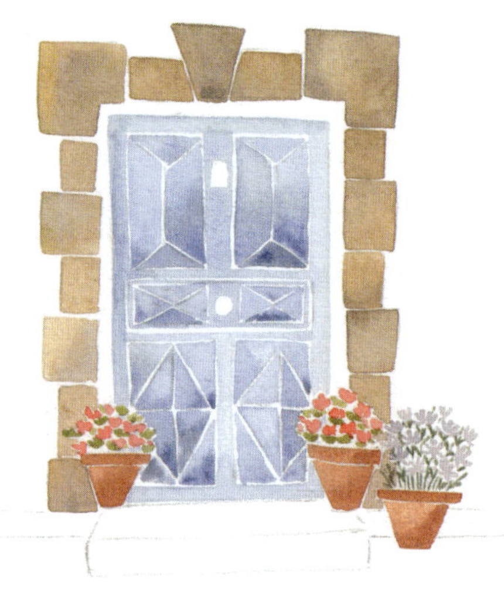 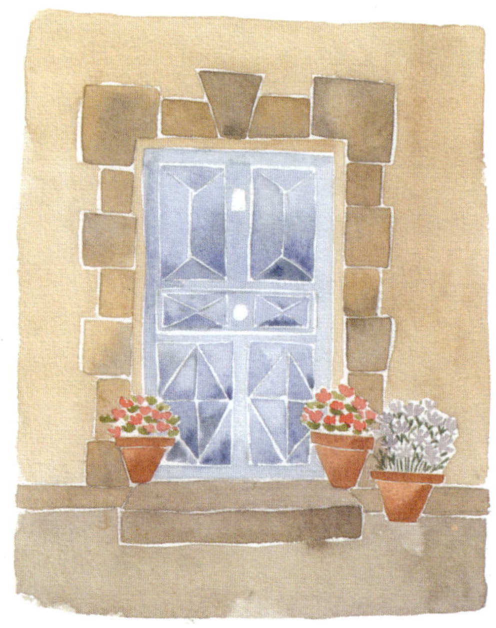

Mix Ultramarine with a tiny bit of Sepia and lots of water to make a muted blue. Also create a separate mixture of Ultramarine with lots of water to make a light blue. Use your medium brush and both mixtures to paint the door. Paint one section of the door at a time with the light blue mix, then add a drop of the muted blue mix while it's wet to add variety. Add more of the muted blue mix to the panels that would appear in shadow. Leave a white space between each individual section of the door.

Create a very watery mixture of Yellow Ochre and Sepia. Using your medium brush, paint the space between the door and the stones. Using your large brush, paint the wall. Add more Sepia to the mixture, and paint the step in front of the door using your medium brush. Add more water, and paint the ground with your small brush. Leave a thin white space between the edges of the step and the ground.

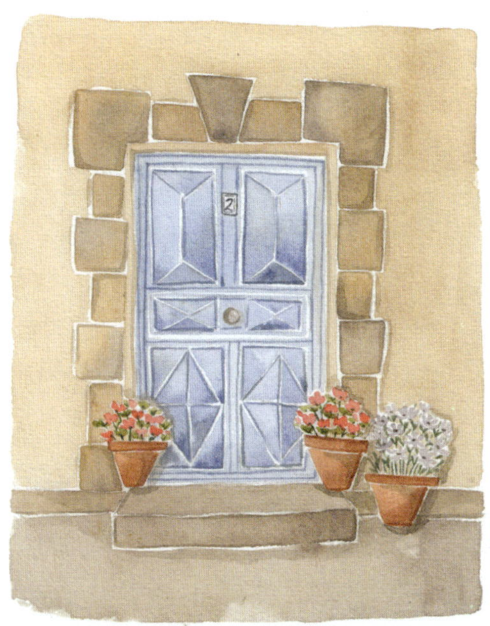

Use Ultramarine and your small brush to paint the detailing on the door. To help you paint thin, neat lines, remove any excess paint from the brush and make sure the paint mixture isn't too watery. Mix Ultramarine with a little bit of Sepia, and carefully paint the door number. Paint the door handle with a watery mixture of Sepia and your small brush. When that's dry, use a darker mixture of Sepia to add a shadow on one side.

Use a watery mixture of Sepia and your medium brush to add shadows under the plant pot, around the edges of the doorstep, and along the edges of the stones around the door. Mix Sap Green with a little bit of Sepia, and use your small brush to paint stems on the geraniums. Use Sepia and your small brush to paint centers in the purple daisies.

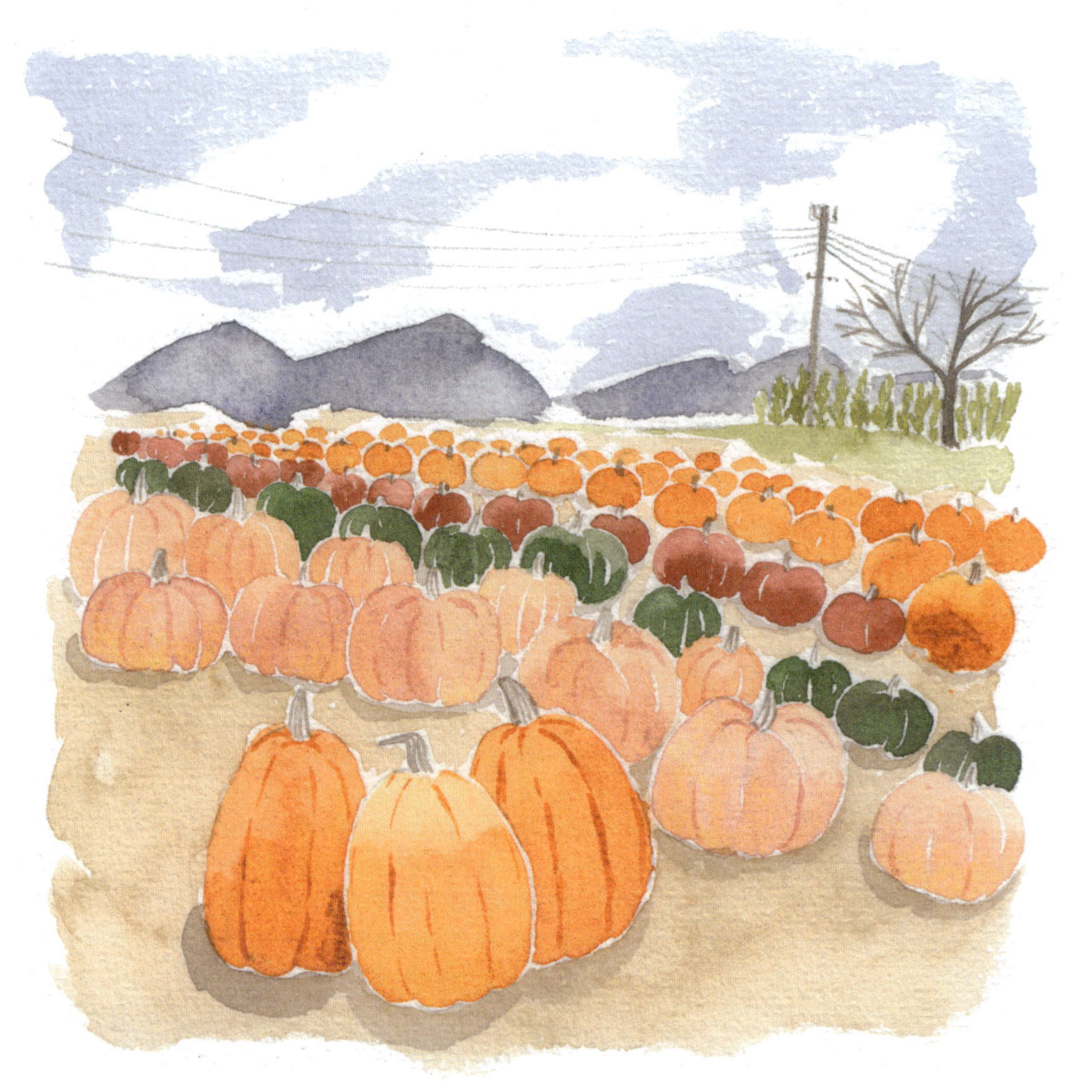

Pumpkin Patch

This piece is inspired by a visit to a beautiful pumpkin patch on a sunny autumn day in California. I was so moved by the beautiful variety of colors and shapes of pumpkins, and the subtle color-mixing capabilities of watercolor are the perfect way to recreate that.

Materials Cold press watercolor paper • Pencil • Eraser • Large round brush • Medium round brush • Small round brush

Colors Used Cadmium Yellow 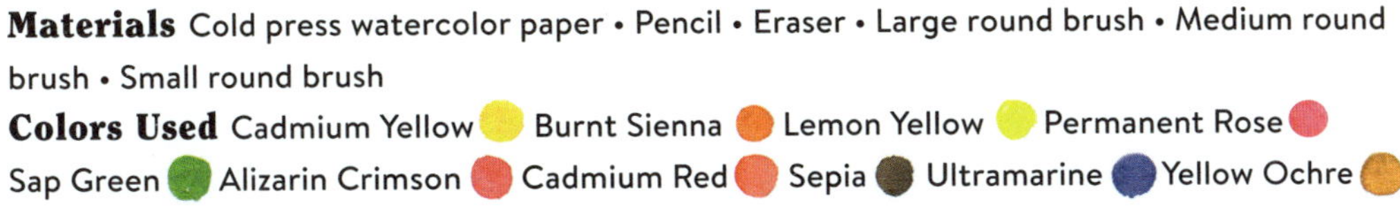 Burnt Sienna Lemon Yellow Permanent Rose Sap Green Alizarin Crimson Cadmium Red Sepia Ultramarine Yellow Ochre

Lightly sketch the design using my sketch as reference. Don't worry about getting a great amount of detail for the pumpkins in the background. You just want to get a sense of the general composition.

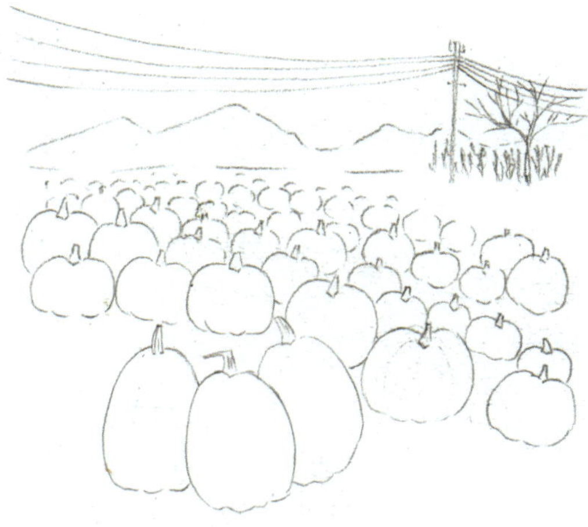

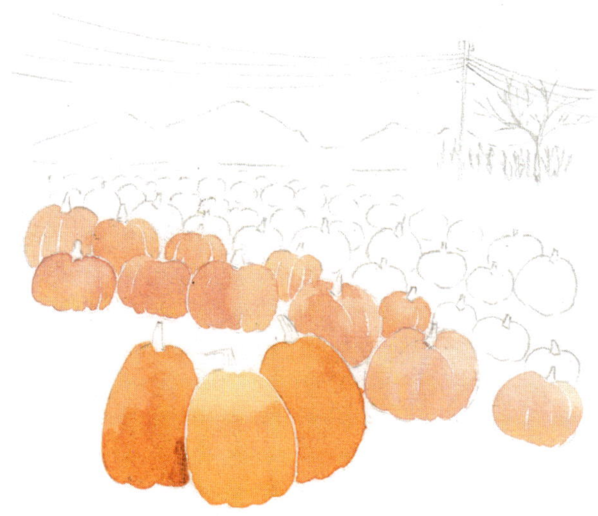

Mix an orange using Cadmium Yellow with a little Burnt Sienna and lots of water. Paint the three pumpkins in the foreground, allowing the color to pool at the bottom of each pumpkin and leaving a thin white space between the pumpkins.

Mix Lemon Yellow with a bit of Permanent Rose and lots of water to create a pale peachy orange. Using this color, paint the next row of pumpkins using your medium brush. Paint each pumpkin using a series of small, curved brushstrokes, pulling the brush down from the top of the pumpkin to the bottom. Leave an occasional bit of white space between the stripes and between the pumpkins. While the pumpkins are still wet, add more pigment at the bottom to create variation.

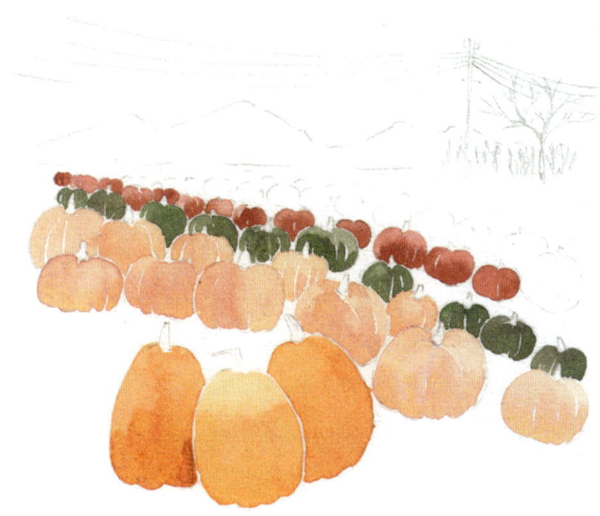

Mix Sap Green with a little bit of Alizarin Crimson to make a dark muted green. Paint the next row of pumpkins behind using the same technique and your small brush.

Mix Cadmium Red with a little bit of Sepia to make a reddish brown, and paint the next row of pumpkins behind using the same technique and your small brush.

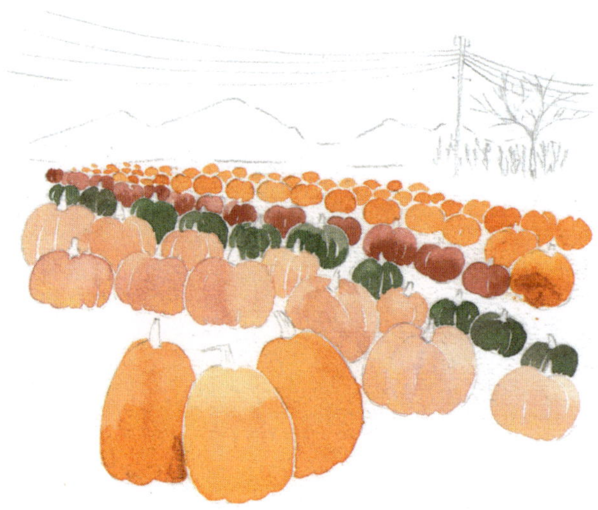

Mix Burnt Sienna and Cadmium Yellow to make a warm orange, and paint all remaining pumpkins using the same technique and your small brush. As they get smaller in the distance, just paint loose circles or semicircles. Don't try to include any detail.

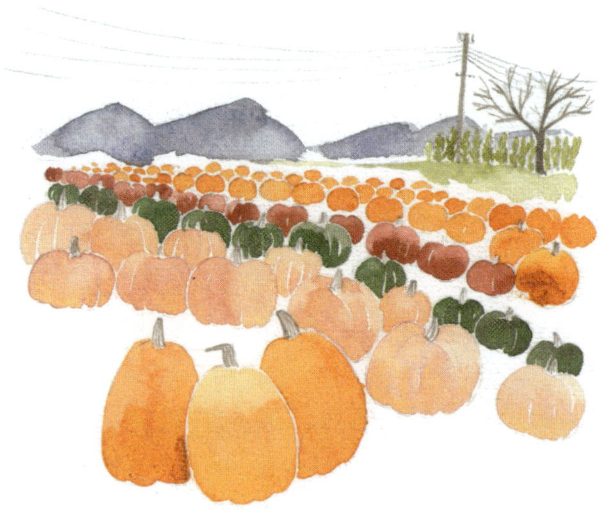

Mix Cadmium Yellow with a little Ultramarine to make a yellowy green. Use a small brush to paint a cornfield in the distance. Add more water to the mixture to loosely paint some grass beneath.

Use your small brush and Sepia to paint thin lines on the stems of the pumpkins. Use your small brush and Sepia to also paint the tree and the telegraph pole.

Mix Ultramarine with Cadmium Red to make a muted purple for the mountains. Using your large brush, loosely paint the mountains in the distance, keeping the edges rough and allowing the color to pool in some areas.

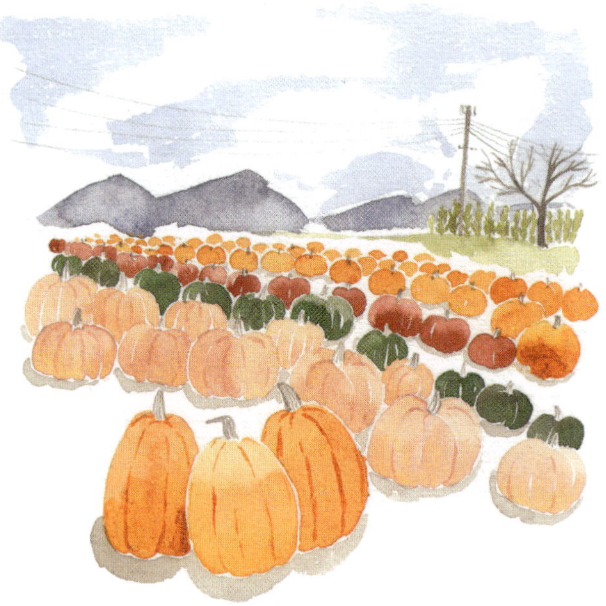

When that's dry, mix some more water and more Ultramarine with the purple mixture you made for the mountains. Loosely paint the sky using your large brush and leaving large white areas to indicate clouds. Less is more; keep the blue areas roughly painted and sparse.

Mix Burnt Sienna with a bit of Cadmium Yellow. Using a small brush, paint a few thin lines on the pumpkins in the foreground to add definition. Mix Lemon Yellow and Permanent Rose, and use this mixture and your small brush to paint a couple of thin lines to add more definition to the next row of pumpkins. Again, less is more; keep the lines thin and delicate. It's easy to make the lines stronger if you think it needs more definition, but it's hard to make them lighter.

Use a watery mixture of Sepia and your medium brush to paint shadows under the pumpkins.

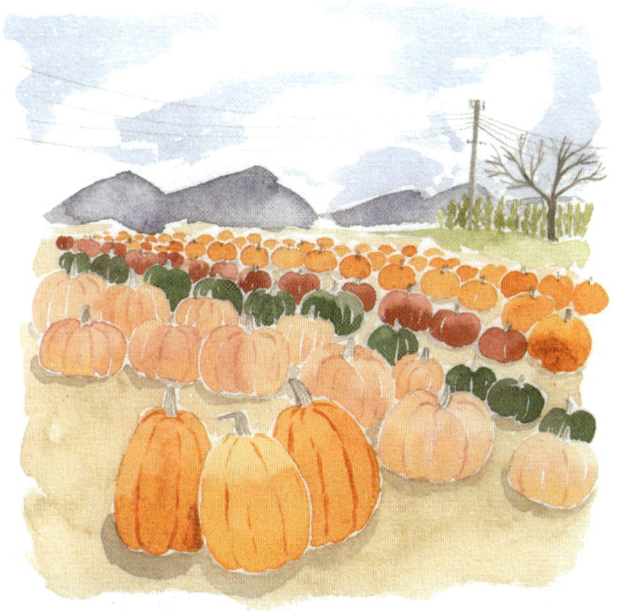

When that's all completely dry, erase any remaining pencil marks. Mix Yellow Ochre, Sepia, and lots of water, and paint the background using your large brush. Keep the background loose, and don't overwork it. Small gaps between the background and the pumpkins are fine. This very watery wash will allow the shadows under the pumpkins to show through. Make sure they are completely dry before you do this step, otherwise they could bleed.

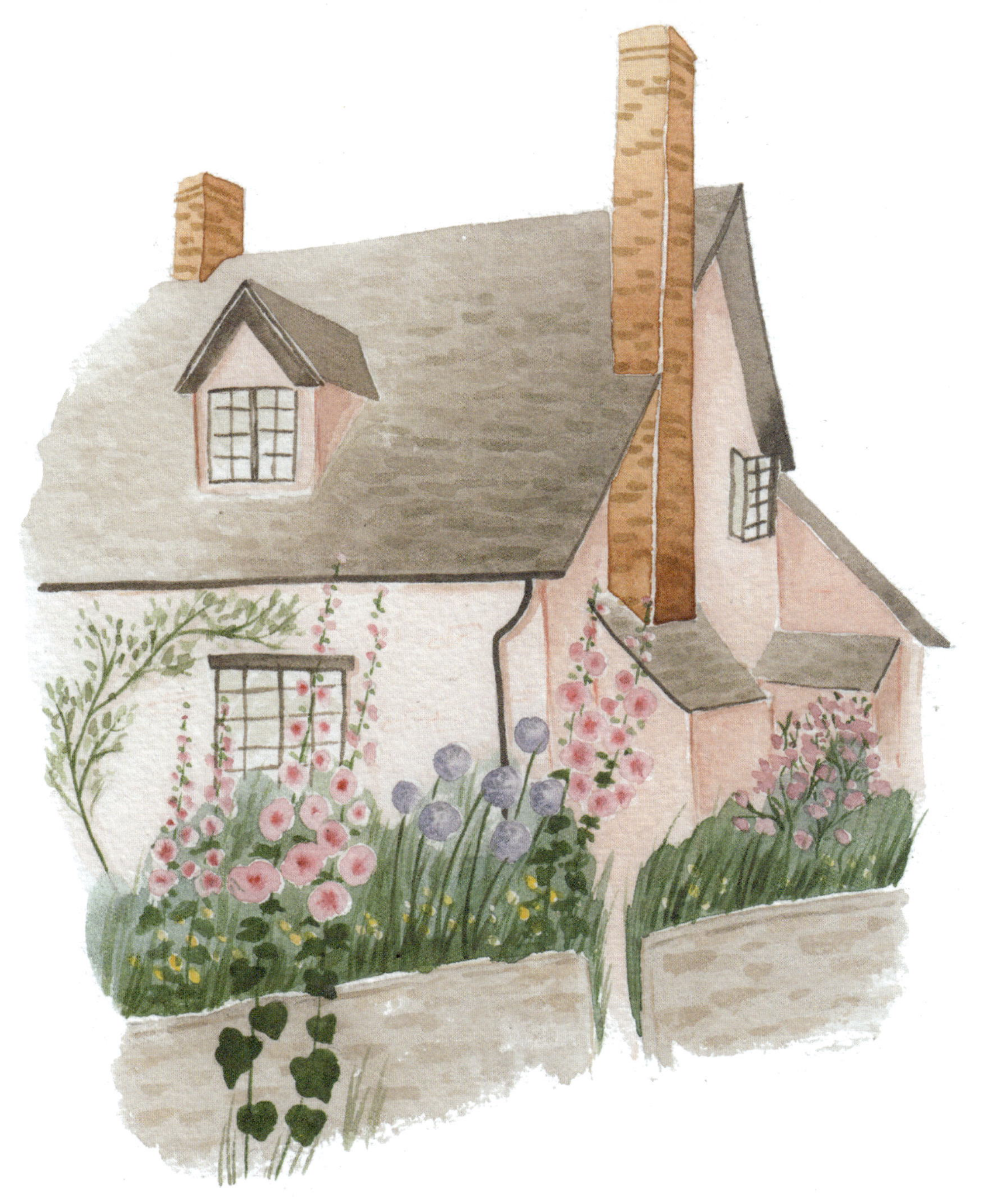

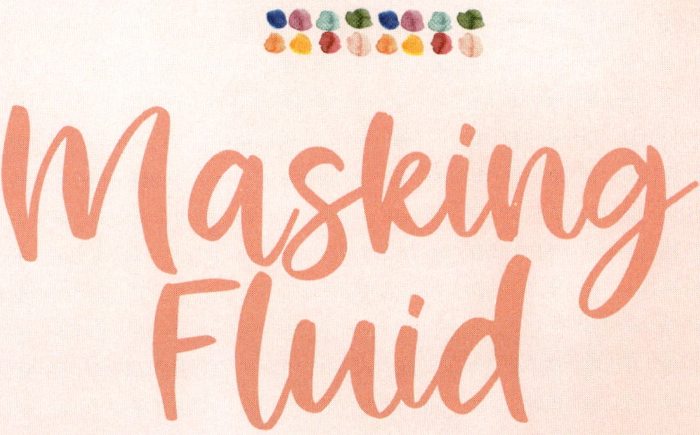

Masking Fluid

Masking fluid creates some beautiful and unique effects, but some painters struggle with when and how to use it. This chapter will show the many creative ways it can be used.

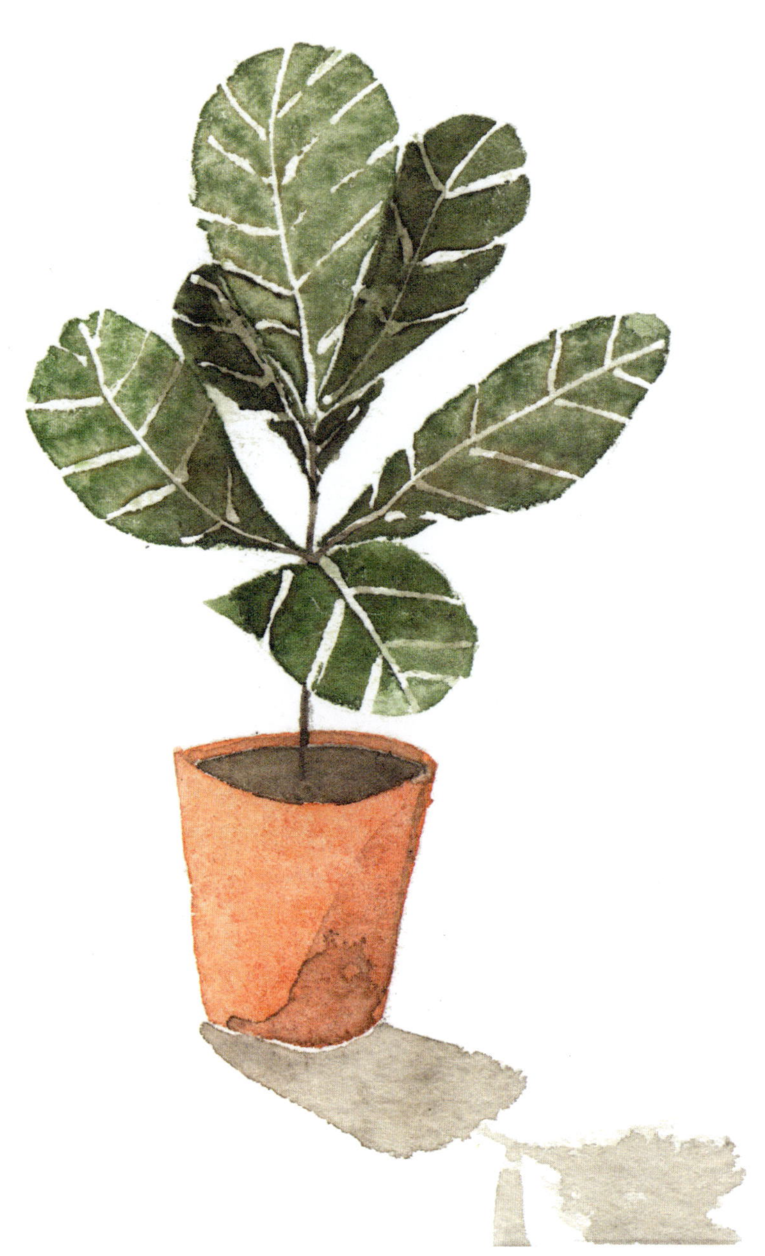

Fiddle Leaf Fig

This simple piece uses masking fluid to create thin white lines. Masking fluid is best used sparingly for small areas, as shown in this project. This piece will be much easier if you have a masking fluid pen, which will help you draw thin lines of masking fluid; if you don't have one, you can use a very small brush instead.

Materials Hot press watercolor paper • Pencil • Eraser • Masking fluid pen • Small round brush
Medium round brush

Colors Used Sap Green ● Alizarin Crimson ● Cadmium Red ● Burnt Sienna ●
Sepia ●

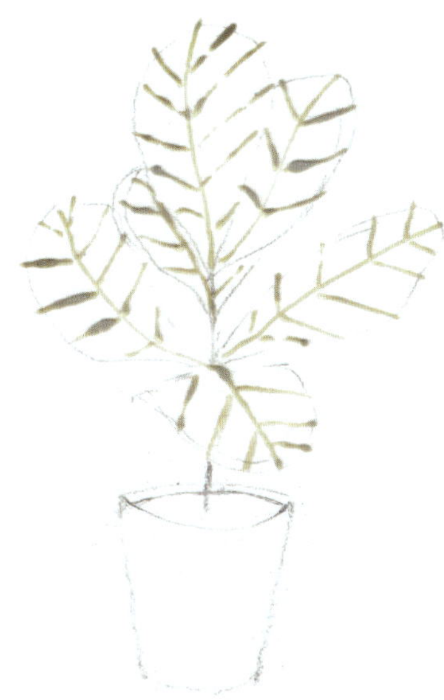

Lightly sketch a fiddle leaf fig using my sketch as reference. I use hot press paper for the projects in this chapter because it's smoother and makes it easier to work with the masking fluid. Using your masking fluid pen or masking fluid and a small brush, carefully paint thin lines on the leaves to show veins.

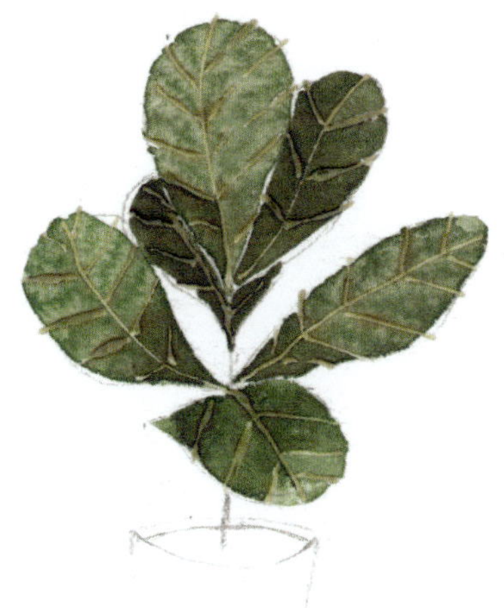

Wait until the masking fluid is completely dry. It will turn translucent and be dry but tacky to the touch. Mix Sap Green with a little Alizarin Crimson to make a muted green. Transfer a small amount of this color to another part of your palette, and add more water to create a lighter version. Use your medium brush to paint the leaves using the lighter mixture of paint; add depth by dropping in some of the darker mixture while it's still wet. Be patient as you paint the leaves. It takes time to make sure they are painted completely and there are no white gaps around the raised masking fluid. Add more of the dark green mixture to the leaves that are behind the others and in shadow.

TIP Always wait for the paint to dry completely before you remove the masking fluid. If you don't, the paint can smudge and ruin the crisp white lines we're looking for. However, don't wait too long! If you leave masking fluid on the paper overnight, you may find it difficult to remove, and it might even rip the paper underneath.

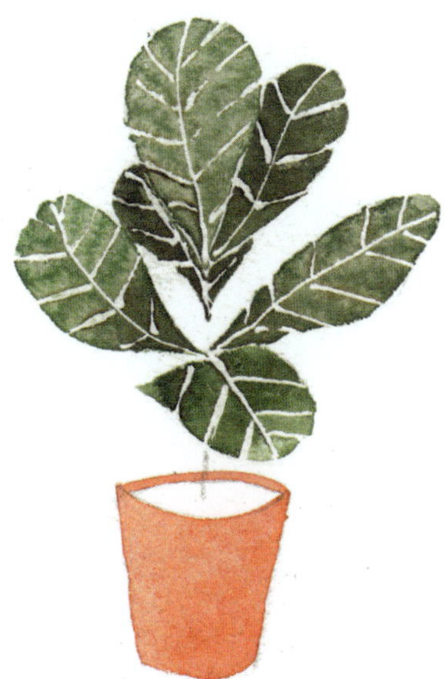

When the leaves are completely dry, very carefully remove the masking fluid using an eraser and gently rubbing at the masking fluid until it peels away.

Mix Cadmium Red with a bit of Burnt Sienna, and carefully paint the pot using your medium brush. Allow more pigment to pool on the right side of the pot.

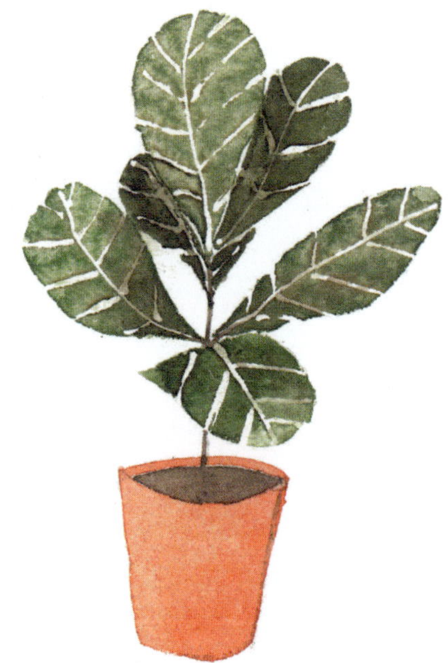

Paint the soil using a watery mixture of Sepia and your medium brush. Use this mixture and your small brush to paint the stems of the plant. Add more water to this mixture and use your medium brush to add shadows on some of the leaves.

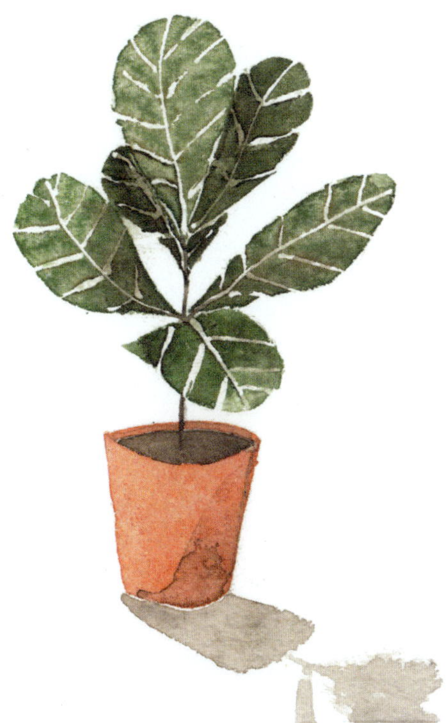

Use the watery mixture of Sepia and your medium brush to paint a shadow on the right side of the pot. On the floor, paint a shadow extending out from the pot showing the pot stems and leaves.

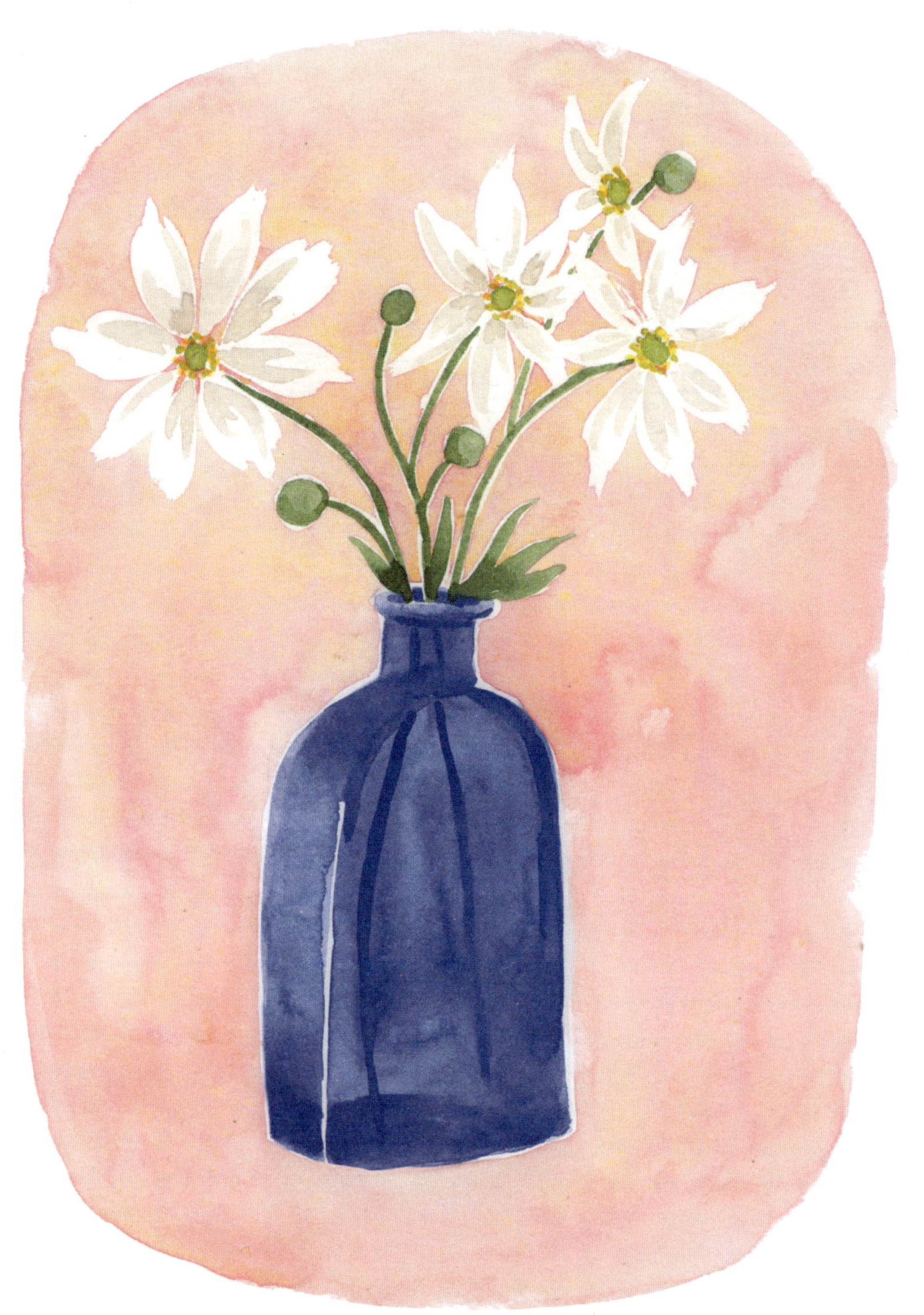

Japanese Anemones in a Vase

This piece is a clever way of doing a colorful painting of some white flowers. Painting white flowers on a white background is always a challenge, so I placed them in a vase on a contrasting colorful background. I love Japanese anemones; they grow wild in my front garden and look lovely in this antique cobalt blue glass bottle. By using masking fluid, we can get perfect crisp white flowers and an even wash of color behind. I've painted this piece using bright blue and a soft peach, but you can try different color combinations.

Materials Hot press watercolor paper • Pencil • Eraser • Old small round brush for masking fluid
Small round brush • Medium brown brush • Large round brush
Colors Used Lemon Yellow ● Permanent Rose ● Ultramarine ● Sap Green ● Sepia ●
Cadmium Yellow ●

Roughly sketch a bottle and plant stems. You can sketch the flowers, too; however, I prefer to paint them freehand using the masking fluid to keep them looking natural. Using an old small round brush, paint the flower stems, leaves, and centers using masking fluid. Paint the petals by placing the tip of the brush at the center of the flower and gently pulling it outward. This should give the petals a slightly rough feathered edge at the tip. The masking fluid is thick, viscous, and sticky, so you will need to work very slowly and carefully.

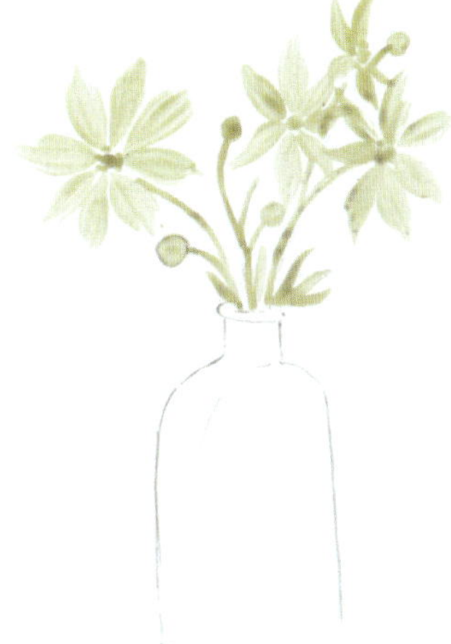

TOP TIP Keep all your old worn-out paint brushes that would otherwise be thrown away, and use them for masking fluid. Unfortunately, masking fluid ruins brushes, but if you use a brush destined to be thrown out anyway, it won't go to waste.

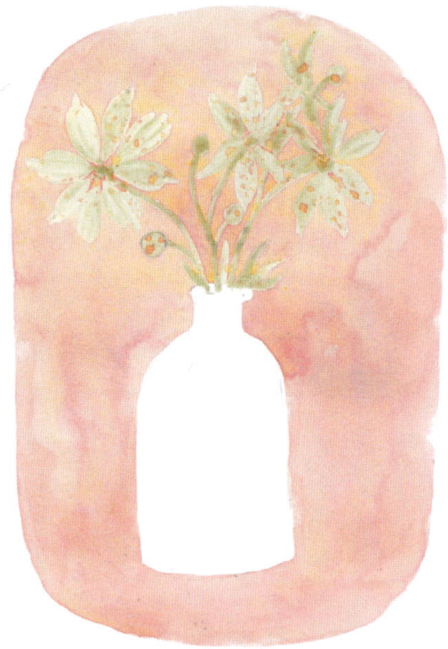 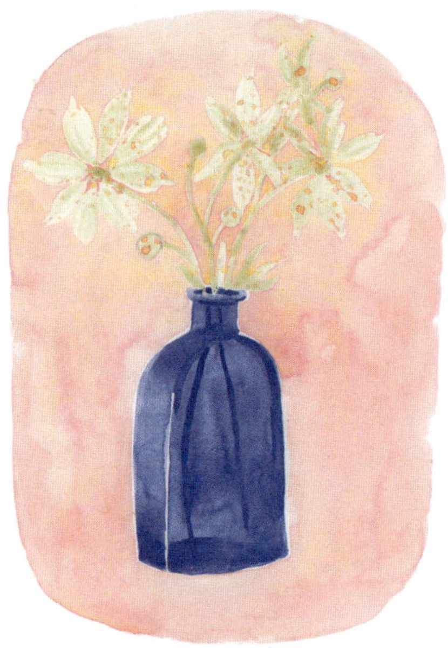

When the masking fluid is dry, completely paint the background. (When dry, the masking fluid should be tacky to the touch and should appear translucent.) Mix Lemon Yellow with Permanent Rose and lots of water to make a peachy background color. Make sure you mix plenty of this color because you don't want to run out halfway through painting the background. Paint the background using a large soft brush, ideally sable, painting straight over the masking fluid flowers and carefully painting around the bottle.

When the background is completely dry, create a watery mix of Ultramarine. Use your large brush and this mixture to loosely paint the bottle, leaving a thin white strip of paper along the corner of the bottle. While the paint is still wet, use your medium brush and a darker mixture of Ultramarine to add shadows to the base of the bottle, around the rim, the sides, and to paint the stems seen through the bottle. These details painted with the darker mixture of Ultramarine should blend slightly in some parts where the paint is still wet and remain distinct in others where the paint below is dry.

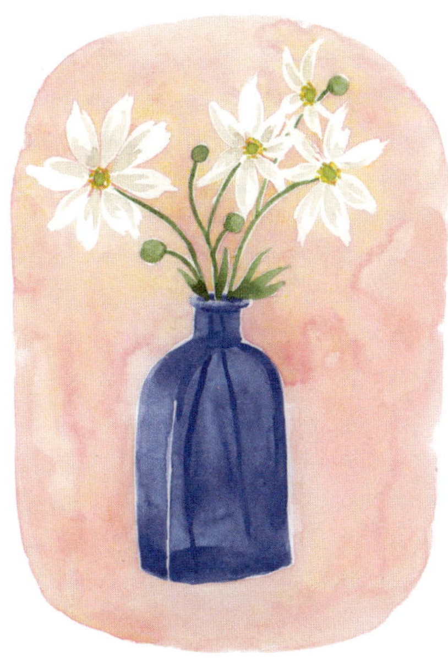

When that's all completely dry, very carefully remove the masking fluid. My favorite method for doing this is to use an eraser to carefully remove the masking fluid starting at the bottom and working your way up. Sometimes, trying to remove it with your fingers can lead to smudging the paint, and removing it with a craft knife can scratch the surface of the paper.

Once all the masking fluid is removed, paint the stems and leaves using a mixture of Sap Green with a little bit of Sepia and your medium brush. Add a drop more of this mixture to the base of the leaves. Add a second layer of color around the base of the flower buds.

Mix Sap Green with a little bit of Cadmium Yellow and a tiny bit of Sepia, and paint the flower centers. Add small dots around the center using Cadmium Yellow and Sap Green and your small brush. Mix a little bit of the background color (Lemon Yellow and Permanent Rose) with a tiny bit of Sepia and lots of water to make a warm shadow color. Use your small brush to paint a few shadows on the white petals. Less is more, so keep the shadows light and sparing. You can always add more if you need to.

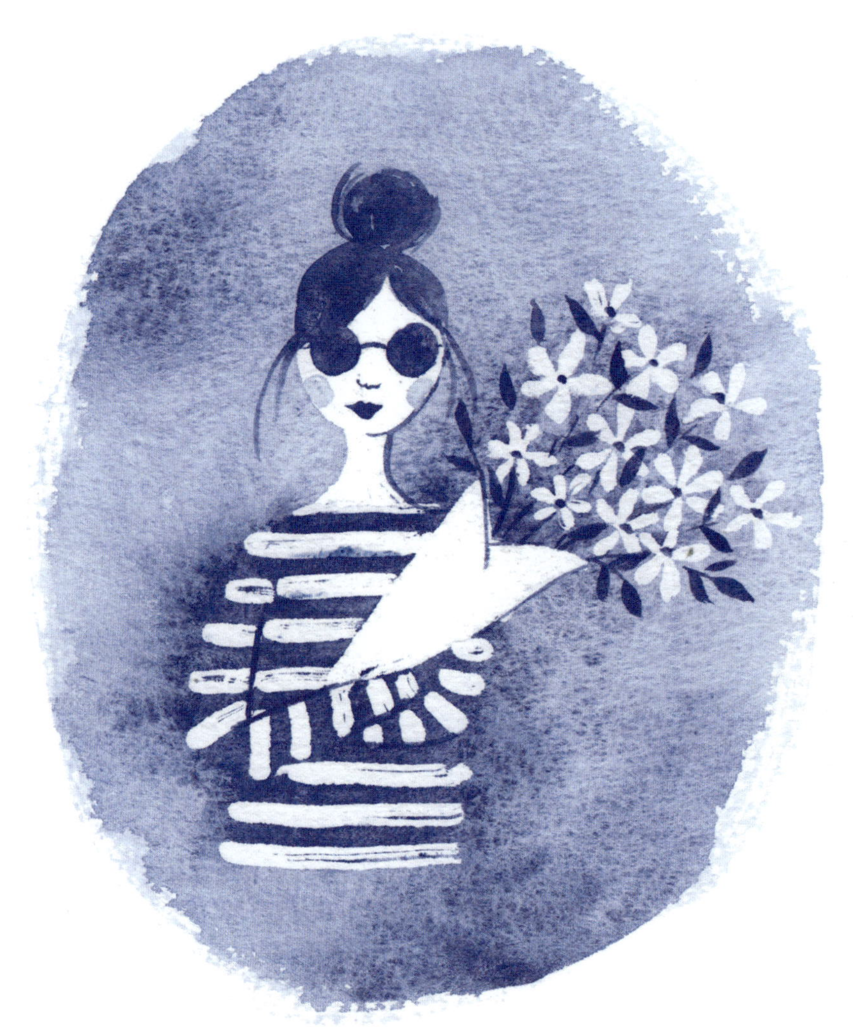

Lady in Blue

This fun piece uses masking fluid and a very limited color palette to paint a stylish woman holding some flowers. All you need is Ultramarine or any other strong color of your choice. This piece is all about the contrast of the white daisies, the medium blue background, and the darker blue of her hair, sunglasses, and stripey shirt. If you're feeling a little bit nervous about painting people, try not to worry. This woman is wearing large, dark sunglasses and has her arms folded, hiding her hands, which means you don't have to tackle painting hands or eyes, two things that people find difficult.

Materials Cold press watercolor paper • Masking fluid • Pencil • Eraser • Old small round brush Small brown brush • Medium brown brush • Large round brush
Color Used Ultramarine ●

With your pencil, lightly sketch a woman wearing sunglasses and holding flowers wrapped in paper. Use my sketch as a reference. I haven't skipped the flowers, just the stems and paper.

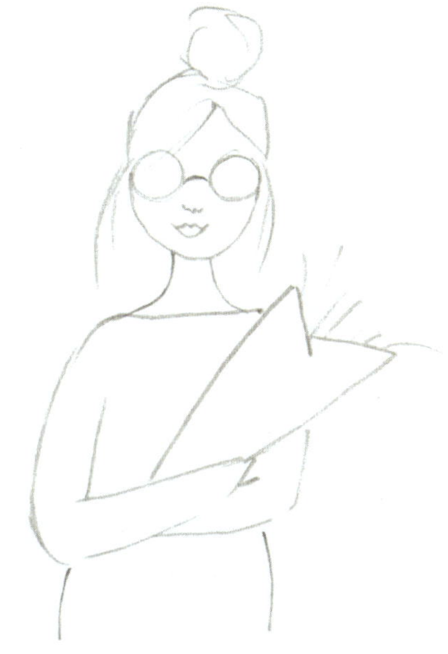

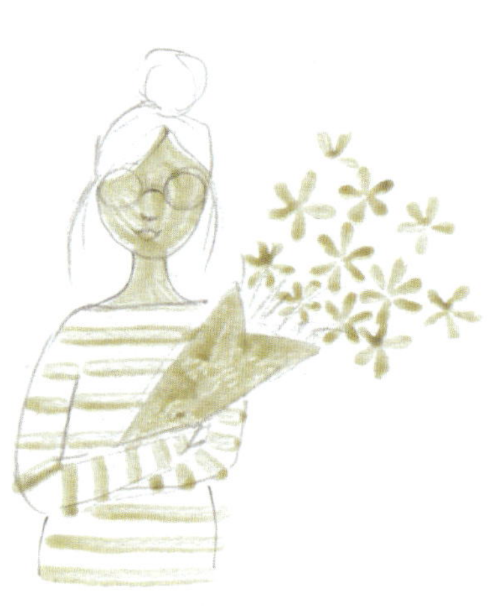

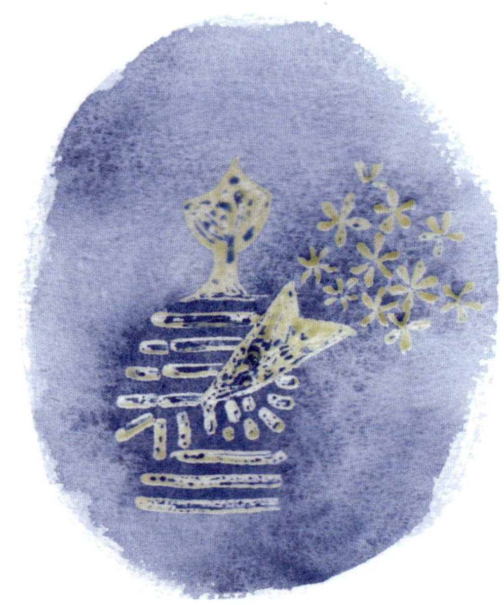

Using masking fluid and a small old brush, paint the woman's face, stripes on her shirt, the paper surrounding the flowers, and simple daisies. Take your time with the daisies. Make sure the petals remain separate and don't merge into each other.

Once the masking fluid is completely dry, paint a watery wash of ultramarine over the surface using your large brush. Paint the wash in an oval shape, and keep the edge of the oval quite rough. Allow color to pool in different areas. Add more Ultramarine to the woman's shirt and bunch of flowers.

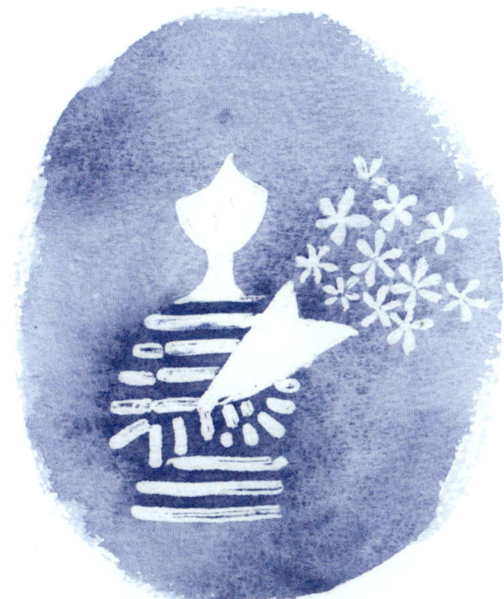

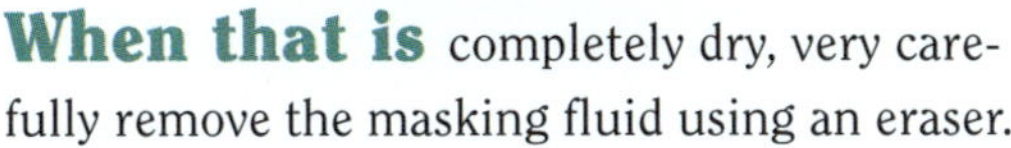

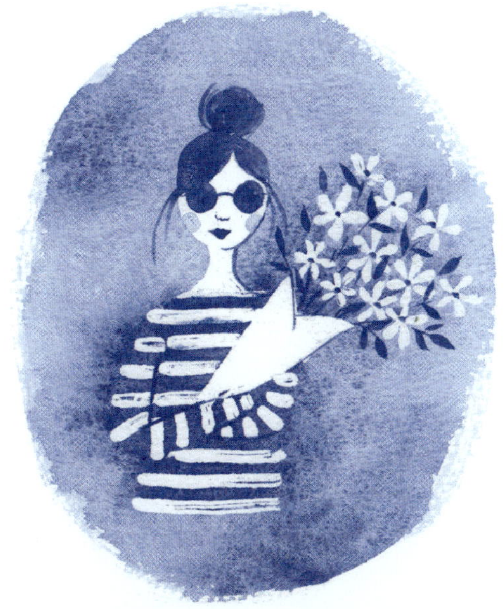

When that is completely dry, very carefully remove the masking fluid using an eraser.

> **TIP** If there is a lot of paint on top of the masking fluid, you can use a damp tissue to carefully remove that before removing the masking fluid. That way, the paint won't smudge as you peel the masking fluid.

Use a dark mix of Ultramarine with only a little bit of water and your medium brush to paint two circles for the woman's sunglasses and loosely paint her hair in a messy bun. Use the dark mixture of ultramarine and your small brush to paint centers, stems, and leaves on the flowers. Use your small brush to paint the woman's nose and lips, and add a couple of lines to her folded arms and the side of her face. Use a more watery mixture of Ultramarine to carefully paint cheeks using your small brush.

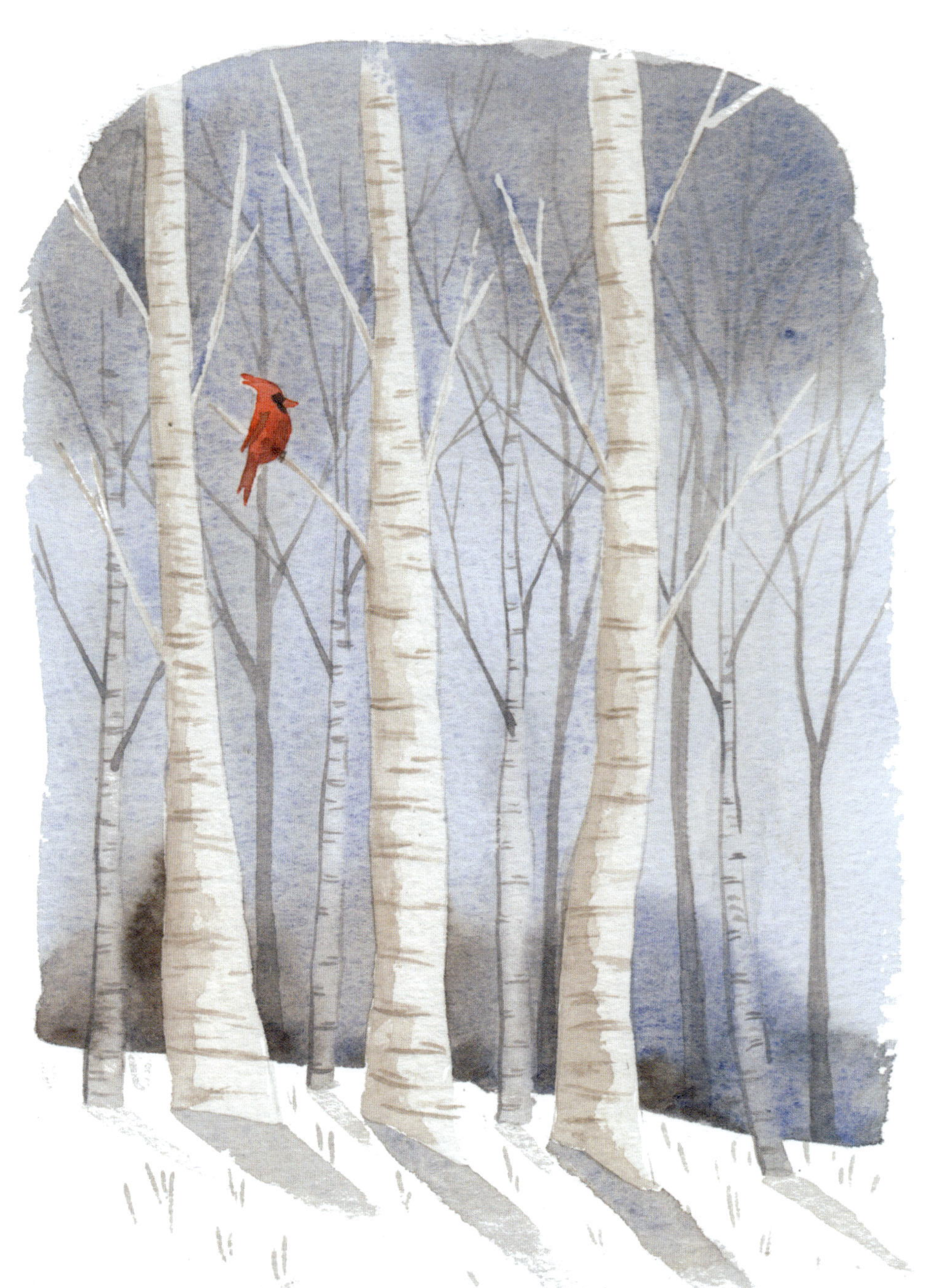

Silver Birches in Winter

This atmospheric piece uses masking fluid and a limited color palette to create silver birches in a snowy forest. The red cardinal provides the perfect pop of color in this wintery scene.

Materials Cold press watercolor paper • Masking fluid • Pencil • Eraser • Large paintbrush
Medium round brush • Small round brush
Colors Used Ultramarine ● Sepia ● Alizarin Crimson ● Cadmium Red ●

Lightly sketch three silver birches and a cardinal in pencil.

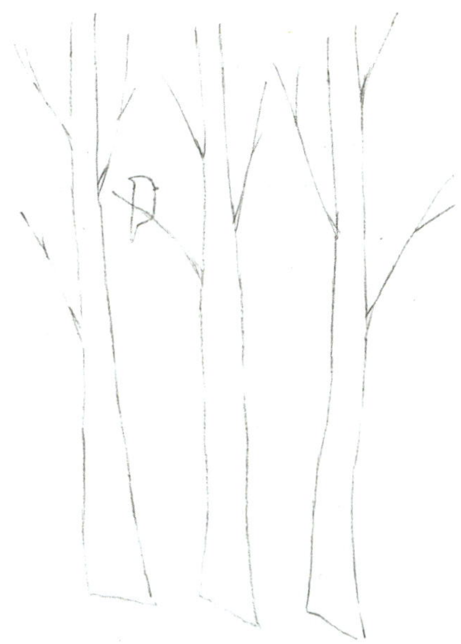

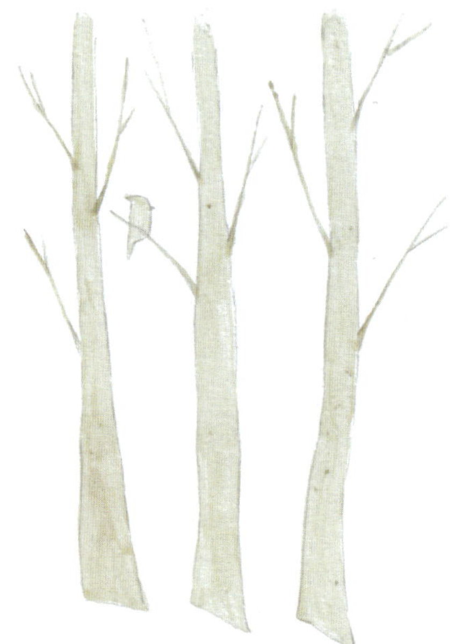

Paint the three tree trunks and the bird using masking fluid and an old small paintbrush. If you have a masking fluid pen, use that for the branches; otherwise, use the very tip of your brush to paint the thin branches.

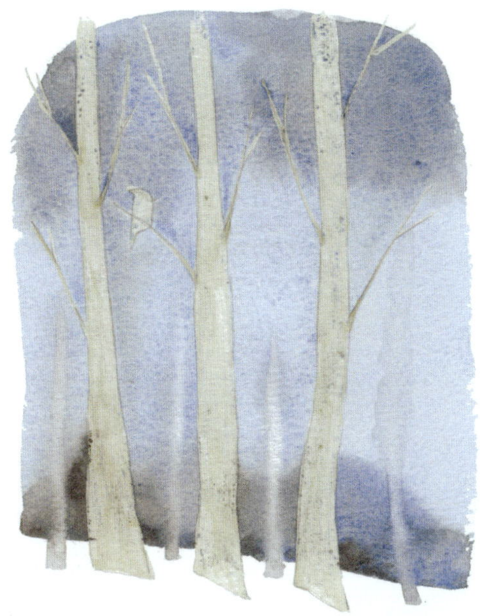

Create a watery mix of Ultramarine. Create another watery mix of Ultramarine with a little bit of Sepia. Create a slightly darker mix of Ultramarine and Sepia. Create a watery mix of just Sepia. When working wet-on-wet, it helps to have all the color mixes prepared beforehand. Once the masking fluid is completely dry, paint the background behind the trees using the watery mix of Ultramarine and your large brush. Finish the wash of blue just above the bottom of the trees at a slight angle, indicating trees in a snowy forest. While the background is still wet, add some of the darker mix of Ultramarine and Sepia and some of the Sepia on its own to the bottom of the wash behind the trees. Add some of the lighter mixture of Ultramarine and Sepia to the top of the wash.

Use a very light mixture of Ultramarine and Sepia with lots of water and your medium brush to paint smaller trees in the distance. Paint the base of the tree starting in the snow just below the bottom of the wash, and then pull upward. Wash your brush, and use your clean damp brush to continue to pull up, displacing the wet paint of the wash, giving the impression of white trees in the distance.

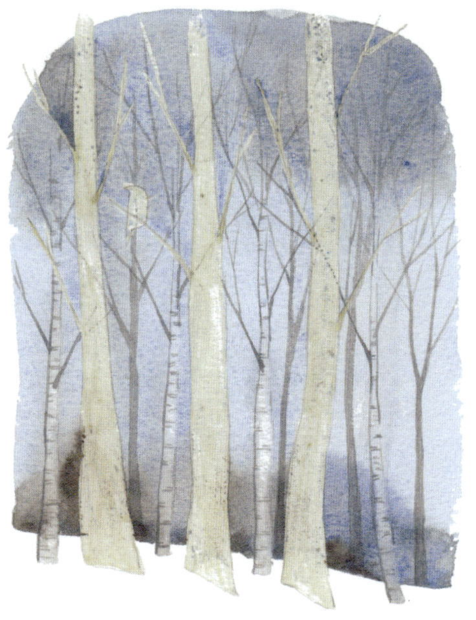

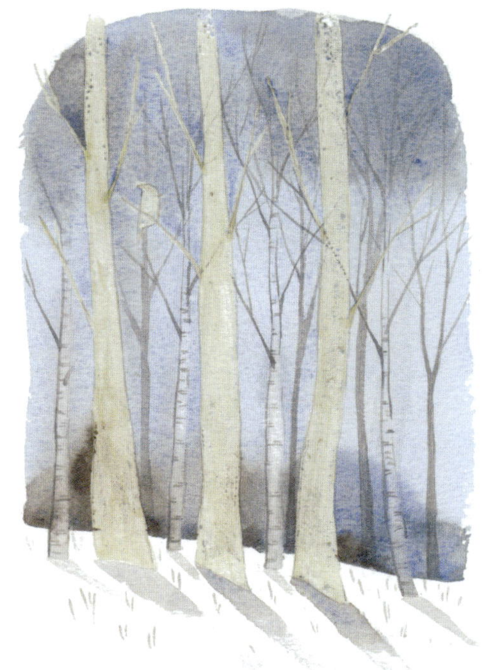

Using your small brush and the darker mixture of Sepia and Ultramarine, outline the trees in the background, painting thin horizontal lines to show the texture of the bark and adding thin branches.

Use the same mixture and your small brush to paint more trees farther in the background; allow the branches to overlap.

Using the watery mixture of Ultramarine and Sepia and your medium brush, paint shadows extending from the bottom of the trees diagonally toward the bottom of the page. Add more paint to the shadow at the base of the trees. Use this color mix and your small brush to paint a few blades of grass poking through the snow.

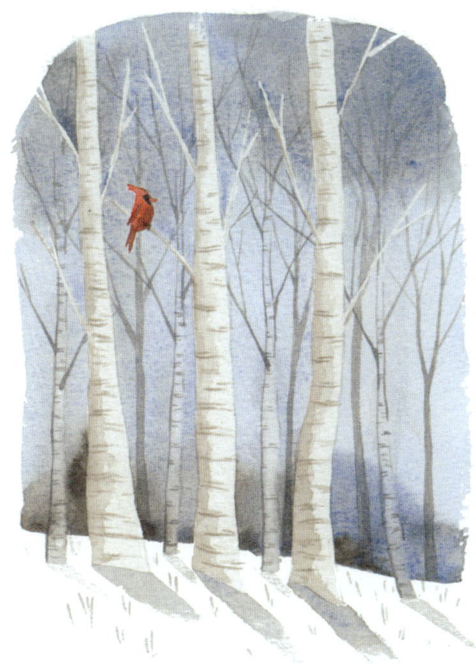

When that is dry, very carefully remove the masking fluid using an eraser and working from the bottom of each tree trunk upward. Once all the masking fluid is removed, use a watery mixture of Sepia and your medium brush to paint shadows along the left side of the tree trunks. When that's completely dry, use your small brush and a slightly darker mixture of Sepia to paint horizontal lines across the tree trunks.

Create a mixture of Alizarin Crimson and Cadmium Red, and using your small brush, paint the cardinal sitting on the branch. Add a little bit of Sepia to the red mixture on your palette, and paint shadows on the bird's wing, tail, and chest. Use a dark mixture of Sepia and your small brush to carefully paint markings on the bird's face and the bird's feet.

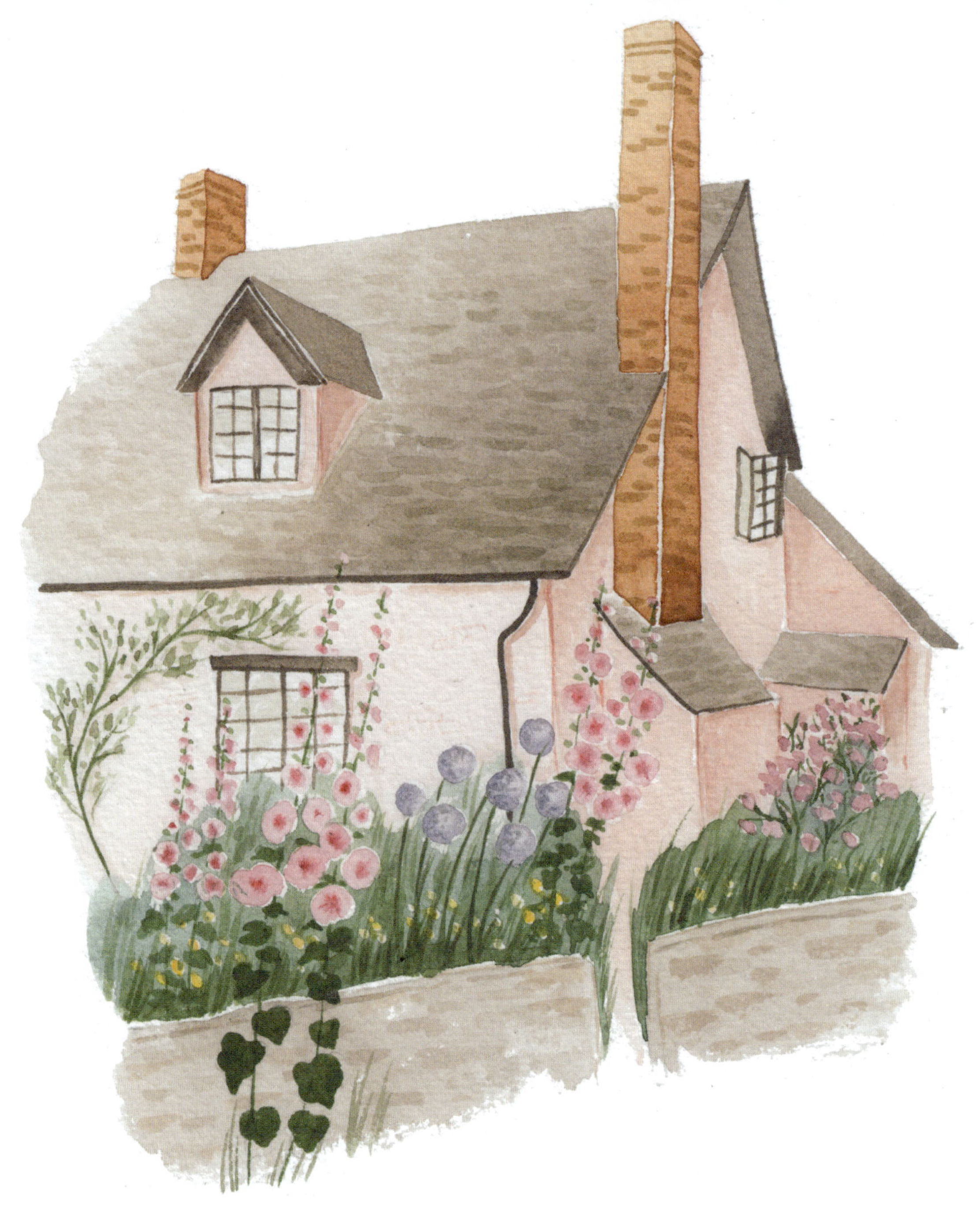

Pink Cottage

This piece is inspired by summers spent with my parents in Suffolk, on the east coast of England. Suffolk is famous for its beautiful chocolate-box cottages, often painted in pink. This piece uses a small amount of masking fluid to great effect. By masking out the flowers first, we can concentrate on painting the house and greenery before turning our attention to the flowers as the finishing touches.

Materials Cold press watercolor paper • Pencil • Masking Fluid • Small old brush • Small round brush • Medium round brush • Large round brush

Colors Used Cadmium Red • Sepia • Burnt Sienna • Yellow Ochre • Viridian Green • Alizarin Crimson • Sap Green • Ultramarine • Cadmium Yellow

Lightly sketch the cottage in pencil using my sketch as reference. You might notice that the sketch looks unfinished in the bottom half. This is to allow room for expressive brush-strokes for the greenery and flowers.

Using a small old brush and masking fluid, fill in the flowers. Paint rough circles for the large stems of hollyhocks and alliums, and create random dots of masking fluid just above the garden wall to indicate small flowers.

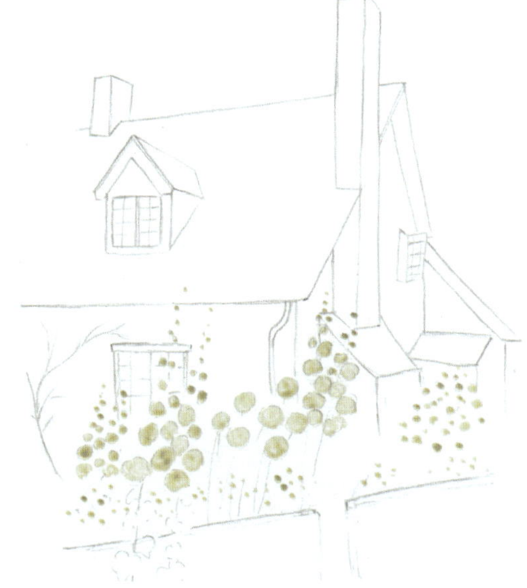

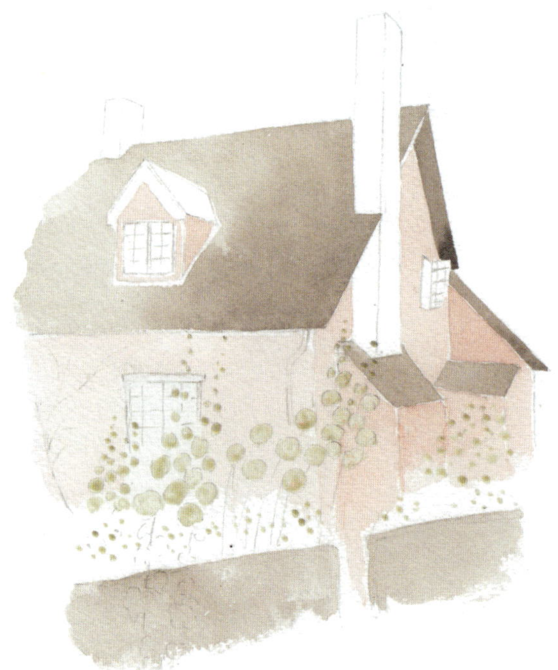

Create a light pink using Cadmium Red, a tiny bit of Sepia, and lots of water. Paint the walls of the house using your large brush, keeping the edges loose and adding more pigment to the walls on the right side. I like the color to fade out at the bottom, where it will meet the greenery.

Create a watery mixture of Sepia. Using your large brush, paint the roof. Add more pigment to the right side. Use this watery mixture and your large brush to loosely paint the garden walls, keeping the bottom rough. Using your medium brush and this paint mixture, paint the smaller roofed areas and the gables. Add more pigment to the bottom of the gables.

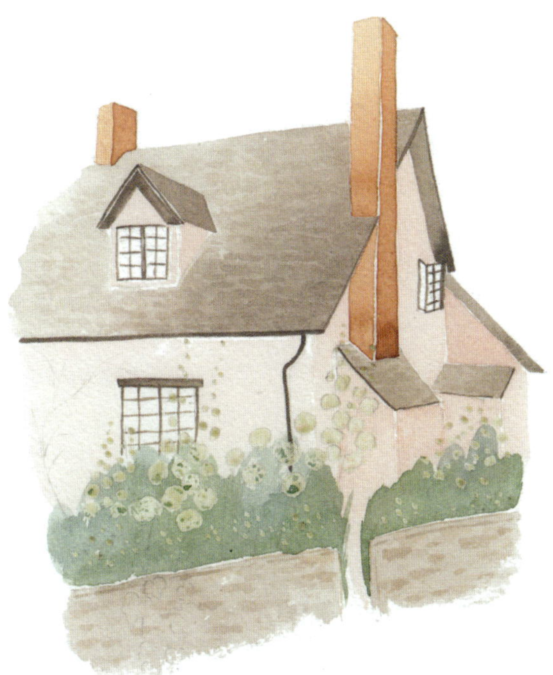

When that is dry, use a dark mixture of Sepia and your small brush to outline the edges of the roof, the gutters, the windows, and the gables. Using a watery mixture of Sepia and your medium brush, paint slate roof tiles by adding little horizontal brushstrokes across the roof. Create similar horizontal brushstrokes on the front wall to give the impression of a rustic slate wall.

Mix Burnt Sienna with a little bit of Yellow Ochre and a little bit of Sepia to make a color for the chimney. Using your medium brush, paint the chimney, allowing more color to pool at the bottom. Paint one side at a time, adding more paint to the right side of the chimney so it appears in shadow.

Create a mixture of Viridian Green with a little bit of Alizarin Crimson and lots of water. Create another mixture of Sap Green with a little bit of Sepia and lots of water. Use your large brush to loosely paint greenery behind the garden wall and in front of the house. Use the two green mixtures, and allow them to blend on the page. Create large, loose brushstrokes that go straight over the masking fluid. We will be building more detail on top later.

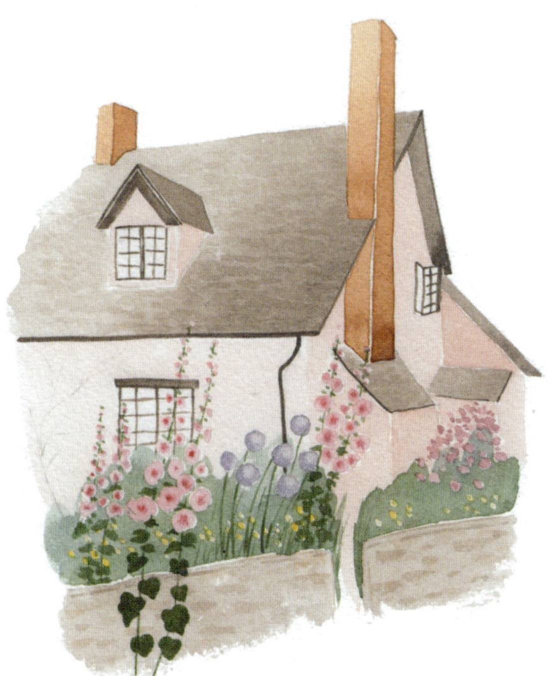

 completely dry, very carefully remove the masking fluid. Paint the hollyhocks with a watery mixture of Alizarin Crimson and your medium brush. Add a dot of darker crimson to the center of each flower while it's still wet.

Mix Sap Green with Sepia to create a dark green. Using your small brush, paint the leaves and stems of the hollyhocks. Mix Alizarin Crimson with Ultramarine to make a purple.

Use your small brush to paint the alliums; add more pigment to the left side. Mix Alizarin Crimson with a bit of Viridian Green and lots of water to make a purple, and paint the flowers on the right side of the building. Paint the remaining small flowers with Cadmium Yellow. Use the dark green mixture of Sap Green and Sepia and a small brush to paint stems on the alliums, and paint a few thin brushstrokes for blades of grass.

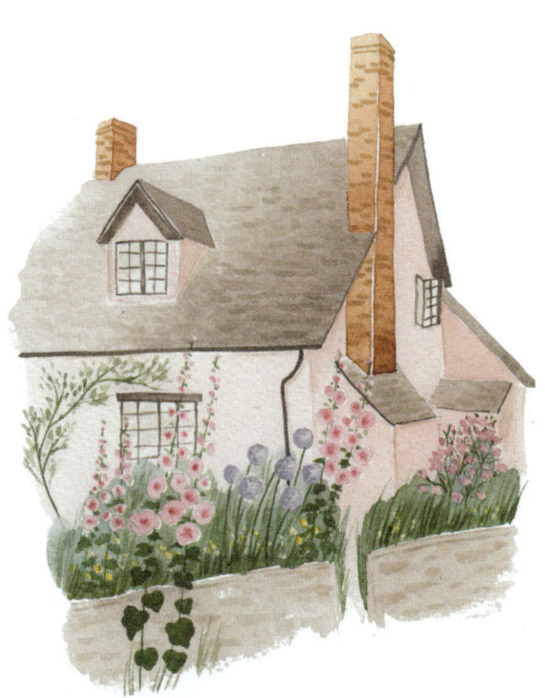 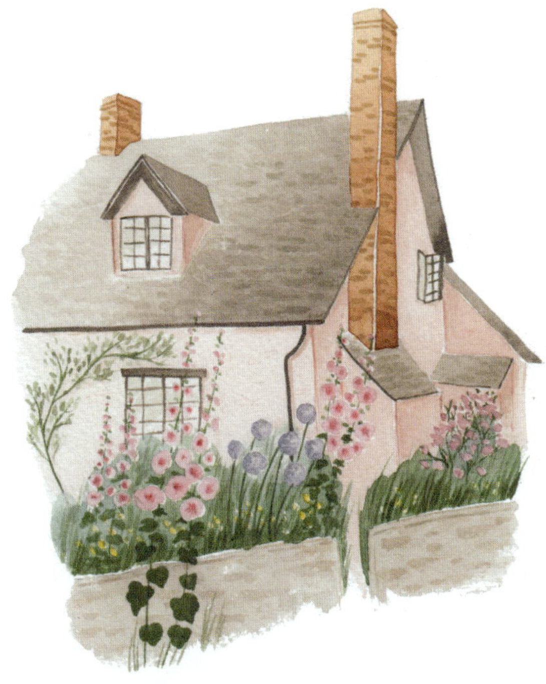

Using a mixture of Sap Green and Sepia and your small brush, paint the vine on the left wall of the house. Use this mixture and your small brush to paint stems on the bush of purple flowers on the right side of the house. Create a green with a mix of Sap Green and a bit of Sepia and Yellow Ochre. Use this color and your small brush to paint lots of blades of grass coming from behind the garden wall and a couple just in front. Paint these by starting the brushstroke at the bottom and pulling upward, leaving a thin line that ends in a point. Use this light mixture of green to paint little leaves on the vine on the side of the house.

Use a very watery mixture of Sepia and your medium brush to add a little bit of shadow to the windows. Also use this mixture and your medium brush to add a few more roof slates, overlapping those already there.

Mix Cadmium Red with a bit of Sepia, and use your small brush to outline the edges of the walls. Add more water to this mixture, and use your medium brush to add a little bit of shadow anywhere you feel the house needs more definition.

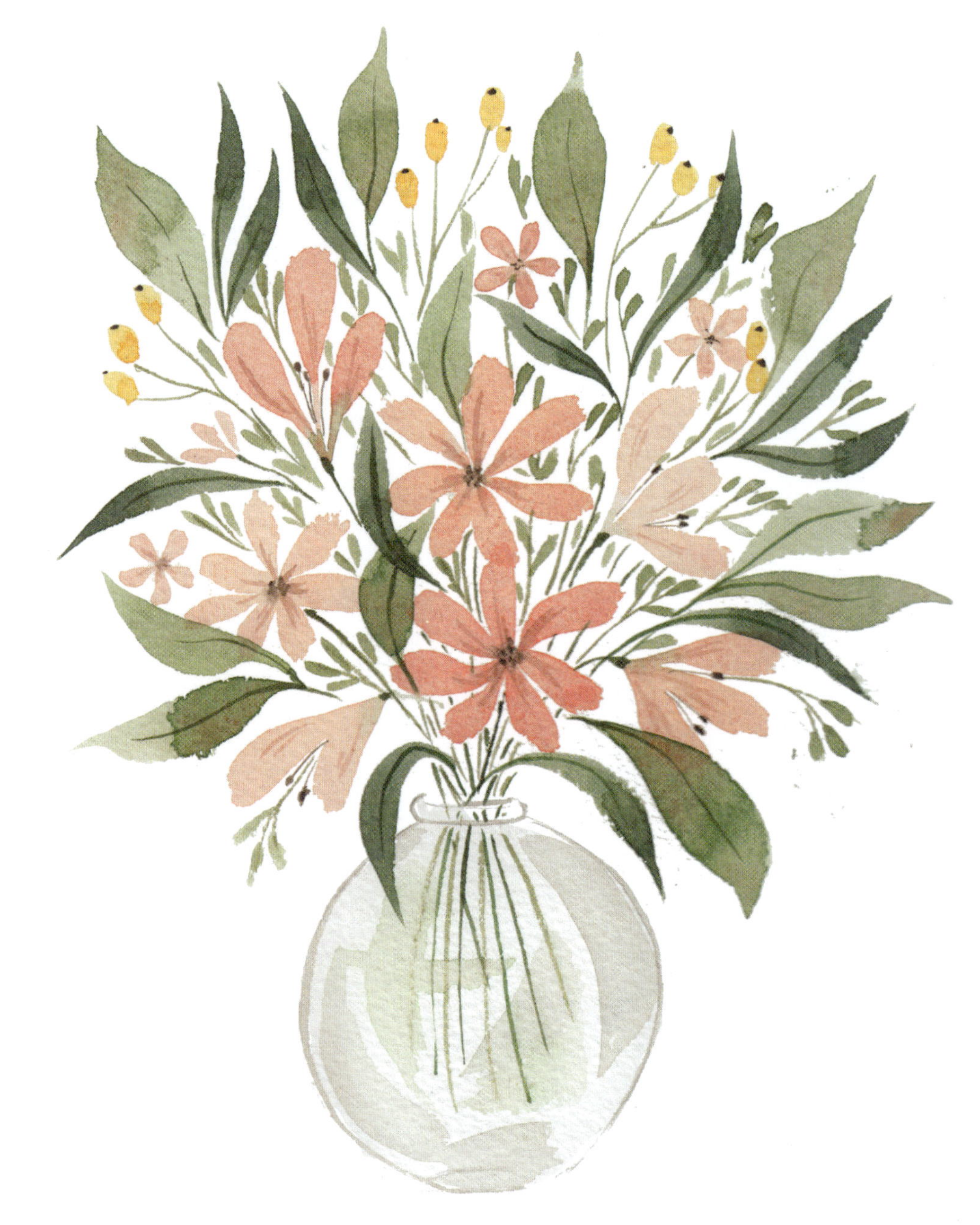

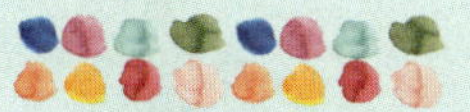

Expressive Brushstrokes

This chapter uses both round and angled brushes and a variety of expressive brushstrokes to create many different effects.

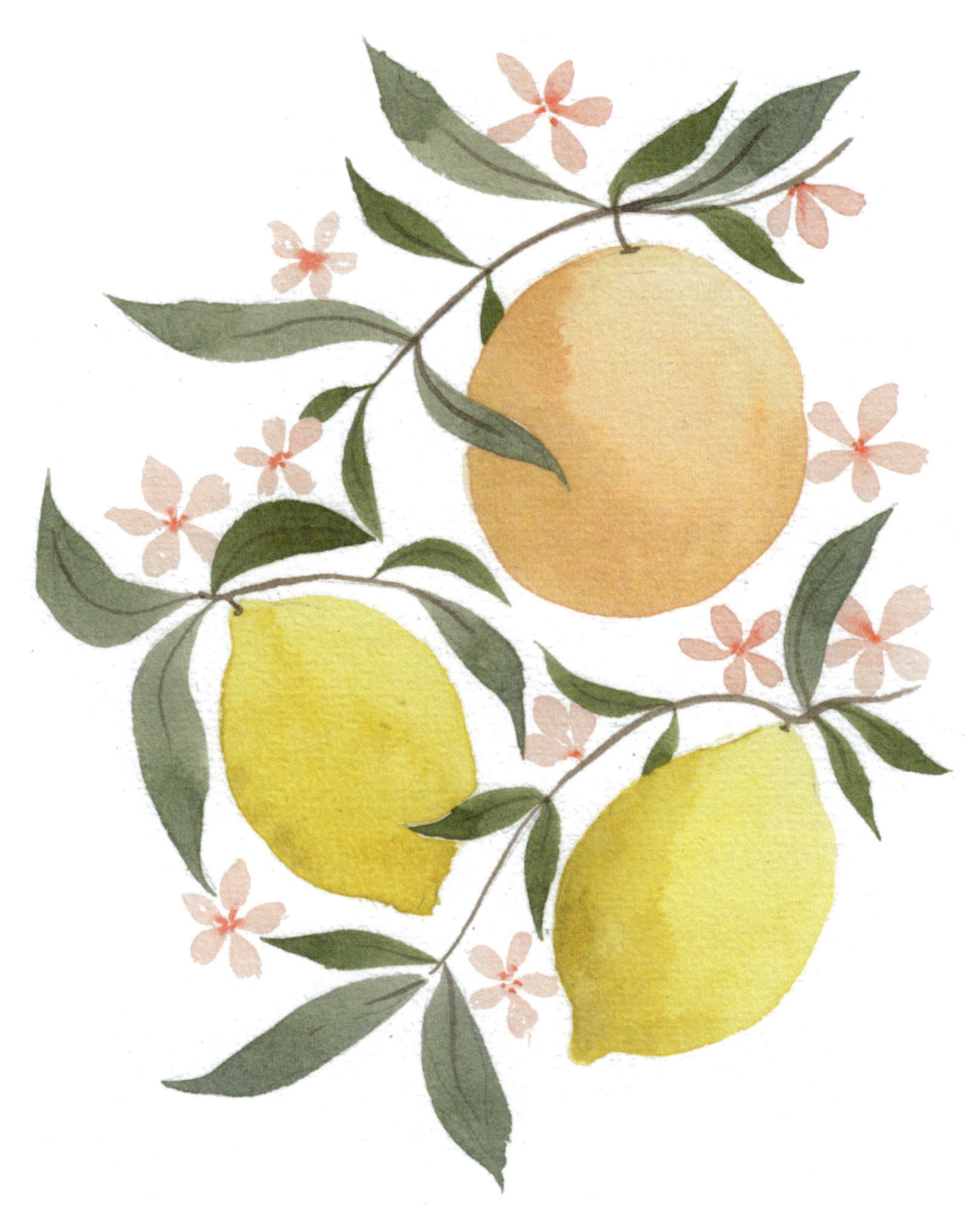

Oranges and Lemons

This simple piece makes great use of expressive brushstrokes to paint the leaves on the oranges and lemons. I find pieces like this very calming and meditative to paint, as creating the perfect leaf with a single brushstroke takes great concentration but is also incredibly satisfying. Make sure you repeatedly practice the leaf technique before applying it to your final piece. Once you've mastered this piece, try your own composition with a variety of fruits.

Materials Cold press watercolor paper • Pencil • Eraser • Large sable paintbrush • Medium round brush • Small round brush

Colors Used Ultramarine ● Cadmium Yellow ● Sap Green ● Cadmium Red ● Sepia ● Lemon Yellow ●

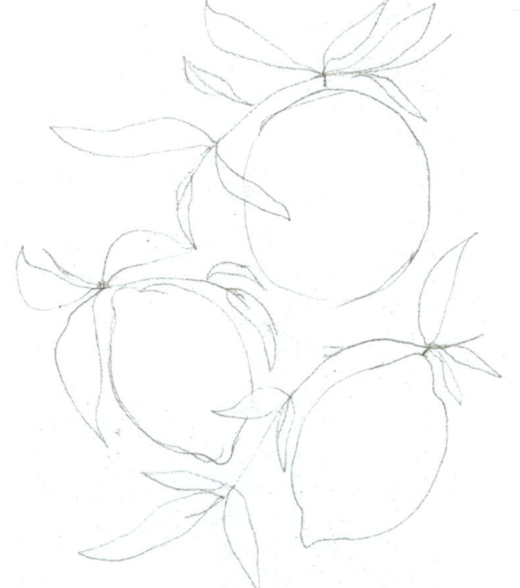

Very lightly sketch the design using a pencil. Don't worry about making the leaves or fruit perfect; you want them to look natural.

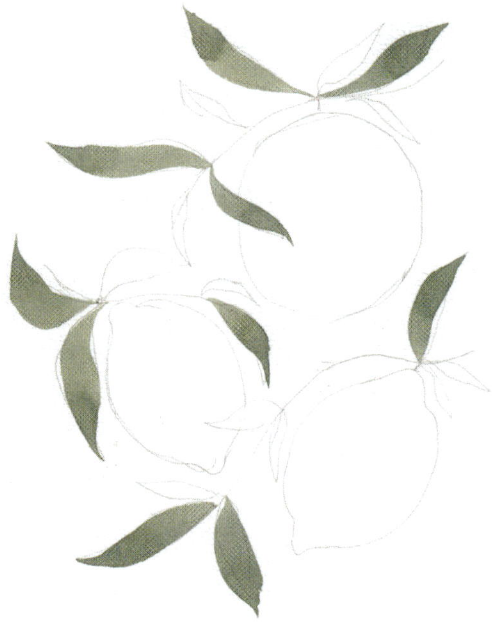

Mix a dark green using Cadmium Yellow and Ultramarine. Using your large sable brush, paint the large leaves starting with light pressure where the leaf meets the branch, applying more pressure as the leaf becomes broader, and then gently lifting the pressure off at the tip of the leaf so the brushstroke becomes thin again. Practice it a few times on a separate piece of paper until you feel confident with the motion. It's really important to keep the pressure steady and slow. Don't rush and lift the brush from the paper too quickly. Don't worry about following the pencil lines exactly; just go with the flow. Make sure you pick up plenty of paint on your brush when doing this technique because it won't work well with a dry brush.

TIP This technique works best with a sable brush because the belly of the brush will hold a lot of paint, it will have a fine point, and the soft bristles will create beautifully curved shapes.

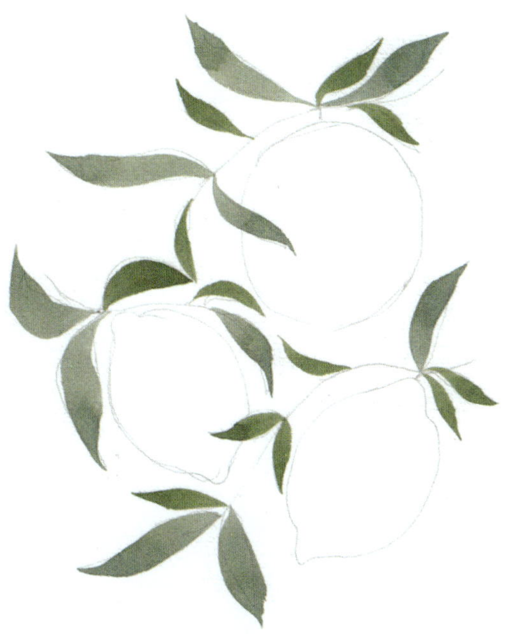 

Mix Sap Green with a little bit of Cadmium Red to make a lighter green, then paint the small leaves with your large sable brush using the same technique. You can turn the paper around to help you avoid putting your hand in any wet paint and to help you pull the brush at a natural angle.

Create a watery mixture of Cadmium Yellow and Sepia, and paint the lemons with your large sable brush, painting around the overlapping leaf. Allow the color to pool at the bottom and left side of the lemons. While the paint is still wet, add more Sepia to the left side.

Mix a light orange using Lemon Yellow, Cadmium Red, and lots of water, and paint the orange using your large sable brush. Add a little bit of Sepia to the orange mixture, and add shadow to the bottom left side while it's still wet.

When everything is dry, use an eraser to remove any excess pencil lines around the leaves or fruit. Create a watery mixture of Cadmium Red, and use your medium brush to paint the blossoms, making sure to leave white space between the petals so they are defined. While the flowers are still wet, add a drop of stronger Cadmium Red to the center using your small brush.

Use your small brush and Sepia to paint the branches and small veins on the leaves.

Create a mixture of Sap Green and Cadmium Red, and use your small brush to paint in a few extra leaves tucked behind the orange, the lemon, and the flower to balance the composition.

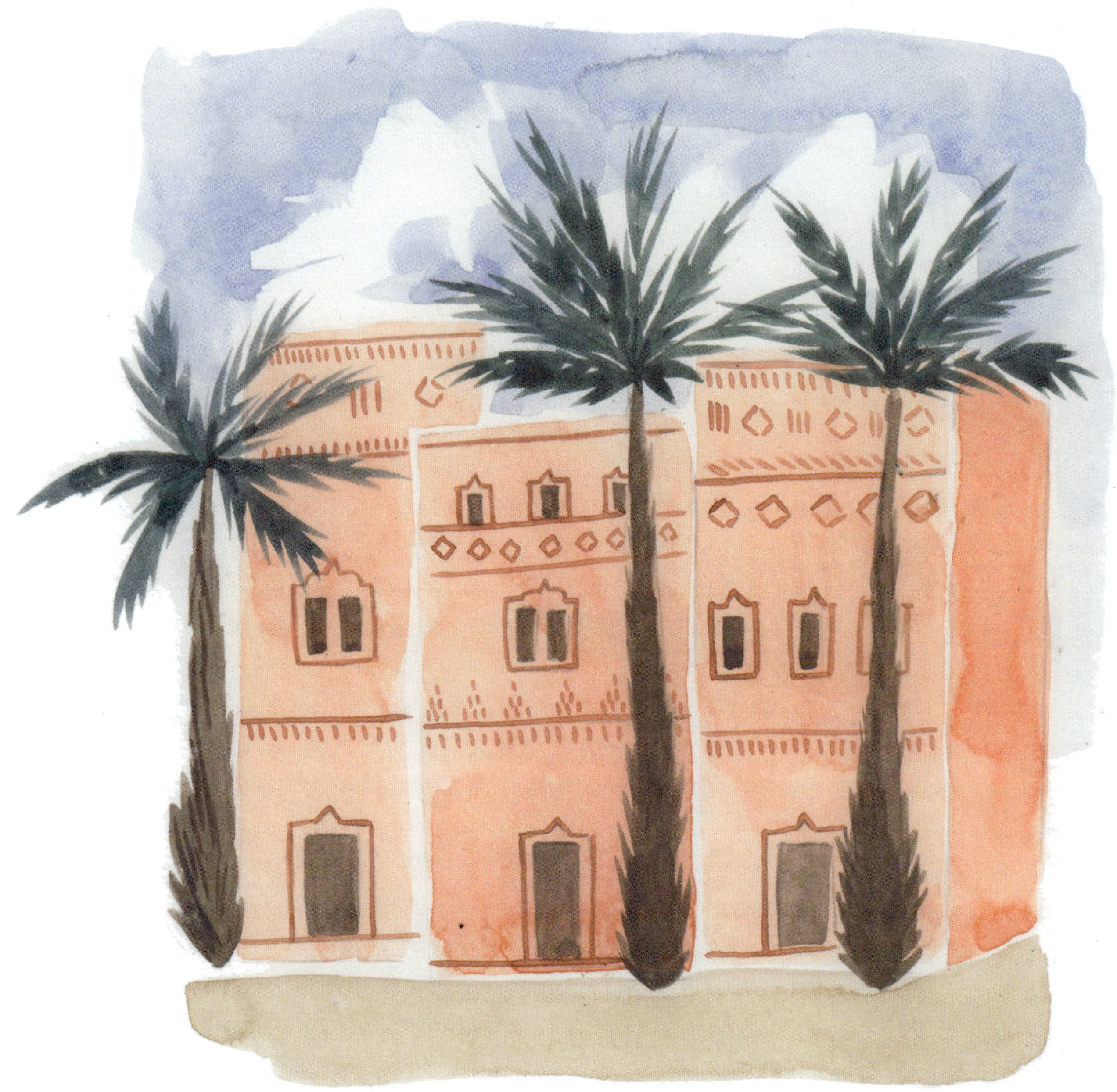

Moroccan Building with Palm Trees

Apart from the small details, this piece is painted almost entirely with an angled brush. The angled brush gives some wonderfully expressive effects and is truly versatile. It's great for creating broad washes of paint and painting large areas using the flat of your brush, but it's also great for creating expressive spiky shapes using the point of your brush, perfect for the fronds of palm trees.

Materials Hot press watercolor paper • Pencil • Eraser • Medium angled brush • Small round brush
Colors Used Cadmium Red ● Burnt Sienna ● Ultramarine ● Sepia ● Cadmium Yellow ● Lamp Black ● Yellow Ochre ●

Very lightly sketch the three tall Moroccan buildings and three palm trees. I've kept the palm tree sketches very minimal and will be adding more details as I paint them.

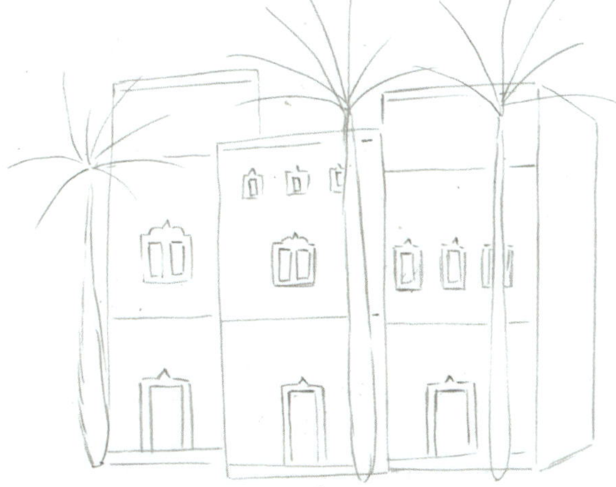

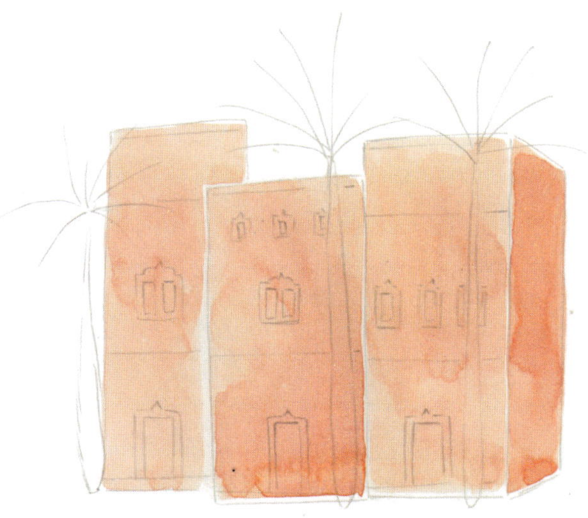 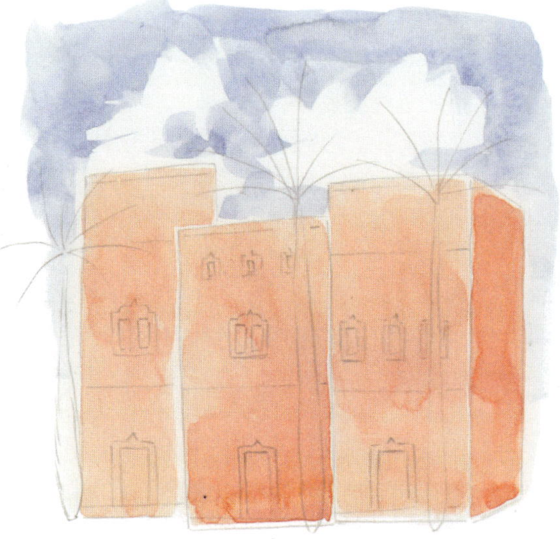

Create a watery mixture of Cadmium Red and Burnt Sienna, and paint the buildings using the flat of your medium angled brush. Paint the side of the right building with a more concentrated mixture of the paint.

Use a watery mixture of Ultramarine to loosely paint the sky behind the buildings using the flat of your angled brush; leave white spaces for clouds.

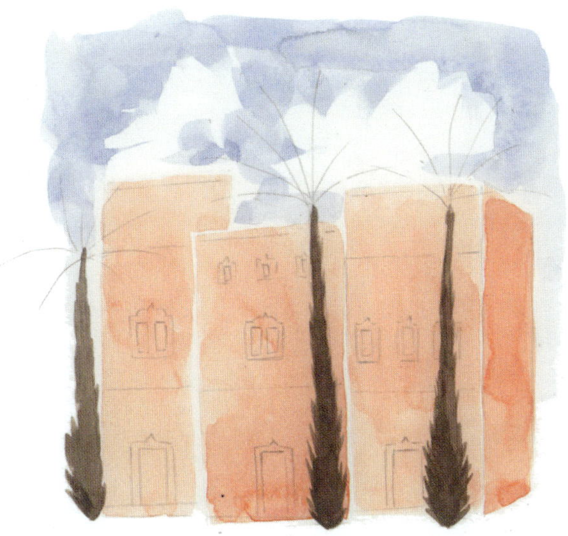

Use a slightly watery mixture of Sepia to paint the palm trees. Start at the bottom of the palm tree trunk and pull the point of the angled brush upward to create a short-pointed shape. Keep building up these short-pointed shapes to create a rough, tapered trunk.

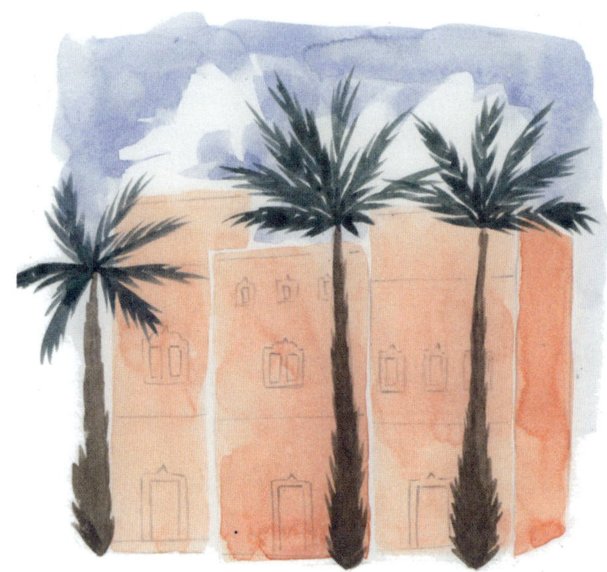

Mix Ultramarine with a little bit of Cadmium Yellow to make a dark bluish green.

Paint the palm fronds using your angled brush. Place the tip of the brush on the pencil line you've drawn and pull outward, creating a thin, sharp-pointed shape. Continue doing this along the length of the pencil line to create the palm frond. Continue for the rest of the palm branches, thinking about varying the angle of the palm leaves. As we are using a dark mixture of green, there should be no problem with painting straight over the building and sky in the background.

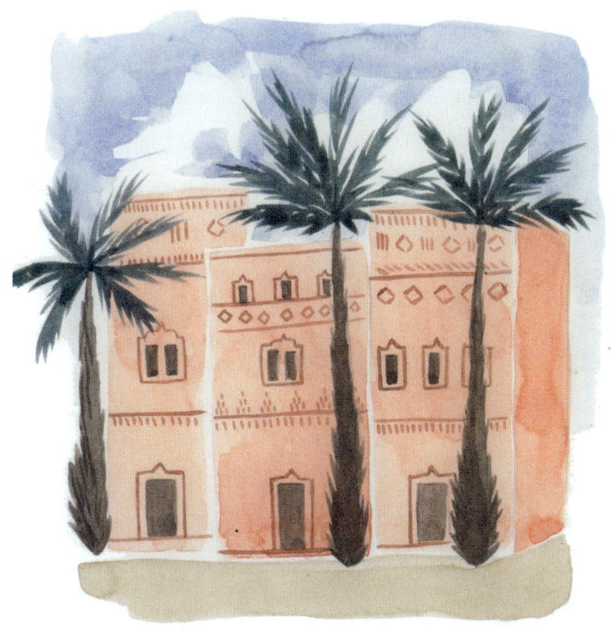

Mix Cadmium Red and Burnt Sienna, then add a tiny bit of Lamp Black. Use your small round brush and this color to add details to the building by following my painting for reference. Add lines, dashes, and outlines around windows and doors. Use Sepia and your small round brush to paint the doors and windows. Add a few upward Sepia brushstrokes to the palm trees to add details.

Mix Yellow Ochre with a little bit of Sepia and lots of water, and use your medium angled brush to paint the ground below the buildings.

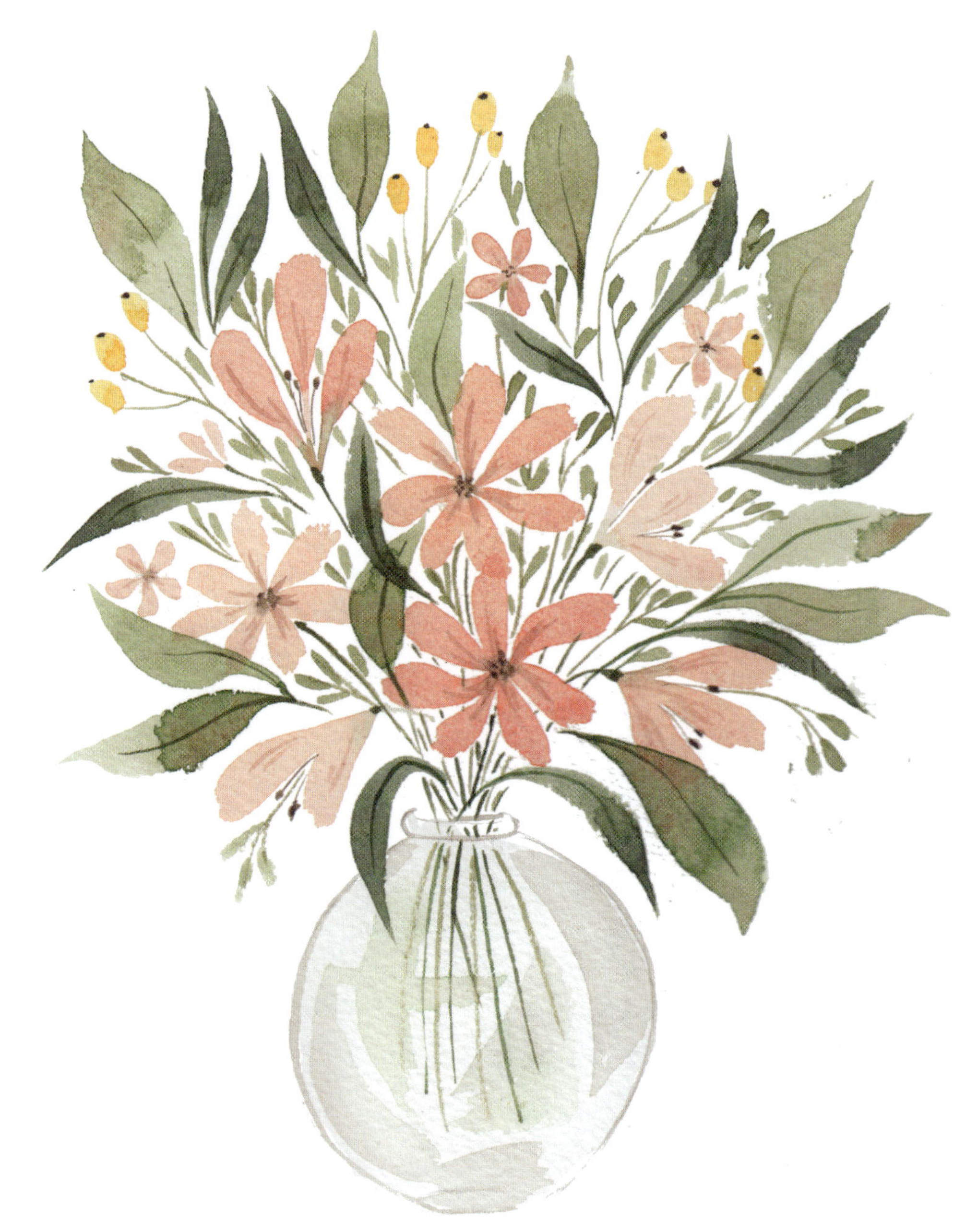

Alstroemeria in a Vase

This piece uses two types of expressive brushstrokes. We use a single brushstroke from a large sable brush to create both individual rounded petals and pointed leaves, which gives the piece an energy and vitality. Initially, these brushstrokes can be tricky to master, but once you get the hang of it, they are incredibly satisfying and meditative to do. Make sure you spend lots of time practicing these brushstrokes before attempting the final piece.

Materials Cold press watercolor paper • Pencil • Large sable paintbrush • Medium round brush
Small round brush

Colors Used Cadmium Red ● Cadmium Yellow ● Sap Green ● Sepia ● Ultramarine ●

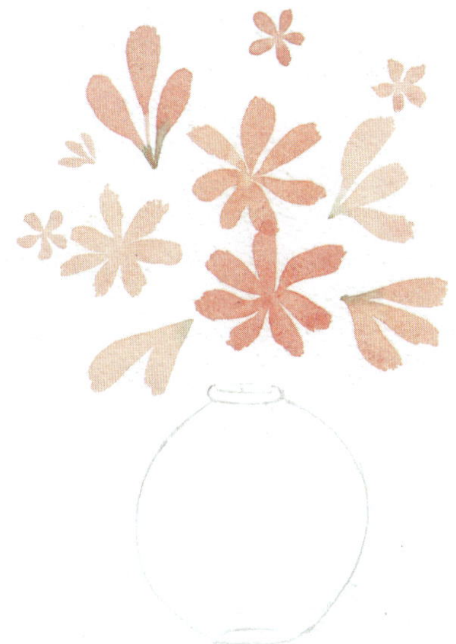

Very lightly sketch a round vase in the bottom half of your paper. I am not going to sketch the flowers, leaves, and stems because I want to add them intuitively rather than carefully following pencil lines.

Create a watery mixture of Cadmium Red with a little bit of Cadmium Yellow. Using a large round sable brush, practice making petal shapes on a piece of scrap paper. To create the petal shape, start with the tip of the brush at the center of the flower. Gradually apply more pressure as you pull the brush out toward the outside of the flower. When the bristles are spread wide on the paper, slowly lift the brush straight up. This should give you a petal shape that is pointed at the beginning and finishes with a rounded shape, a bit like a teardrop. Spend some time practicing this brushstroke; it takes a bit of getting used to. The key to getting the rounded end of the petal is to slowly lift the brush straight up rather than pulling it outward as you lift up, which would result in a point.

Once you're comfortable with this technique, paint some flowers facing toward you, turning the paper as you go. Add slightly more water to the mixture for some of the flowers to make them lighter. Use the same paint mixture and technique to paint some flowers facing away, showing just two or three petals. While these flowers are still wet, add a drop of Sap Green using your medium brush to the base of the petals. Use your medium brush and the same paint mixture to paint a few smaller flowers.

Mix Sap Green with a little bit of Cadmium Red and lots of water to make a muted green. Practice painting some leaves on your scrap paper using your large sable brush and this paint mix. Start with the tip of the brush at the point of the leaf, apply more pressure while pulling the brush so the bristles spread out across the paper, and gradually lift the pressure off

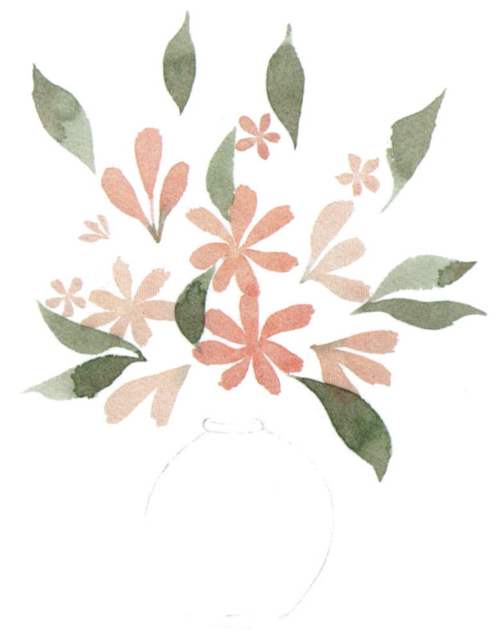

while continuing to pull the brush in a straight line. This should create a pointed leaf shape. This technique is very similar to the one we used for the petals. The difference is that when we lift the brush off the page, we keep pulling it to create a point rather than lifting it straight up to create a round shape.

Once you are happy with this technique, use it to paint some leaves around the flowers. Work intuitively, filling in the spaces between the flowers, varying the size and angle of the leaves, and vary the amount of water used.

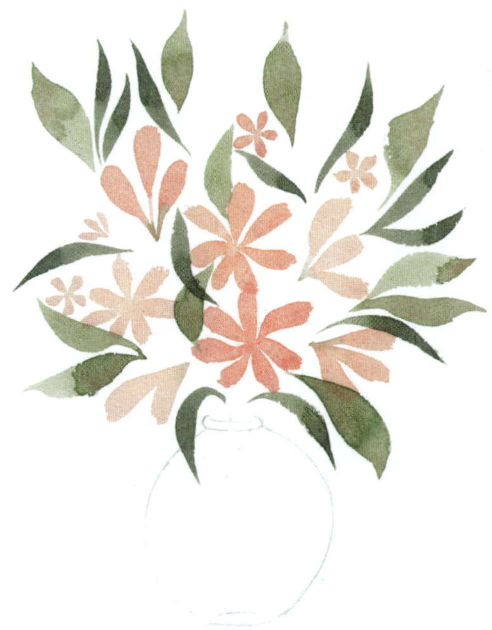

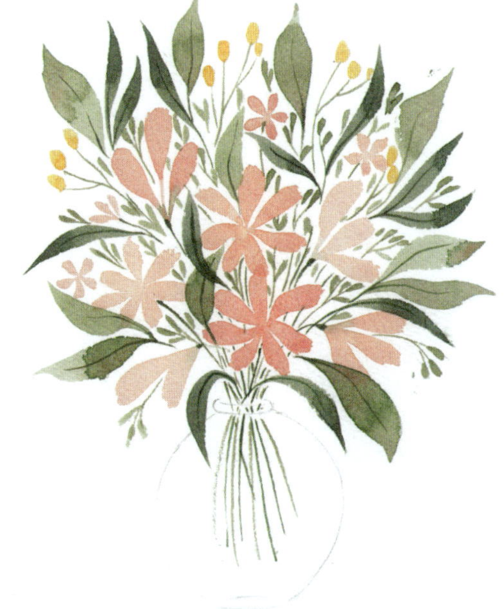

Mix Sap Green with a little bit of Sepia and Ultramarine to make a darker blue green, and use the same technique to paint thin pointed leaves using your large brush. To make the leaves thinner, just apply less pressure to the brushstroke.

Use this darker green and your small brush to paint in stems from the vase to the leaves and flowers. Add some stems that don't connect to a leaf or flower; we will add berries and leaves to these later. Add more stems using the lighter green mixture and your small brush.

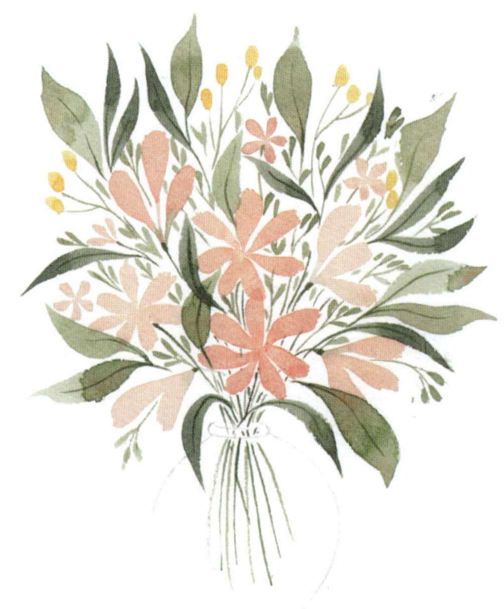

Create a warm yellow using Cadmium Yellow with a little bit of Cadmium Red, and use your medium brush to paint berries at the ends of some of the stems. At the end of the remaining stems, paint small, rounded leaves using your medium brush and the light green mixture. Place the tip of your brush at the end of the stem, and gradually apply more pressure, pulling the brush away from the stem and then lifting off to give a teardrop-shaped leaf. Paint these small leaves around the flowers and larger leaves, filling in the composition.

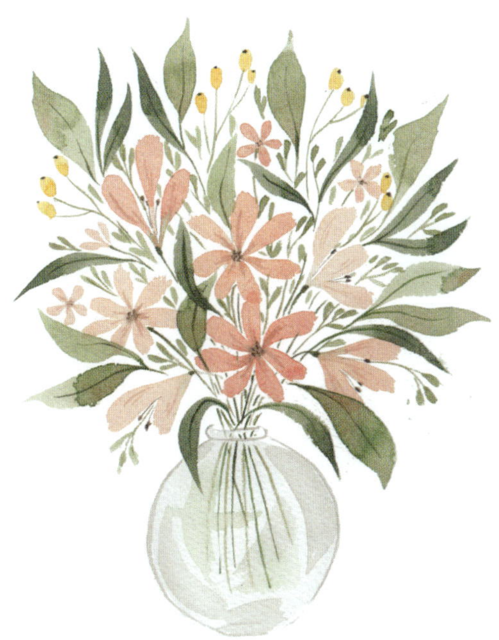

Create a gray using Sepia with a bit of Ultramarine and lots of water. Using your small brush, outline the glass vase. Using your large brush, paint broad expressive sweeps of the gray color onto the glass to create a curved effect. Add more water and a little bit of Sap Green to this mixture, and paint a few broad brush curved strokes, showing the shape of the vase and the level of the water.

Mix Cadmium Red with a tiny bit of Sepia and lots of water, and using your small brush, paint thin lines on the petals of the open flowers. Using a clean wet brush, make the center of the flowers a little bit damp. Use Sepia and your small brush to paint dots in the centers of the open flowers; because the paper is damp, these should bleed slightly. Use Sepia and your small brush to paint stamens in the center of the flower that is facing to the side, and add a small dot of Sepia to the top of the yellow berries.

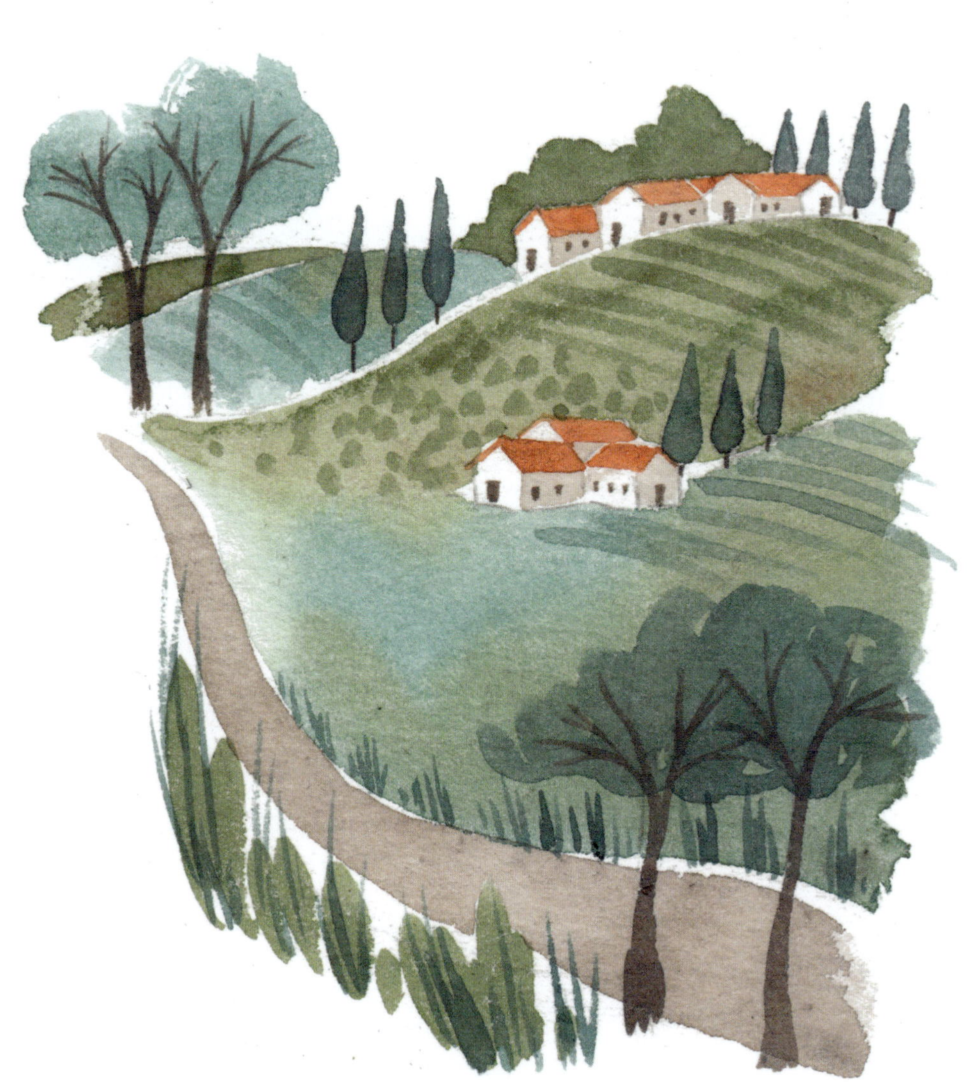

Tuscan Hills

This piece is inspired by the beautiful rolling hills of Tuscany. It's a very simple piece with only a few colors, which really allow the beautiful brushstrokes and blending of watercolor to take center stage.

Materials Cold press watercolor paper • Pencil • Large sable paintbrush • Medium round brush Small round brush

Colors Used Viridian Green ● Alizarin Crimson ● Sap Green ● Cadmium Red ● Sepia ● Burnt Sienna ●

Using my sketch as a reference, lightly sketch a couple of rolling hills, simple houses, trees, and a curved dirt track leading down to the foreground.

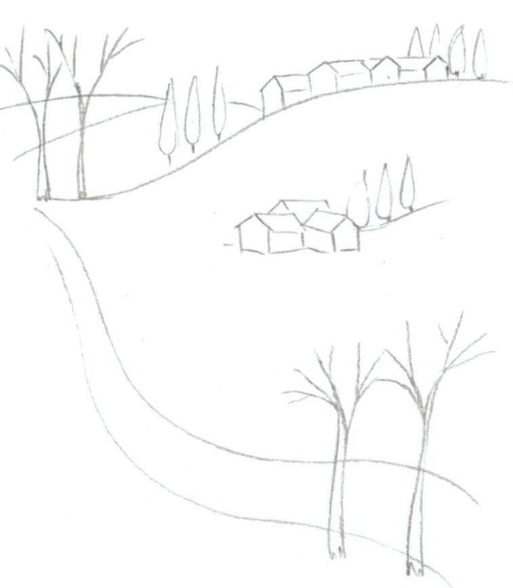

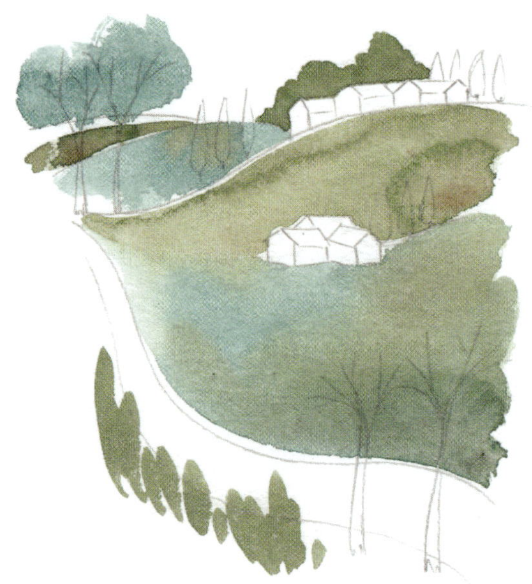

Create a watery mixture of Viridian Green and Alizarin Crimson to make a deep bluish green. Mix Sap Green, Cadmium Red, and lots of water to create a grassy green. Make sure you create plenty of both of these color mixes.

Use a large sable brush to paint the two trees on the left side using the blue-green mixture. Swirl the tip of your brush on the paper to create loose, curving shapes. Paint one of the hills below the trees with a broad sweep of your brush. Use the Sap Green mixture and your large round brush to paint a small hill behind the trees, a larger hill under the village, and a broad brushstroke of paint in the foreground. While that is still wet, add more of the blue-green mixture to the center using your large brush. Allow the two different greens to mix on the paper. Use your medium brush and the Sap Green mixture to paint greenery behind the houses on the top of the hill. Use this Sap Green mixture and your large brush to roughly paint brushstrokes at the bottom of the path, pulling your brush up from bottom to top for each brushstroke.

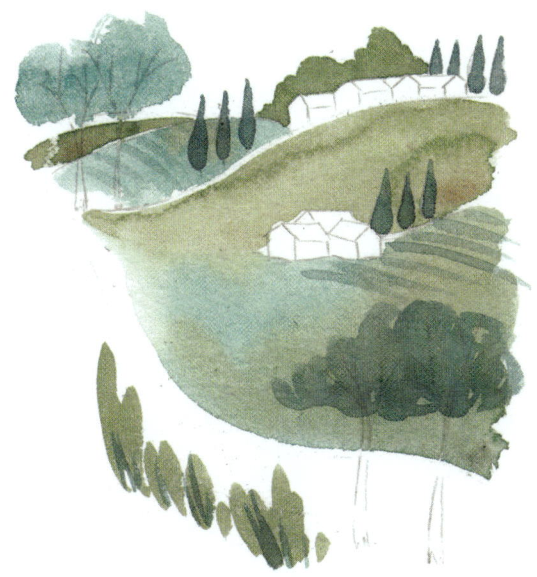

When that's completely dry, use the Viridian Green mixture you've already made and your medium brush to paint broad, curving stripes across the hills to indicate fields. Use this color and your large brush to paint the leaves on the trees in the foreground. Swirl the tip of your brush around loosely to create the shape of the tree. Create another darker mix of Viridian Green with slightly more Alizarin Crimson and less water, and use this mixture and your medium brush to paint the cypress trees. Use this mixture to add a few brushstrokes to the bottom of the picture, over-lapping with the larger brushstrokes already there. As before, pull your brush up from the bottom to the top of the brushstroke.

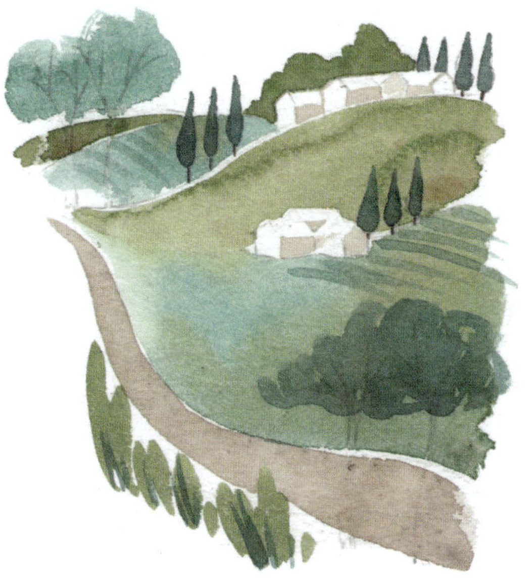 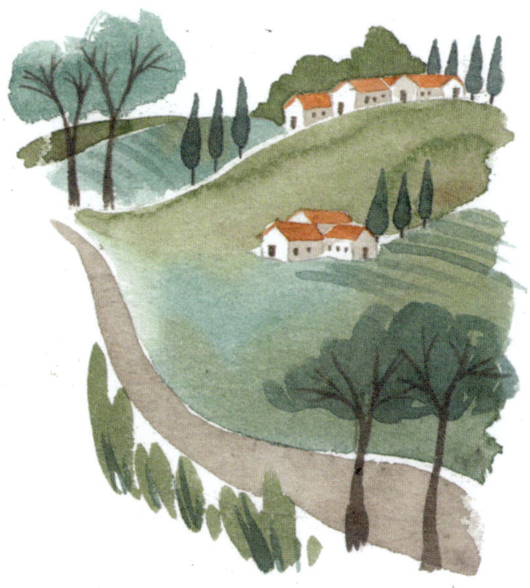

Create a very watery mixture of Sepia. Use this color and your small brush to paint shadows on the right side of the buildings. Use the same mixture and your large brush to paint a sweeping dirt track. Use a darker mixture of Sepia and your small brush to paint thin lines at the bottom of the cypress trees to indicate trunks.

Use Sepia and your small brush to paint the tree trunks on the remaining trees and to paint small doors and windows on the houses. Use Burnt Sienna and your small brush to carefully paint the roofs of the houses.

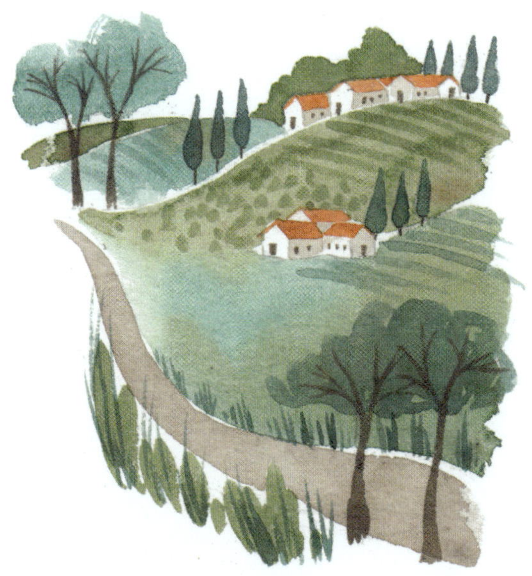

Use the Sap Green mixture and your medium brush to paint broad, curved lines across the top of the hill to indicate fields. On the lower half of the hill, dab your brush to create the impression of bushes or crops. Use the darker Viridian Green mixture and your small brush to add more blades of grass around the dirt track. As before, start with your brush at the bottom and pull it upward to create a long, thin, pointed brushstroke.

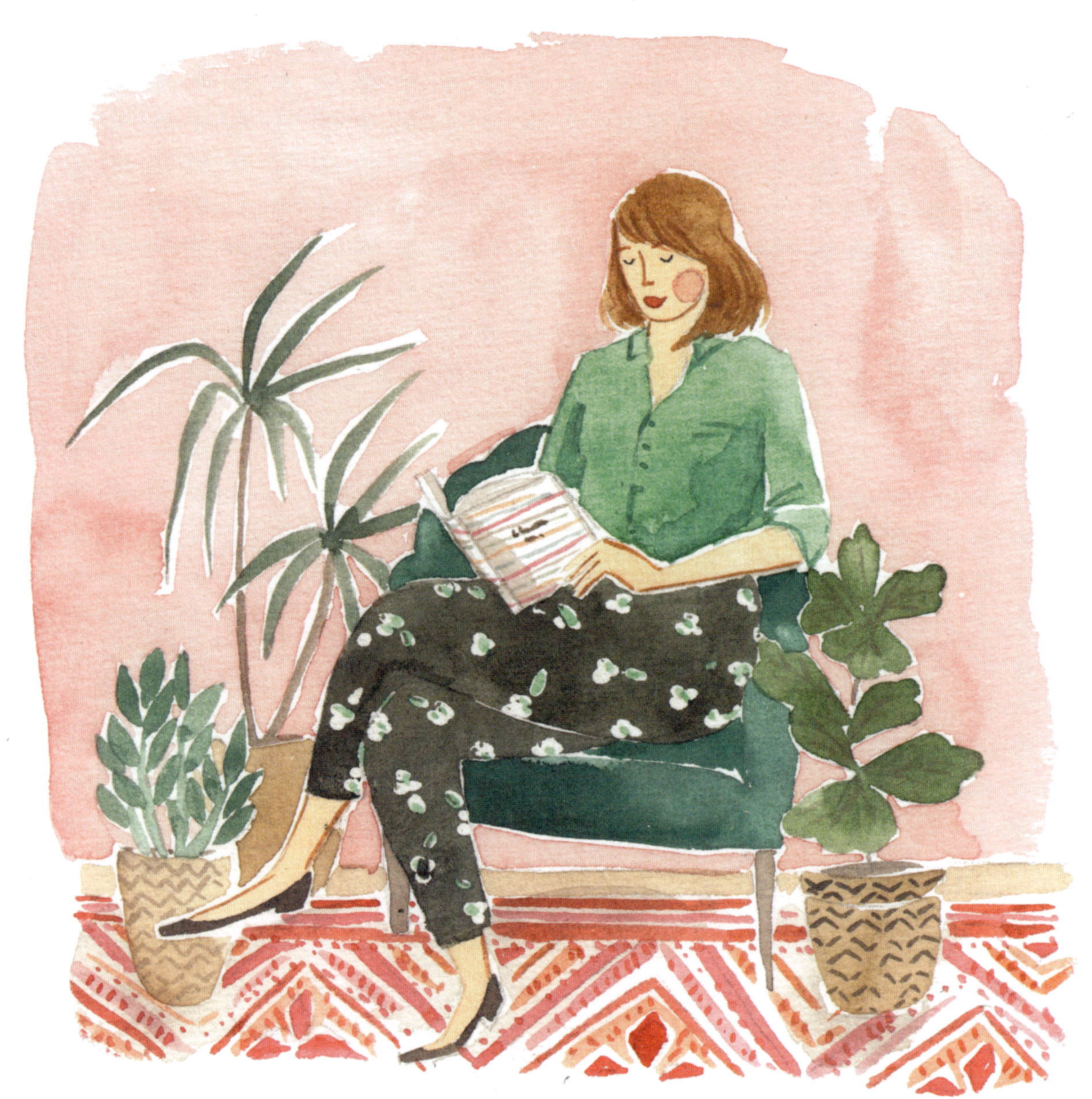

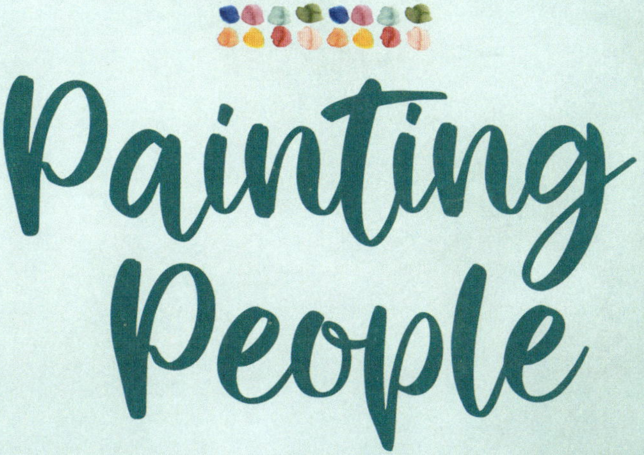

Painting People

Painting people is one of the most challenging yet rewarding subjects for a watercolorist or any artist. By their very nature, people are so complicated; not only do we need to consider anatomy, but we also need to think about body language, emotion, movement, and capturing a likeness, as well as the actual application of paint. It's a lot! Depictions of the human figure are fundamental to art, and creating representations of ourselves and others has been a human instinct since the beginning of time.

This chapter is designed to help you dip your toes into the world of painting people. Painting people is a huge subject, but in this chapter, we are going to look at some of the essential skills you need to be able to paint every variety of people.

Before we can learn to paint people, we need to learn to draw them, and I know this is an area that a lot of people will struggle with. Drawing people is really hard. Don't feel bad if your first attempts don't turn out the way you thought they would. When we start to draw people, there is often an idea that they should look as realistic as possible, and the more realistic the painting, the better it is. But there are many things that make your painting good, and accuracy is just one of them. It's also important to think about creating mood, personality, and gesture, as well as accurately capturing the human form. It is as much of a skill to capture someone's essence with a few well-placed brushstrokes as laboring over shading for hours to create a photorealistic portrait.

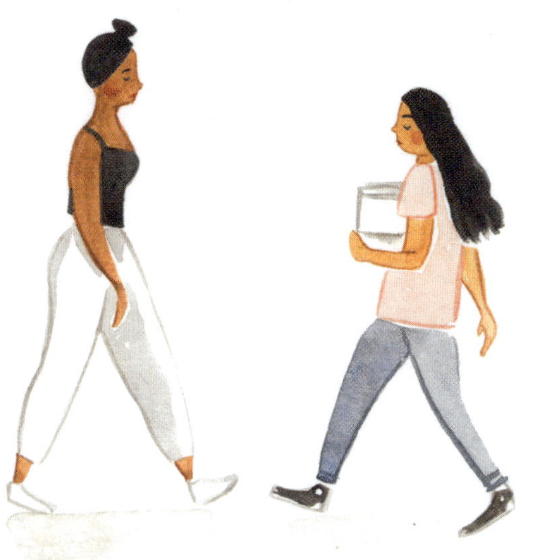

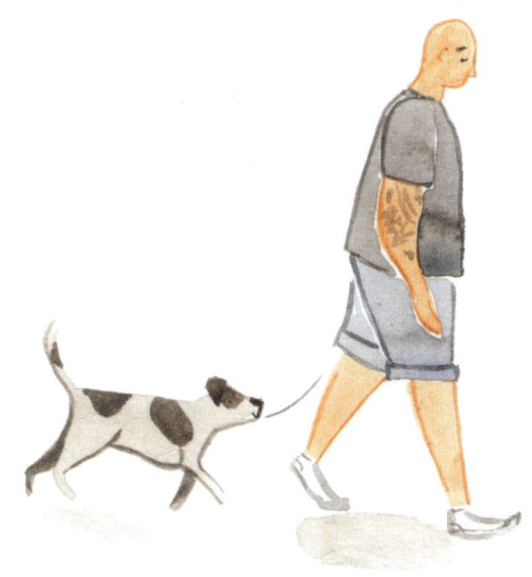

Clearly, the way I draw and paint people is not realistic, but I have my own style, and my people tend to convey a mood or feeling. I do think it's important to first learn the basics of anatomy and then develop your own style. While my work is stylized, I have done years of life drawing while studying art, and I do think there is no better way to learn to draw people than by attending a life drawing class.

Getting Started

The best way to learn to draw people is from life; that could be in a life drawing class, observing people out and about, or asking friends and family to sit for you. Finding a model can sometimes be a challenge, and photos are often a valuable resource for inspiration and reference. Be careful with the photos you choose, though; photos taken from unusual angles or are heavily filtered or cropped won't provide good reference photos. Look for photos that clearly show the subject from a straight-on angle. When working from life or a photo, look at what is actually there. Don't just draw what you think you can see. Spend as much time looking at your subject as drawing.

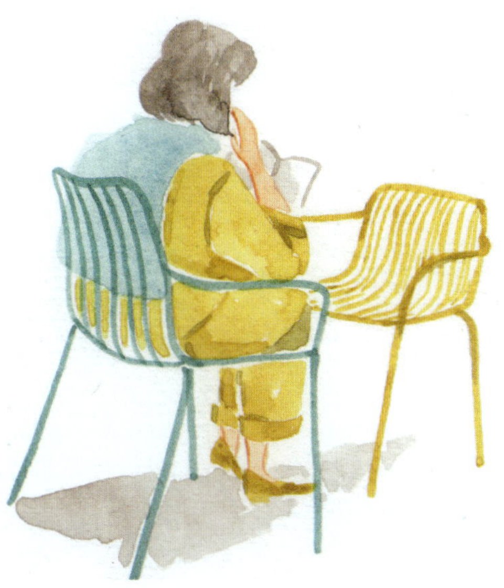

Top Tips for Drawing People

Be an observer of people. One of the most important things that we need to do when we learn to draw or paint is learn to look at the world around us and really see it. The best way to learn to draw people is to become an observer of people. Watch people when you're in a café, on the train, or in a park. Notice their body language, how they move, how they stand, how they dress. People watching often inspires the work in my sketchbook; sometimes I see somebody with a great outfit walking their dog or standing contemplatively in front of a painting in a gallery, and I have to draw them. Keep an eye out for interesting people who inspire you.

Think of the face or body as a whole and not as separate limbs or facial features. Don't pay too much attention to one particular area, drawing it in great detail while neglecting others. For example, it would be a mistake to draw two very detailed realistic eyes, draw an oval around them, and then try to work out where the mouth and nose should go. Sketch the shape of the head first, then roughly sketch in the eyes, nose, and mouth. Once they are in the right place, you can add more detail. All the facial features and body parts work in tandem with each other; think about the relationship between them while you are sketching. Once you have roughly sketched the whole face or the whole body, you can add more details.

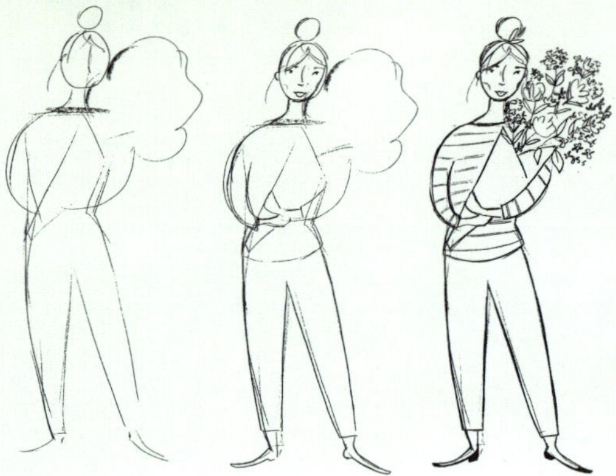

Get some distance from your drawing to see what's wrong. Sometimes we know a drawing isn't right, but we can't quite see what's wrong. A big problem when drawing is that we see what we think is there, not what's actually there. This can make it difficult to spot our own mistakes. A good tip is to turn your drawing or painting upside down. It will be much easier to spot mistakes, like eyes that aren't on the same level or features that are out of proportion. You could also look at your painting in the mirror, take a photo of it, or prop up your painting and then take a few steps back. Get some physical distance from your painting so you can look at the whole thing objectively. If you notice something not right about your drawing, correct it immediately. It's much better to fix mistakes early than to continue adding details to a drawing you know is wrong.

Look at things in relationship to each other.

Look for reference points to help you get things in proportion and in the right place. Facial features and body parts work in relationship to each other, so try not to focus on individual features too much. For example, when you're thinking about how long the arm should be, check how far down the thigh it comes. When you are working out how high the eyes should be on a face, look at where they are in relationship to their ears. You can look at body parts in relationship to other body parts, to the clothes they are wearing, and to the background they are standing in front of. You can even look at the negative space. If someone has their hand on their hip, look at the triangle of negative space created between the waist and the bent arm.

Think about capturing personality, not just a technically accurate portrait.

There is more to creating a portrait than just creating a photorealistic representation of a person. Personality is so important, too. When you think about painting someone you know, think about what makes them "them." Do they have rosy cheeks, freckles, bushy eyebrows, glasses, a beard, a wide nose, thin lips? Your painting might not be photo-realistic, but if you capture some of the key distinguishing features and the personality of your subject, they will surely be recognizable.

Less is more.

Not only can a drawing with a few well-chosen brush marks be lively and engaging; it can also appear more accurate. When we don't have all the details, our brains fill in the gaps, which can help a simple painting look more accomplished. When we draw or paint in a highly detailed, realistic way, it's important to get it really accurate; otherwise, it can look a little bit odd or distracting.

PROPORTIONS

Below is a rough guide to proportions for a man, a woman, and a child. Take the time to look at the person you're actually drawing; very few people have perfect proportions. Generally, the proportion of an adult is such that their height is roughly equal to seven or eight heads, and a young child has a much larger head in proportion to their body. The young child in this example is four heads tall and the baby is two and a half heads tall, but this will vary depending on the child's age.

The younger the child, the bigger their head in proportion to their body.

Of course, these proportions are just a starting point. Almost nobody has these exact proportions; we're all different. Some people have long necks, sloping shoulders, a broad chest, narrow hips, short legs, and so on. When you're observing people, think about how you might represent their body type, posture, and mood in a drawing. Would you use curved lines or more angular lines? Are they upright or slouched? Do they rest their weight on one foot more than the other? The more time you spend carefully observing, the better you become at drawing people. Look at your model or reference picture, and think about where they actually carry their weight. Additionally, we may choose to disregard these proportions to stylize a painting or illustration.

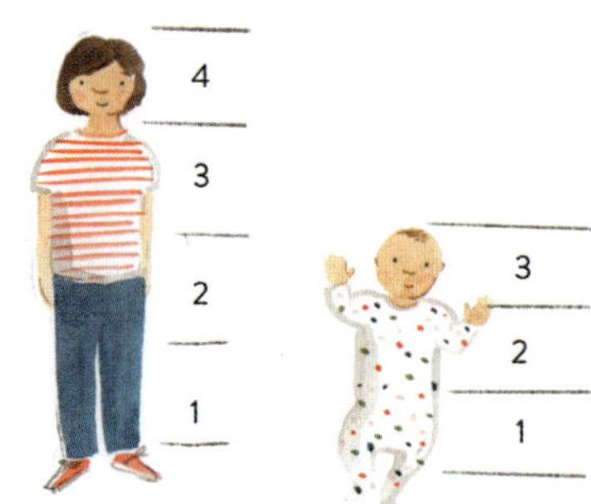

FACIAL FEATURES

Again, here is a rough guide to facial proportions. The eyes are roughly on the midline of the head. The nose is halfway between the eyes and the chin, and the lips are halfway between the nose and the chin. The eyebrows are a quarter of the way up from the eyes to the top of the head, and the ears are level with the eyes. These guidelines are a useful reference when practicing drawing faces, but don't worry about sticking to them too rigidly; everyone's face is different.

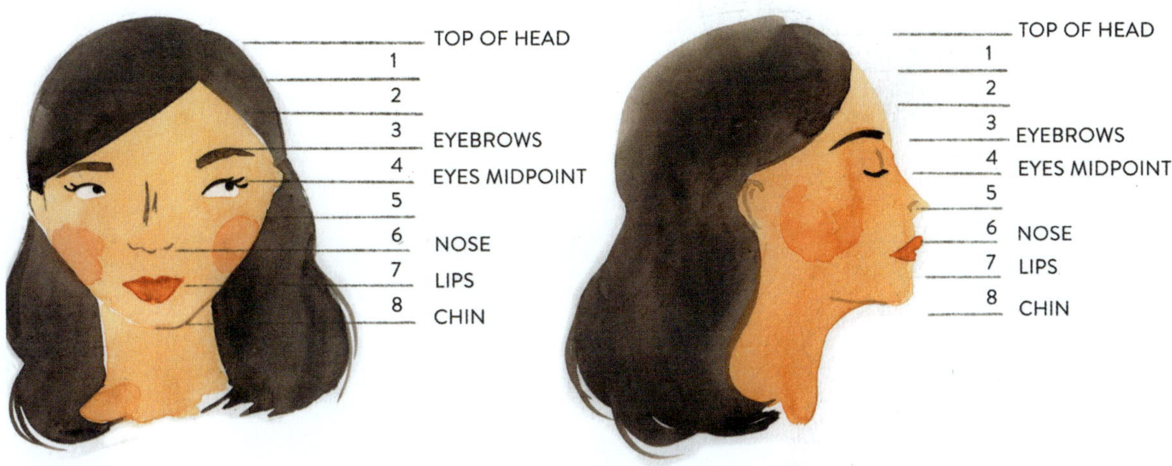

PAINTING SKIN AND HAIR-COLOR MIXING

This color-mixing exercise will show how I simply mix a range of skin tones and hair colors. The key with both mixing skin tones and hair colors is to keep things subtle and natural. Nobody wants a bright pink face and yellow hair!

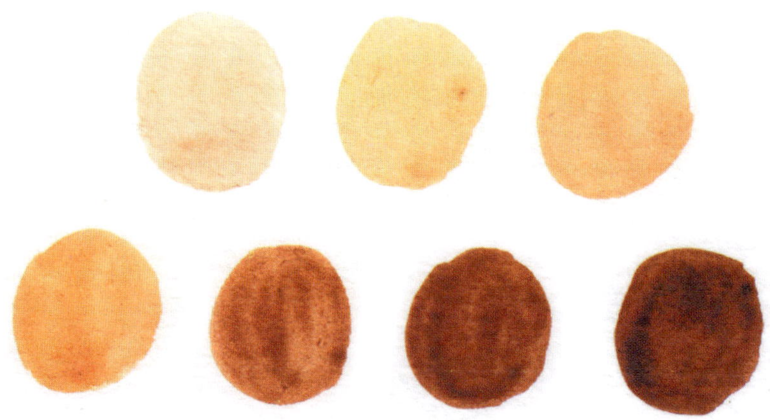

Skin Tones

Painting skin can be intimidating, and many artists have a highly complex way of capturing skin tones, picking out undertones of purple, yellow, and even green and exploring light and shadow on the face. Due to my illustrative style, I have developed a simple method for painting skin tones using Chinese White as a base and then adding varying amounts of Burnt Sienna, Yellow Ochre, and Burnt Umber to create a variety of skin tones. The Chinese White stops the mixture from being too watery even when it is very pale and makes it easier to handle. Using this method, you can make a skin tone darker by adding Burnt Umber, more golden by adding Yellow Ochre, more pink by adding Burnt Sienna, and paler by adding Chinese White.

Materials Any paper • Any brush
Colors Used Burnt Sienna ⬤ Chinese White ◯ Yellow Ochre ⬤ Burnt Umber ⬤

Start by adding a small amount of Burnt Sienna with Chinese White, and paint a swatch. Add Yellow Ochre to the mixture, and paint a swatch next to the first swatch. Add more Yellow Ochre to the mixture, and paint another swatch. Add more Burnt Sienna to the mixture, and paint another swatch. Keep adding both Burnt Sienna and Yellow Ochre at the same time, and paint another two swatches, getting progressively deeper in color. Add a tiny bit of Burnt Umber to the mixture, and paint another swatch. Add more Burnt Umber and Burnt Sienna to the mixture, and paint another swatch. Continue adding more Burnt Umber, and paint another two swatches, getting progressively deeper in color. Paint a final swatch using just Burnt Umber.

TIP I always start by adding Burnt Sienna to the Chinese White base because it is the warmest of the earth colors and will work in most skin tones.

Hair Colors

Materials Any paper • Any brush

Colors Used Lamp Black ● Sepia ● Cadmium Red ● Prussian Blue ● Burnt Sienna ● Yellow Ochre ● Burnt Umber ● Alizarin Crimson ●

Black hair. When painting black hair, I simply use Lamp Black straight from the palette or occasionally mix it with Sepia. If you want to have a go mixing your own black that is warmer or cooler, you could try mixing Cadmium Red with a little Prussian Blue. Slightly more Cadmium Red will be warmer; slightly more Prussian Blue will be cooler.

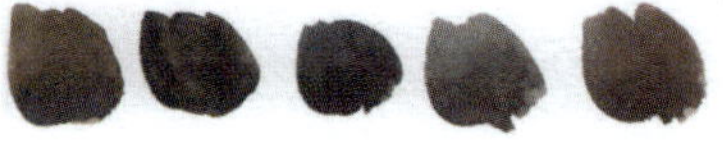

Brown hair. For dark brown hair, I normally use Sepia or Burnt Umber. If you want to mix a dark brown and don't have any Sepia or Burnt Umber in your palate, you could try the following paint mix: Yellow Ochre, Cadmium Red, Lamp Black. Combine Cadmium Red and Yellow Ochre until you've made a warm orange, and then gradually add Lamp Black until you g

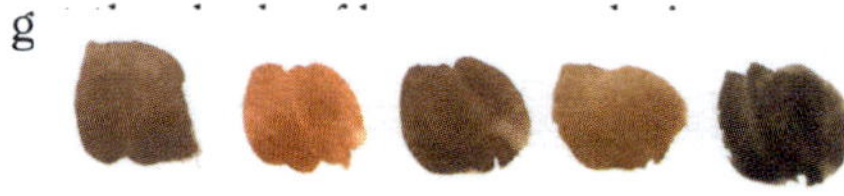

Blond hair. Blond hair is perhaps the most difficult to paint because it's the most multi-tonal and subtle. What you definitely don't want to do is create bright yellow hair. Generally, I find the cooler the blond hair is, the more natural it looks. Try mixing Yellow Ochre with a tiny bit of Sepia and lots of water to create a blond hair color. Allow it to pool in different areas to add depth. When it's dry, add a few individual strands with a light brown pencil.

For a strawberry blond, try mixing Yellow Ochre with a bit of Burnt Sienna and lots of water.

For platinum blond or bleached blond, add plenty of water and allow white areas of paper

:ool

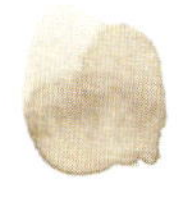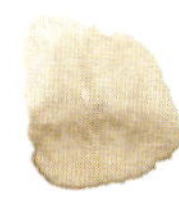

Auburn hair. Burnt Sienna straight out of the palette is great for red hair, or you can mix a subtle red using a mixture of Yellow Ochre and Alizarin Crimson.

Gray hair. For gray hair, you can use Lamp Black for a cooler gray and Sepia for a warmer gray. Add lots of water, and keep it really multitonal. Leave white areas of paper to show light reflecting on the hair, and allow color to pool in some areas where the hair might be in shadow.

Dyed hair. It can be a lot of fun painting hair that has been dyed unnatural colors. Dyed hair can be any color of the rainbow! The key with painting this hair is, as always, to keep it more multitonal so it doesn't look too flat. You can pool color in different areas and show highlights on the hair by leaving white space.

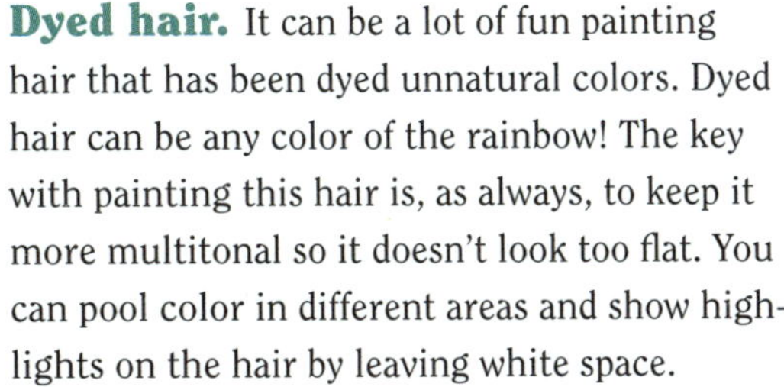

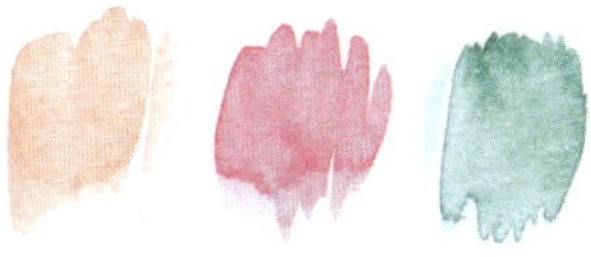

TOP TIPS FOR PAINTING HAIR Think about the direction that you are pulling your brush. Generally, I always start my brush at the scalp and pull it down toward the shoulders or forehead. Usually, hair is going downward, so it makes sense to use vertical brushstrokes, not horizontal. Also, as you pull the brush in the direction of the hair, you will create feathery brush marks at the end of the brushstroke that look like hair. For curly hair, lightly swirl the tip of your brush on the paper to create spirals. For textured hair, use a very dry mixture of paint, and apply it in a light dabbing motion with your brush to create a soft, full texture. When painting more complicated hairstyles like braids, ponytails, or buns, think about the direction of the hair, and paint your brushstrokes in that direction.

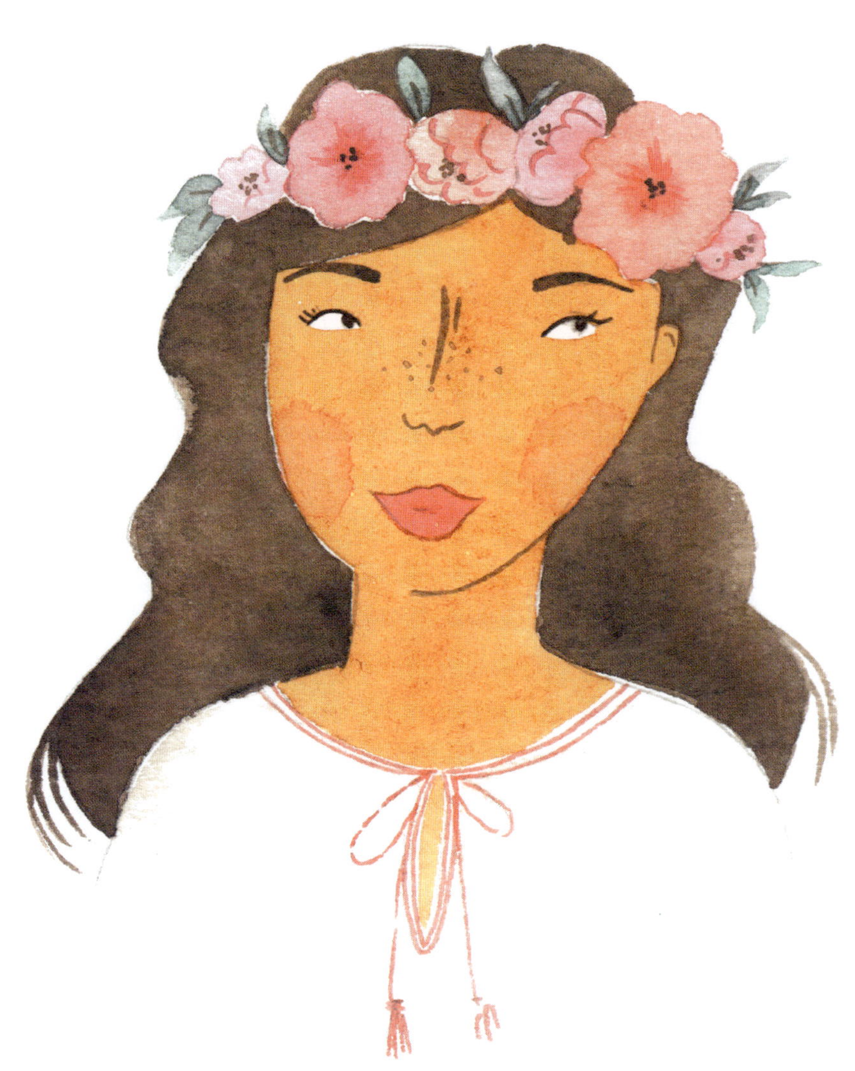

Girl with a Flower Crown

This beautiful decorative painting will help you practice painting faces and capturing hair and skin tones. It's really easy to adapt this piece with whatever skin tone and hair shade you prefer.

Materials Cold press watercolor paper • Pencil • Large round brush • Medium round brush Small round brush

Colors Used Yellow Ochre ● Burnt Sienna ● Burnt Umber ● Alizarin Crimson ●
Sepia ● Viridian Green ● Lamp Black ●

Lightly sketch the girl's face using pencil. Pay attention to the placement of the eyes and eyebrows.

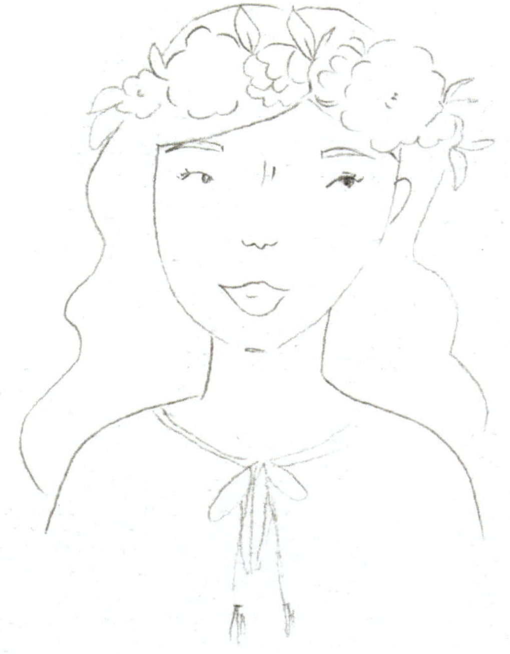

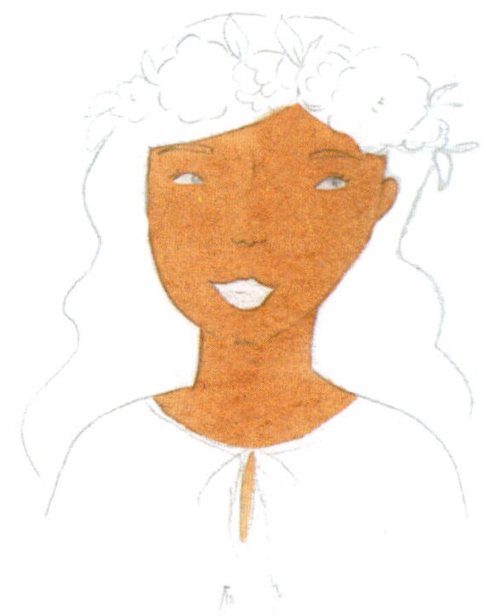

Mix Yellow Ochre, Burnt Sienna, Burnt Umber, and lots of water to create a warm brown. Paint the girl's face using your medium round brush, being careful to leave white space for the eyes and the lips.

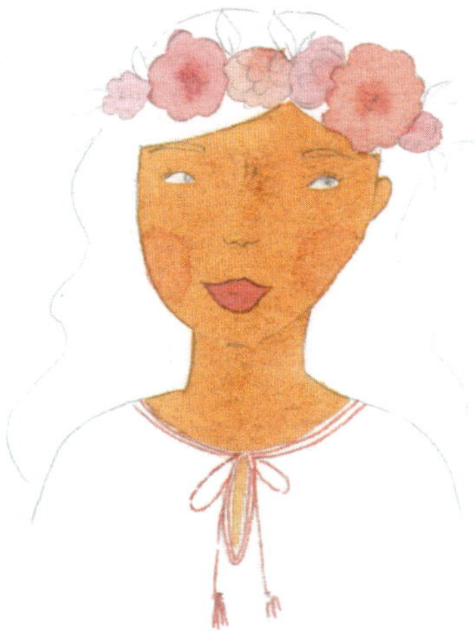

Mix Alizarin Crimson and Burnt Sienna to create a warm pink, and paint the lips carefully using your small brush. Use the same color and a small brush to paint the embroidery on the woman's blouse. Add more water to the color, and paint the cheeks using your medium brush. Paint several of the flowers using the same mixture. Add more of the paint mix to the center of the flowers. Use a watery mixture of Alizarin Crimson to paint the remaining flowers. Add a drop of darker Alizarin Crimson to the center while it's still wet.

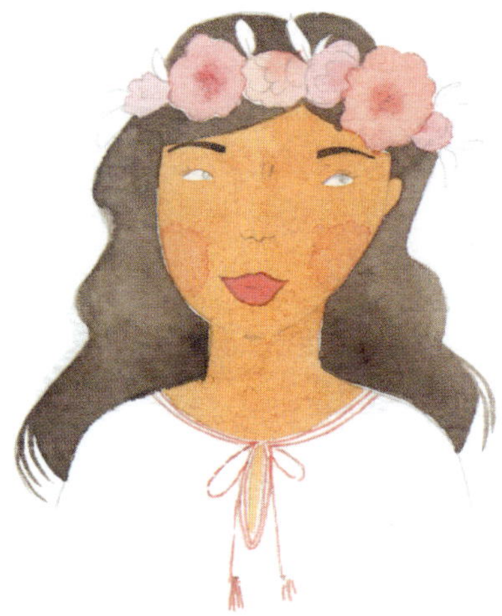

Use Sepia and your small brush to carefully paint the woman's eyebrows. Add more water to the mixture, and paint the woman's hair. Paint carefully around the flowers and leaves using your small brush, then switch to the large brush for the rest of the hair. Use a very wet mixture, and allow color to pool in some areas, such as around the neck and under the flowers.

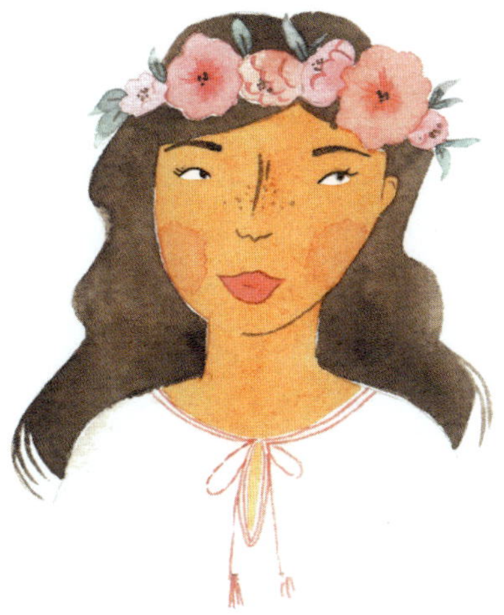

Create a muted green using Viridian Green, Alizarin Crimson, and lots of water, and carefully paint the leaves using your small brush. Allow more color to pool where the leaf meets the flower crown. Use Sepia and your small brush to paint the woman's nose, chin, and ear, and add some freckles with a more watery mixture of Sepia. Use a very watery mixture of Sepia and your medium brush to add subtle shadows to her blouse, working loosely; less is more. Paint her eyes using your small brush and Lamp Black. Take your time, and think about the direction in which you are pulling the brush.

Use Sepia and your small brush to add stems to the leaves and dots to the centers of the flowers. Use a watery mixture of Alizarin Crimson and your small brush to paint petals on some of the flowers and a little shadow in the middle of the woman's lips.

TIP Really take your time with the eyes; this will make your painting come to life.

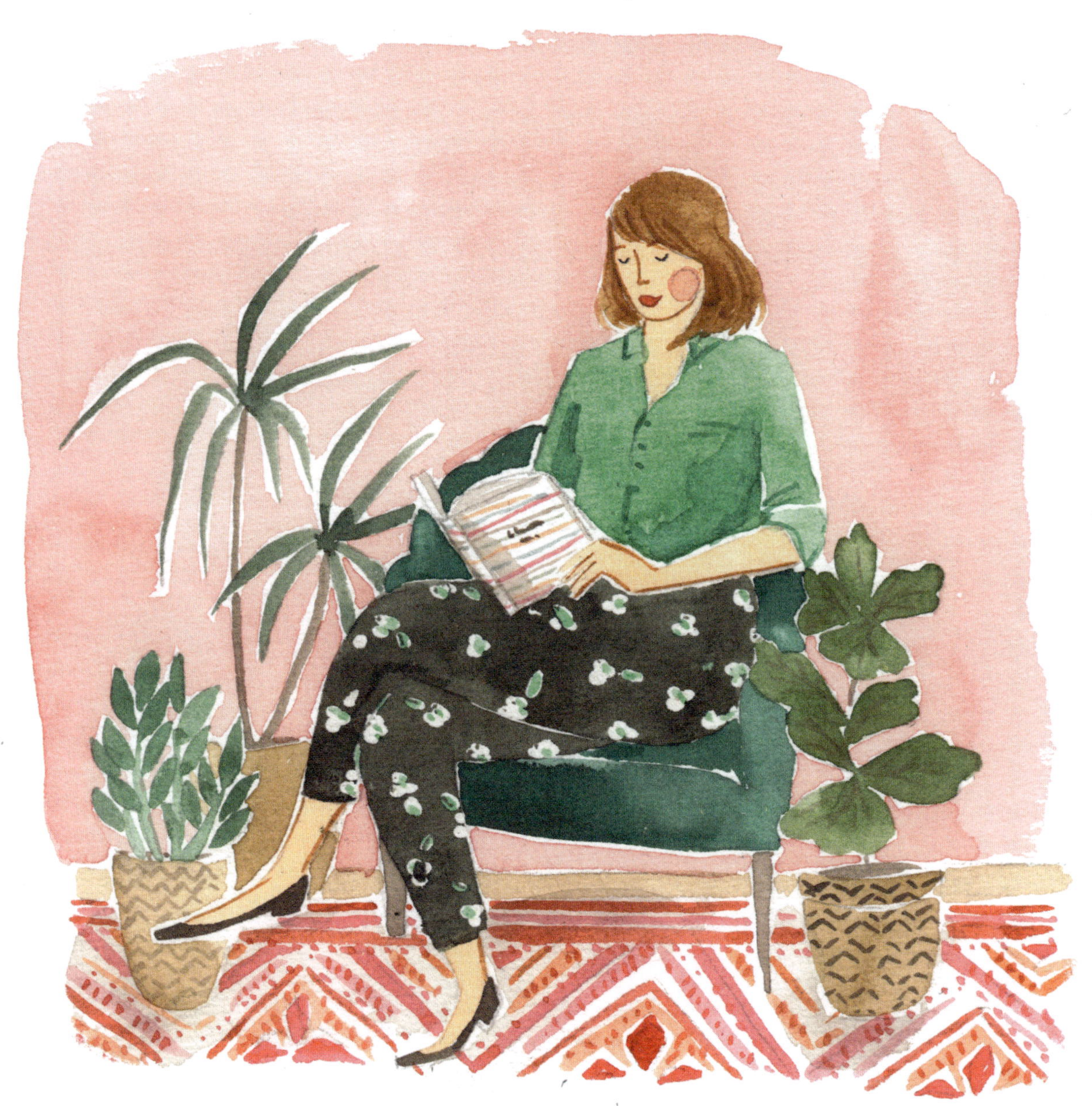

Woman Reading with Plants

In this piece, we explore placing a figure in their surroundings rather than just floating in space. This piece uses a limited complementary color palette and a bit of masking fluid to help with the details. This work is similar to that of Matisse, with its layering of pattern on pattern and the placing of a female figure in a busy decorative scene.

Materials Cold press watercolor paper • Pencil • Eraser • Masking fluid • Old small round brush for masking fluid • Small round brush • Medium round brush • Large sable brush
Colors Used Chinese White   Burnt Sienna ● Lamp Black ● Sap Green ● Viridian Green ●
Yellow Ochre ● Cadmium Red ● Sepia ● Burnt Umber ● Alizarin Crimson ●

Sketch a woman sitting on a chair using my sketch for reference. Pay attention to her proportions, and build up the figure using a mixture of straight and curved lines, simplifying the form as much as possible.

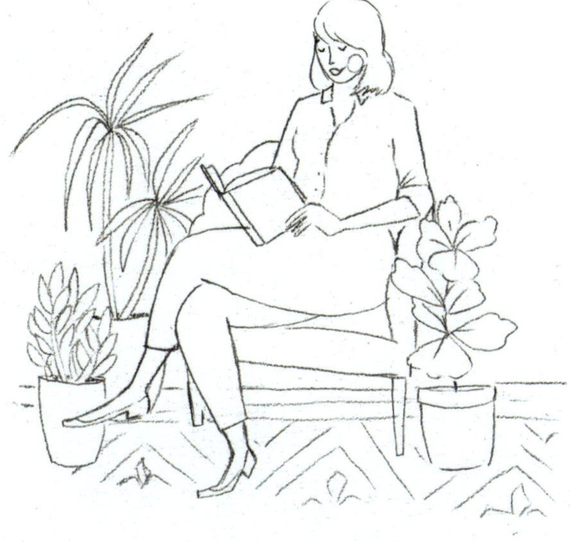

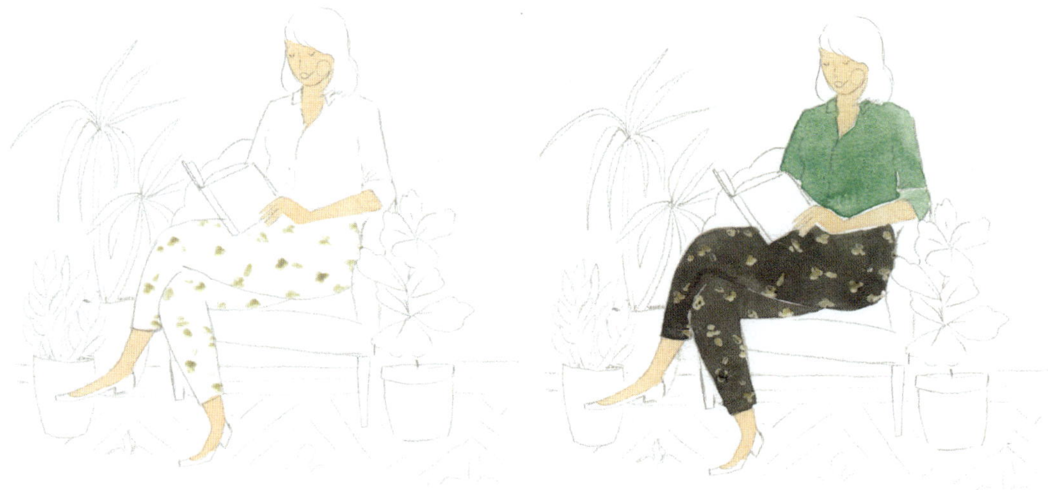

Paint little flowers and leaves on the trousers using masking fluid and an old small brush. While that is drying, mix Chinese White with Burnt Sienna to make a pale skin color. Paint the woman's face, hand, and ankles with another small round brush.

When the masking fluid is dry, paint the woman's trousers using a mixture of Lamp Black and a bit of Sap Green using your large brush. Allow the color to pool where there would naturally be shadows.

Mix a green using Viridian Green, Yellow Ochre, and a little Chinese White. Paint the woman's shirt using your large paintbrush. Add more water to the mixture when painting the rolled-up sleeves.

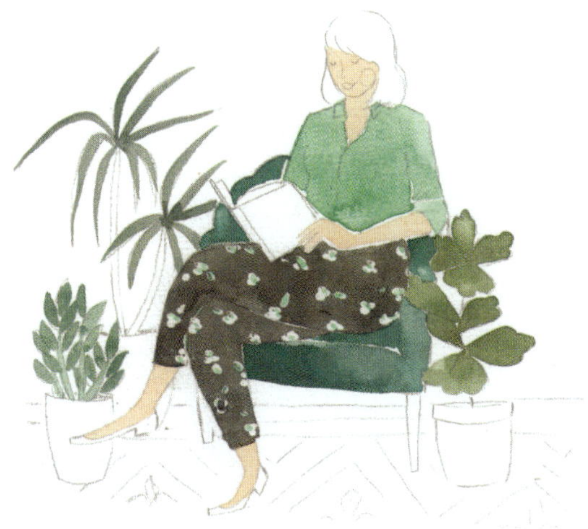

 completely dry, carefully remove the masking fluid. Mix a deep emerald green using Viridian Green with a bit of Cadmium Red. Add more water to one side of the paint mix on the palette to lighten it. Paint the chair using your medium brush and the lighter shade first, then add more deep green where shadows would naturally fall—on the seat, under the woman's arm, and behind her leg.

Mix Sap Green with a bit of Sepia, and paint the fiddle leaf fig on the right with your medium brush, allowing more color to pool in different parts of the leaves. Mix Viridian Green with a little Sepia to make a deep green, and paint the tall plant at the back with your small brush. Paint each leaf with a single brushstroke, varying the pressure to create the tapered leaf shape. Add more water and more Viridian Green to the mixture, and paint the plant in the foreground, adding more water when painting the stems.

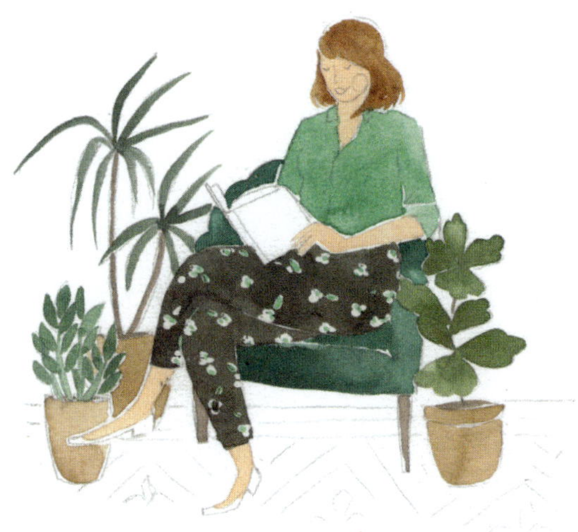

Mix Yellow Ochre and a bit of Sepia to make a light brown. Using your medium brush, paint the plant pots. You can work quite loosely and allow a bit of white space to show when painting around leaves. Allow the color to pool in some areas.

Paint the legs of the chair, the stems of the tall plants, and the soil in the plant pot using Sepia and your small brush. Use a mixture of Burnt Umber and Yellow Ochre and your small brush to paint the woman's hair. Add more Burnt Umber to the woman's hair where it might naturally be in shadow.

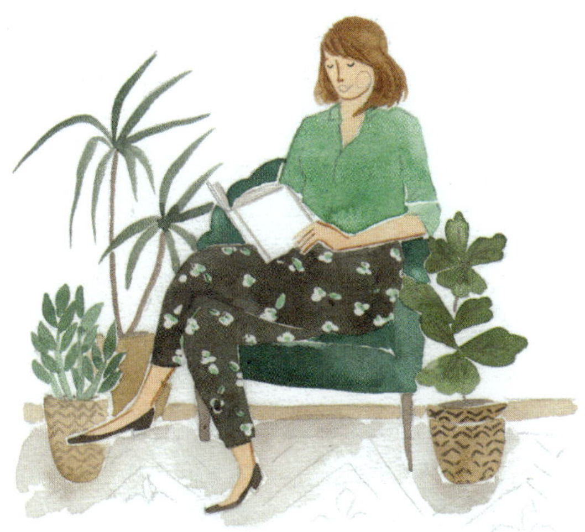

Use Sepia and your small brush to paint zigzags on two of the plant pots. Use a darker mixture of Sepia and your small brush to paint the woman's shoes. Use a very watery mixture of Sepia to outline the book she is reading. Use the mixture of Sepia and Yellow Ochre to paint the strip of floor between the rug and the wall. Use Burnt Umber and your small brush to carefully outline the woman's nose, ankles, and arm and to add more detail to her hair. Use Sepia and your small brush to paint her eyes.

Using a very watery mixture of Sepia, loosely paint shadows underneath the woman and the plant pot. We will be adding detail on top of this later, so keep it light.

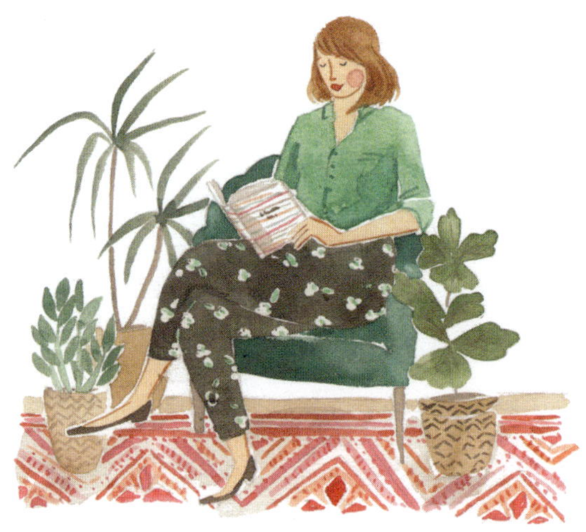

Mix Alizarin Crimson with a little bit of Burnt Sienna to paint her lips with your small brush. Use the same color with more water to paint her cheeks.

Paint the Peruvian rug using the mix of Alizarin Crimson and Burnt Sienna and pure Alizarin Crimson and pure Burnt Sienna in varying concentrations. Build up the pattern using a series of lines, dashes, and dots. Don't worry about being too precise; keep the design loose and playful.

Use a mix of watery Sepia and your small brush to add veins to the leaves of the fiddle leaf fig.

Use Alizarin Crimson, Burnt Sienna, a watery mixture of Sepia, and some of the greens still on your palette to paint the stripes on the book with your small brush. When dry, add shadows using watery Sepia, and add text to the front of the book using a stronger mixture of Sepia. Mix Viridian Green with a little bit of Sepia and lots of water. Add details to the woman's shirt, and add shadows around the arms using your small brush.

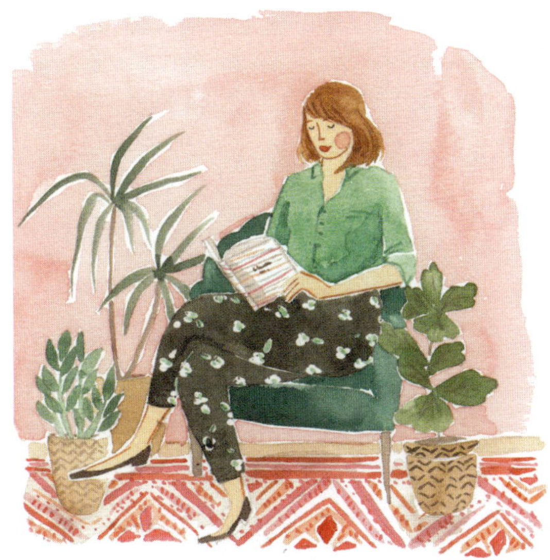

When that's all completely dry, use an eraser to remove any remaining pencil marks. Mix a large amount of Alizarin Crimson and Burnt Sienna with lots of water. We are using this color for the background, and because you don't want to run out halfway through, mix more than you think you need. Paint the background using a large round sable brush.

TIP Sable brushes are great for this kind of work because they can fill in large areas but also have a fine point for small details, which means you won't have to swap brushes often. Work quickly and loosely. Don't worry about leaving white space around the plants or the woman. The little slivers of white space keep the painting fresh and lively and prevent it from looking overworked. Add slightly more paint to areas of the wall that might be more in shadow, and keep the edges of the background rough and loose.

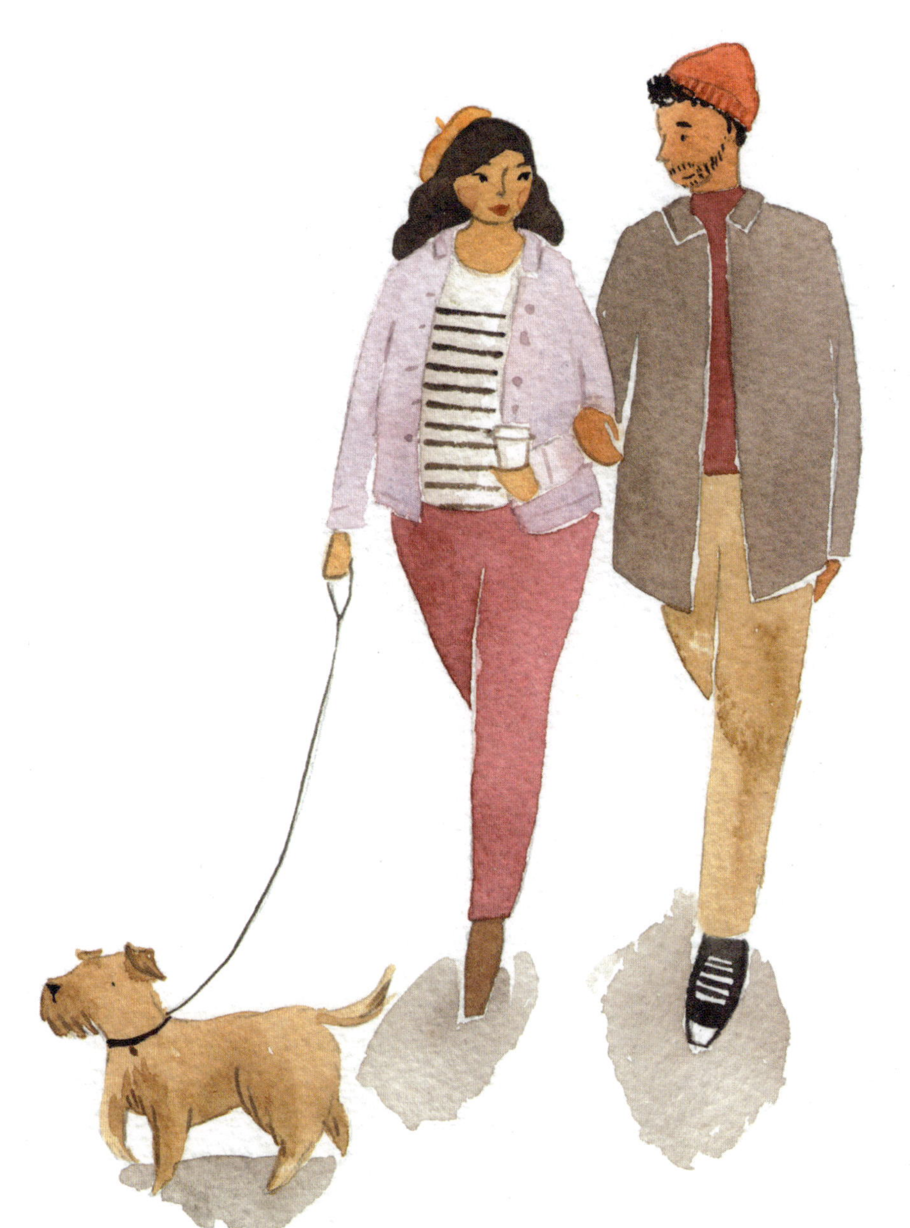

Dog Walkers

This piece deals with a few things that you might find tricky—showing movement, drawing people at a slight angle, and drawing people interacting with each other. It utilizes a limited color palette, which makes the piece stylish and cohesive. Pieces like this normally come about after people watching and sketching from life. Next time you're at the park, take time to watch people walking, take in their outfits and body language, and try to translate it to a painting when you get home.

Materials Cold press watercolor paper • Pencil • Eraser • Medium round brush • Small round brush
Colors Used Burnt Umber ● Yellow Ochre ● Sepia ● Alizarin Crimson ● Burnt Sienna ● Lamp Black ● Ultramarine ●

Start by sketching the couple and the dog in pencil. Spend some time getting the sketch right. This piece involves some perspective, which gives the sense of the man, woman, and dog walking toward us. With the couple, one leg comes toward us and one is tucked behind, giving the impression that they are walking toward us. Make sure the man, woman, and dog are all in proportion to each other.

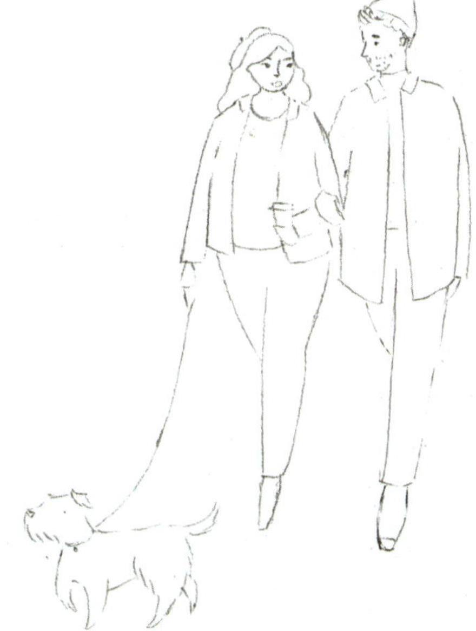

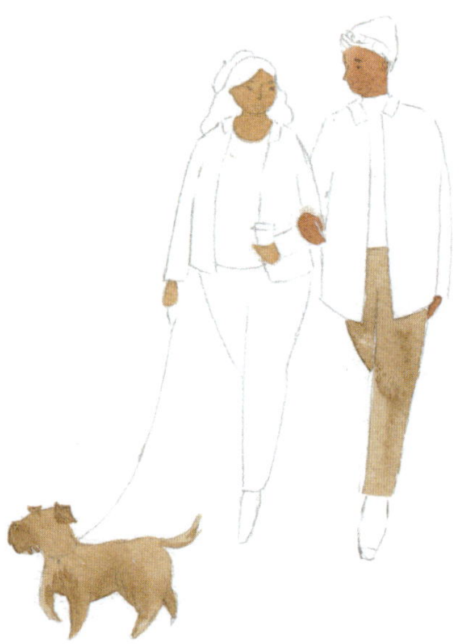

Paint the man's face and hand using Burnt Umber and your small brush.

Mix Yellow Ochre with Sepia and plenty of water to create a muted light brown color. Use this color to paint the woman's face and the man's pants. Leave a tiny white gap between the front and back legs, and add more color to the back leg. Add more water to one side of the brown paint mix to create a lighter version. Paint the dog using your medium brush and the lighter paint mix.

TIP Paint the dog's fur the same way you would paint human hair, pulling a brush in the direction of the fur, especially around the tail and nose. While that's still wet, add some of the darker paint mix to the ears, muzzle, and around the legs.

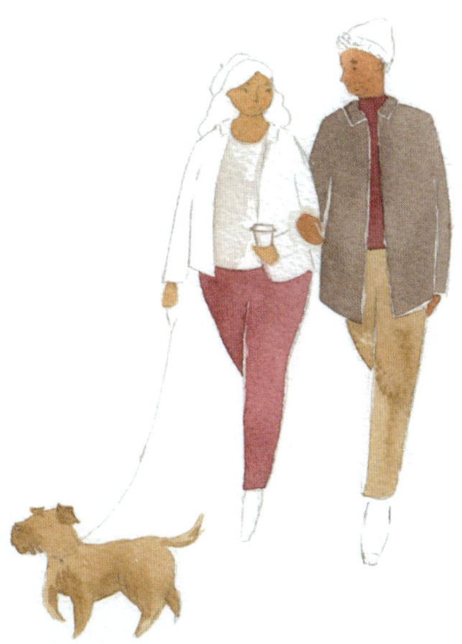

Create a deep burgundy by mixing Alizarin Crimson with a bit of Sepia. Using this color, paint the woman's pants and the man's T-shirt. When painting the woman's pants, leave a thin white space between her legs and allow more color to pool in the leg behind.

Paint the man's coat with a watery mixture of Sepia and your medium brush. Add more water to the mixture to paint the woman's T-shirt and coffee cup.

TIP By leaving this thin white line and painting the leg behind a deeper color, we give a sense of the two legs being separate and one being behind the other, without needing to use outlines.

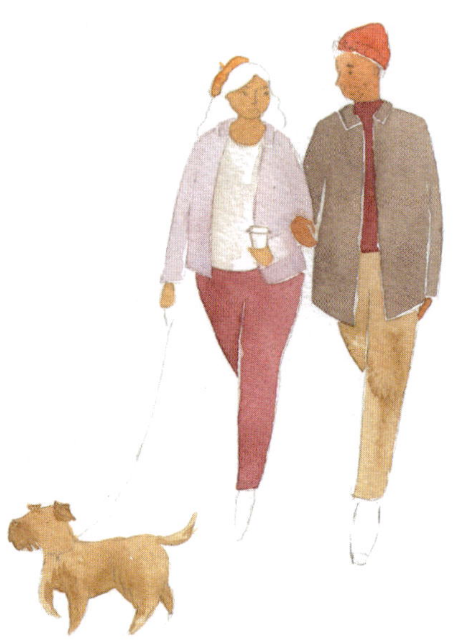

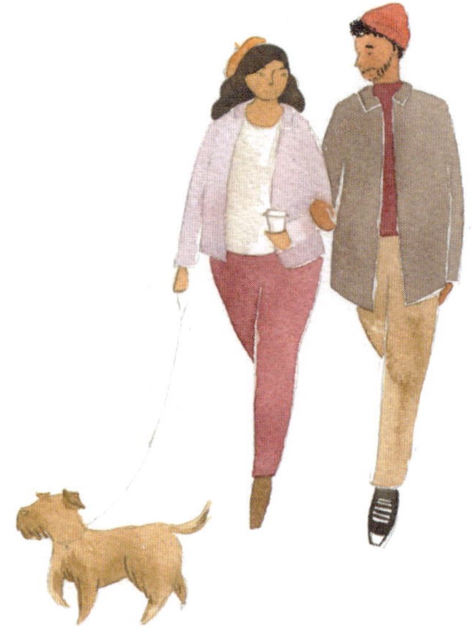

Mix Alizarin Crimson and Burnt Sienna, and paint the man's hat with your small brush.

Paint the woman's hat using Yellow Ochre and your small brush.

Make a light lilac with Alizarin Crimson, Ultramarine, and lots of water. Use your medium brush to paint the woman's jacket.

Paint the woman's hair using Sepia and your small brush. Again using Sepia and your small brush, outline her nose, eyebrows, and chin. Paint the man's beard, eyebrows, and hair using Lamp Black and your small brush. Swirl your small brush to create an impression of curly hair. Use Lamp Black and your small brush to add more details to the dog.

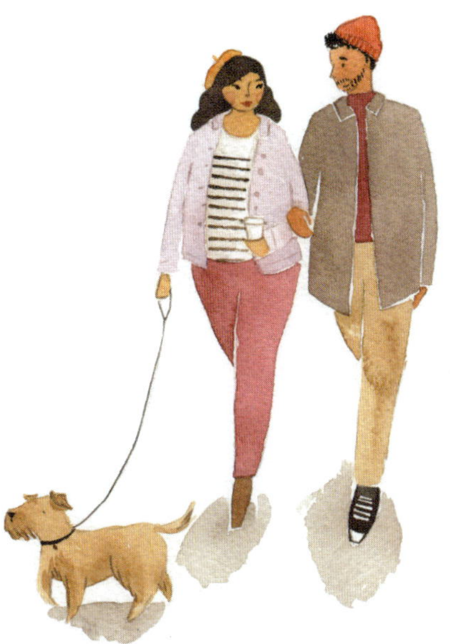

Very carefully paint the man and the woman's eyes using your small brush and Lamp Black. Using the small brush and Lamp Black, paint the dog's nose, eye, and collar. Using Sepia and your small brush, paint the dog's lead and horizontal stripes on the woman's T-shirt.

Mix Alizarin Crimson with Burnt Sienna, and using a small brush, paint the woman's lips and add detail to the man's hat. Add more water to the mixture, and paint the woman's cheeks using your small brush.

Use a watery mixture of Sepia and a medium brush to loosely paint shadows under the feet of the woman, man, and dog.

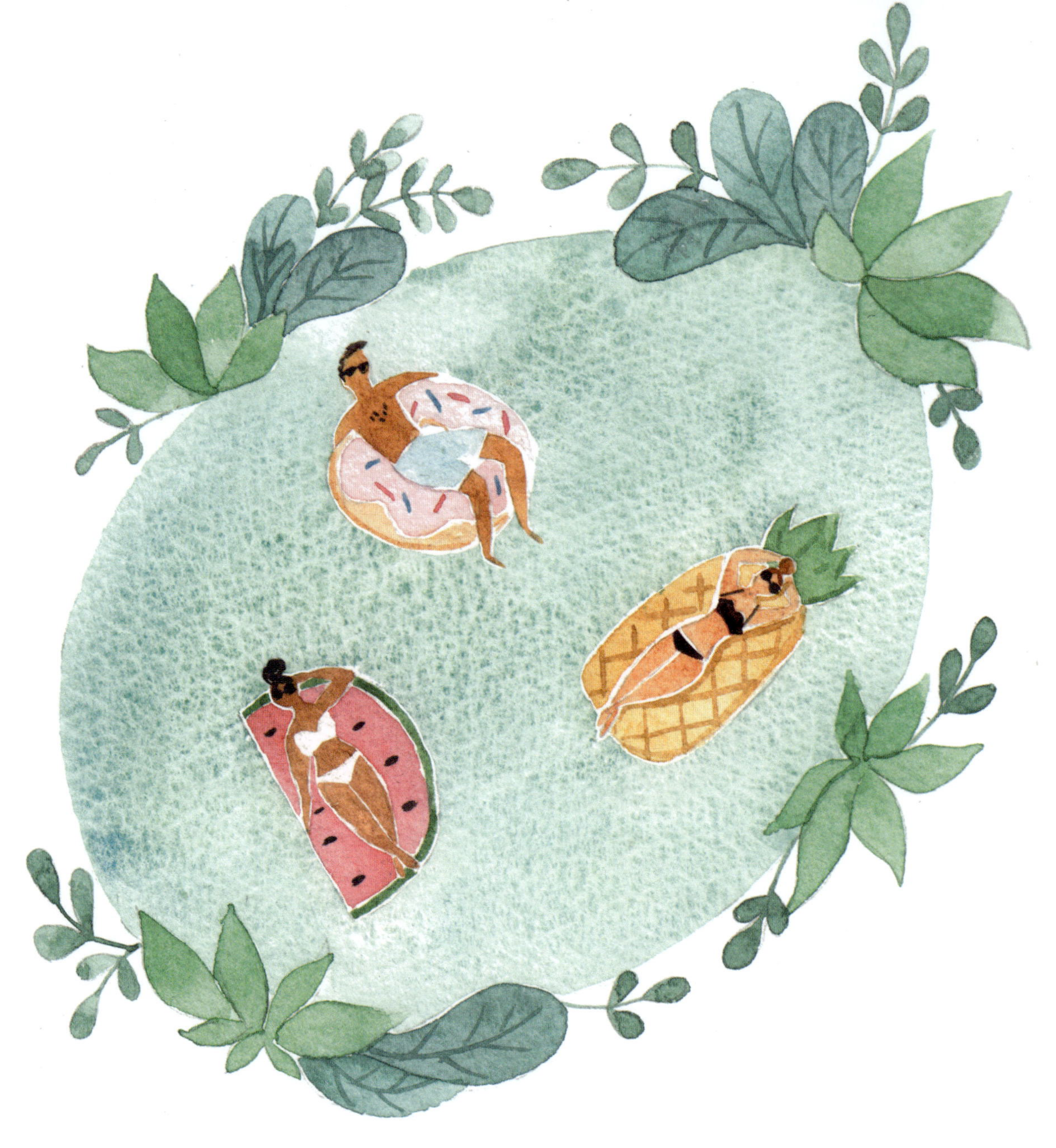

Tropical Pool Party

This piece is inspired by novelty pool toys and swimming pools surrounded by lush tropical plants. We will paint figures on a very different scale; they are part of the overall piece but not the sole focus. Working on a much smaller scale, we don't need to worry too much about painting individual facial features or total accuracy. Creating a fun, atmospheric piece is the aim. We also use masking fluid to create a seamless wash of blue for the pool.

Materials Cold press watercolor paper • Pencil • Eraser • Masking Fluid • Old small round brush
Small round brush • Medium round brush • Large sable brush
Colors Used Cerulean Blue ● Lemon Yellow ● Viridian Green ● Alizarin Crimson ●
Yellow Ochre ● Cadmium Red ● Burnt Umber ● Burnt Sienna ● Lamp Black ● Chinese White

Very lightly sketch a large oval around the edge, and draw large tropical plants. Using my sketch as reference, draw three people on pool floats in the center of the pool. Don't worry too much about getting the people perfect, because we are working on a small scale in which people can just be fleshed-out stick figures.

Carefully paint over the people and the pool floats using masking fluid and a small brush.

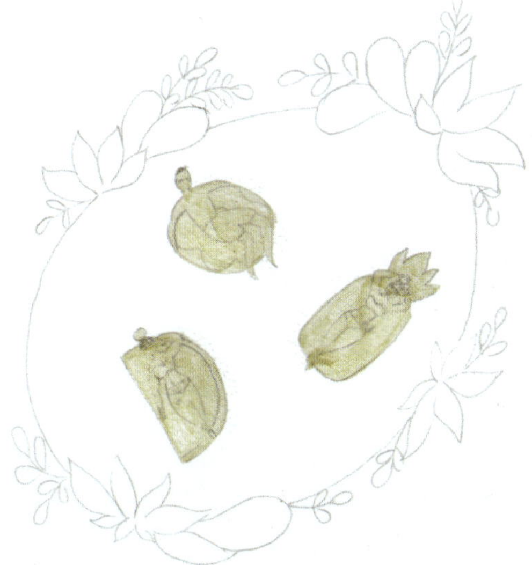

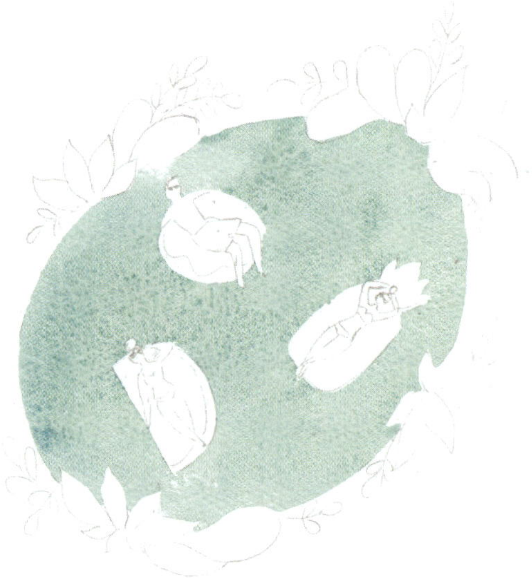 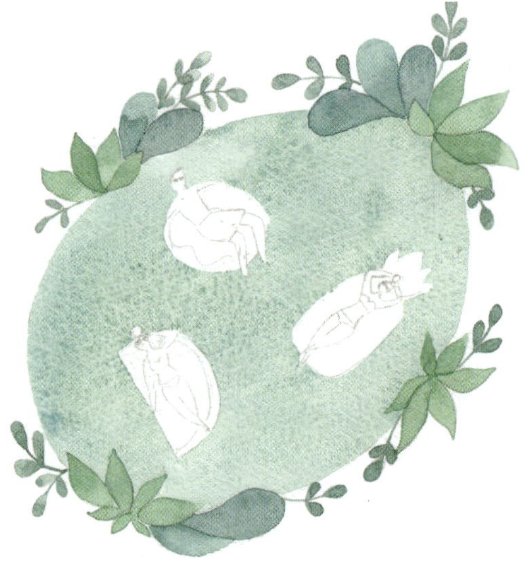

When that's completely dry, mix Cerulean Blue with Lemon Yellow and lots of water to make an aqua color. Use your large sable brush to paint the pool, painting straight over the people and carefully around the plants, encouraging lots of variety of tone.

When that's completely dry, carefully remove the masking fluid from the people.

Mix a bluish green using Viridian Green and a bit of Alizarin Crimson. Paint the large round leaves with your medium brush, allowing color to pool in different areas. Paint the leaves one at a time so they remain distinct. Mix a bright green with Viridian Green and Yellow Ochre, and paint the pointed cactus using your medium brush, again painting each leaf one at a time so they remain separate. Mix a dark green using Viridian Green and Cadmium Red, and paint the small leaves and stems using your small brush, again allowing the color to pool in different areas.

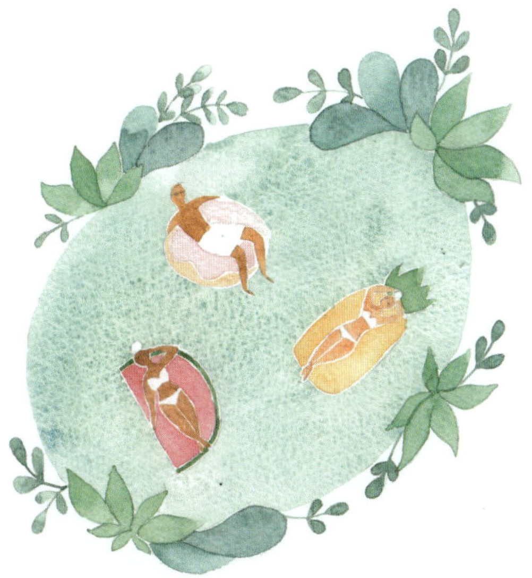

Paint the woman on the watermelon using Burnt Umber and your small brush.

Paint the other woman using a mixture of Burnt Sienna and Chinese White with your small brush.

Paint the man with a mixture of Yellow Ochre and Burnt Umber using your small brush.

Paint the center of the watermelon with Alizarin Crimson with your small brush, leaving a thin white gap between that and the woman. Paint the skin of the watermelon with a mixture of Viridian Green and Yellow Ochre using your small brush.

Paint the pineapple with Yellow Ochre using your small brush.

Paint the icing on the doughnut pale pink using a watery mixture of Alizarin Crimson and your small brush. Paint the doughnut with a mixture of Burnt Sienna and Chinese White.

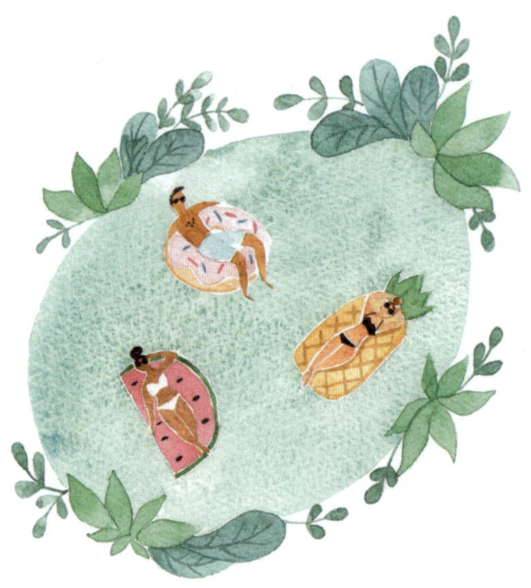

Paint the man's shorts using a watery mixture of Cerulean Blue and your small brush. Use Cerulean Blue and Alizarin Crimson and your small brush to add sprinkles to the doughnut. Paint a criss-cross pattern on the pineapple using your small brush and Yellow Ochre. Paint the bikini of the woman on the pineapple using Lamp Black and your small brush. Using Burnt Umber and your small brush, paint the woman's hair. Using Lamp Black and your small brush, paint sunglasses on all three people, and paint hair on the remaining man and woman.

Mix Viridian Green and Alizarin Crimson to paint veins on the large leaves using your small brush.

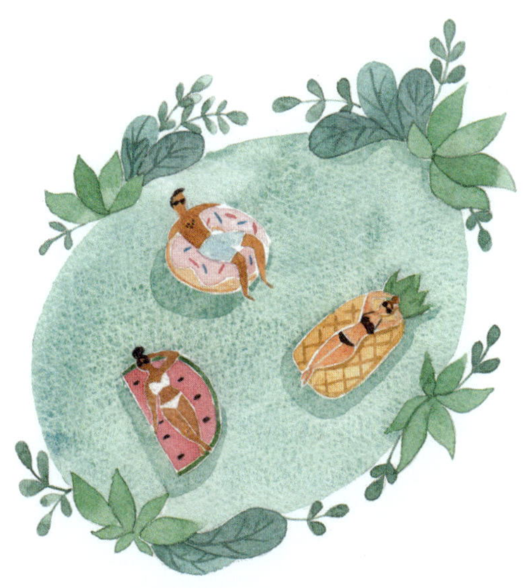

Mix Cerulean Blue and Lemon Yellow
to paint shadows from the pool floats on the
floor of the pool using your medium brush.

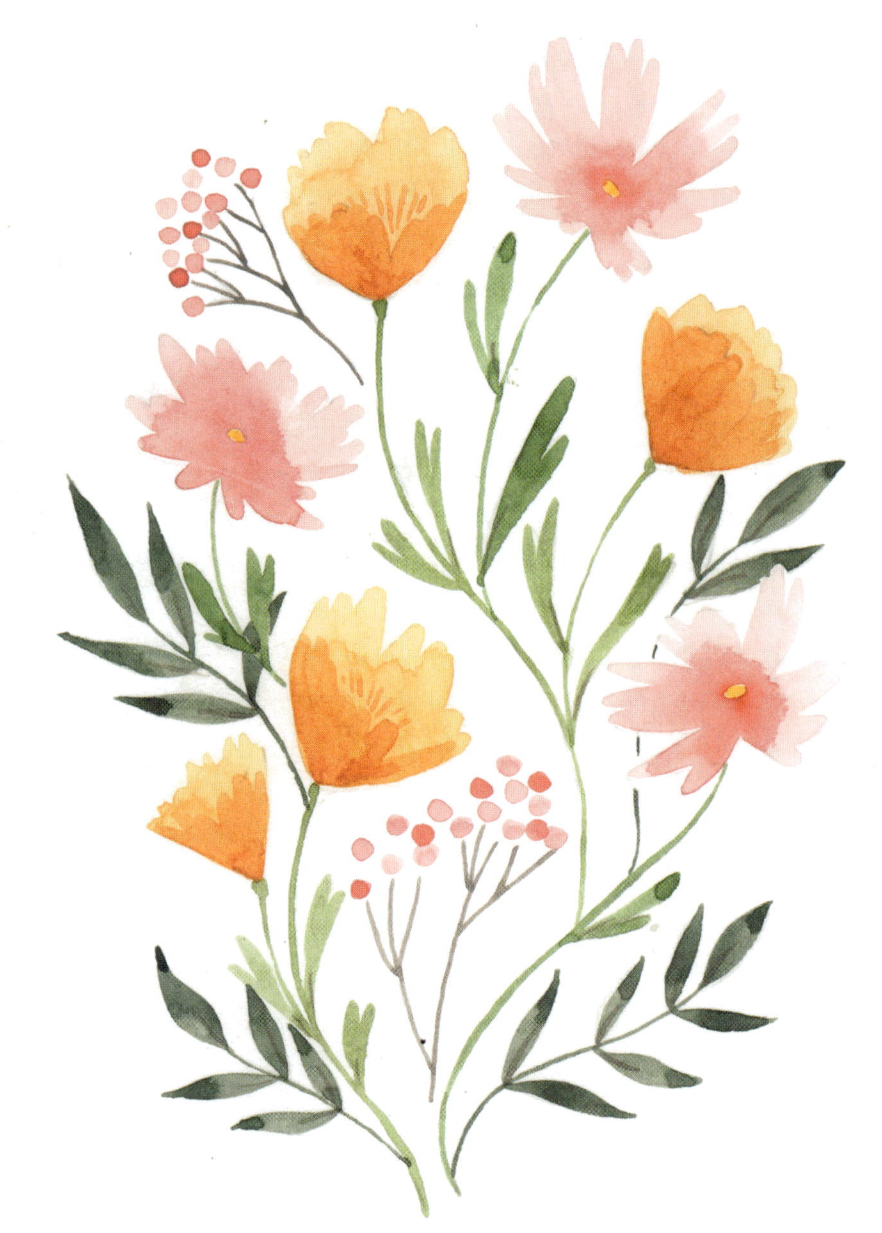

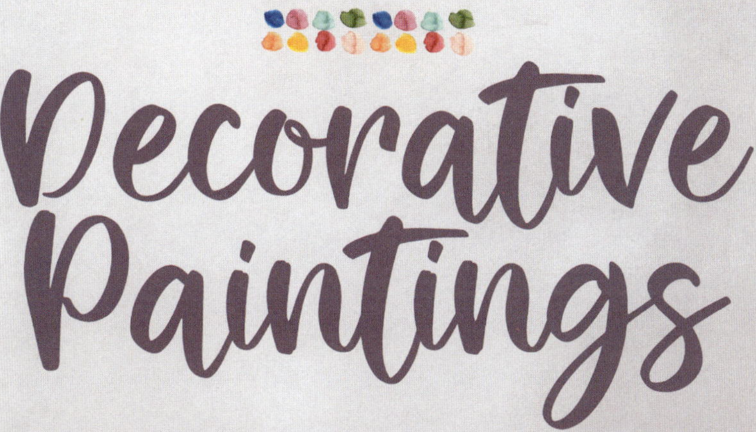

Decorative Paintings

In this final chapter, we are going to be combining some of the skills and techniques we've covered in the earlier chapters to create some beautiful decorative wreaths and designs. These pieces combine observation from nature with a little imagination and a decorative flair. I find these pieces so relaxing and soothing to paint. They would look great on your wall, or you could turn them into a homemade greeting card for a loved one.

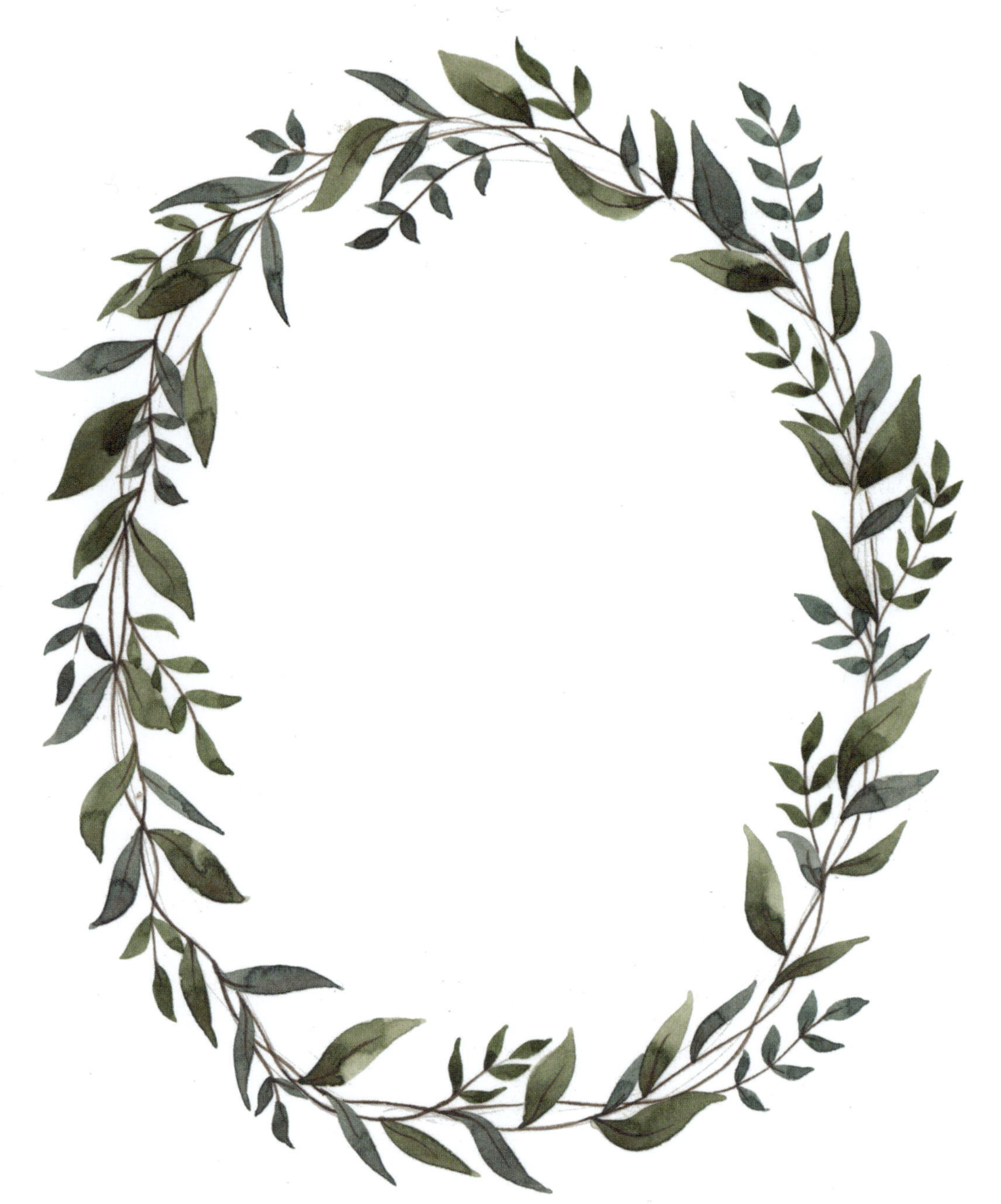

Botanical Wreath

This piece is very simple but far from boring. It's so calming and meditative to paint and to view. Painting lots of beautiful leaves and mixing lovely shades of green are great ways to unwind and practice your color mixing and expressive brushstrokes.

Materials Hot press watercolor paper • Pencil • Eraser • Medium round brush • Small round brush
Colors Used Sap Green ● Sepia ● Viridian Green ● Cadmium Red ●

Start by very roughly sketching an oval in pencil. We want it to be as light as possible. Lightly sketch branches around the oval, and allow some stems to come toward the center of the oval and toward the edge of the paper. Don't get too close to the edge of the paper.

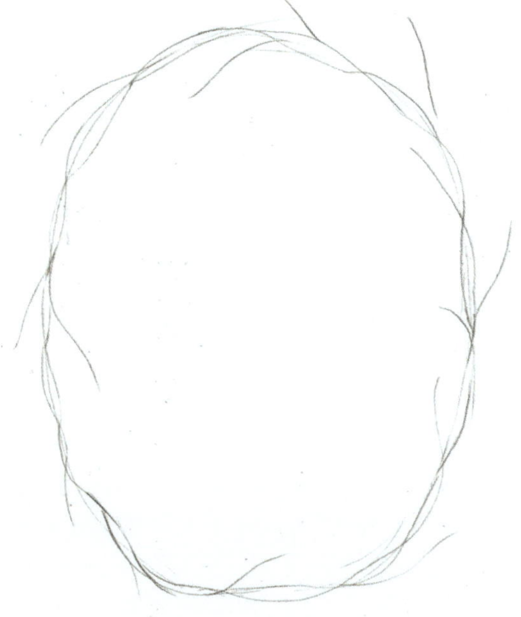

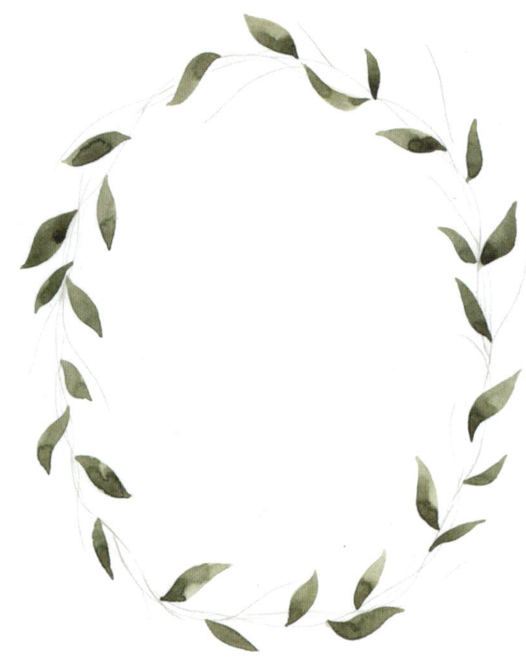

Mix Sap Green with Sepia to create a rich muted green. Add more water to one side of the mix to create a variation in tone. Using your medium round brush, paint leaves around the wreath, using the light and dark green mix to create lots of variation in tone. Take your time when painting these leaves, creating as much variety as possible, varying angle and the way they bend and twist. Remember: Imperfections are good! Space the leaves evenly around the wreath, leaving space for other leaves and occasionally letting the leaves overlap the branches.

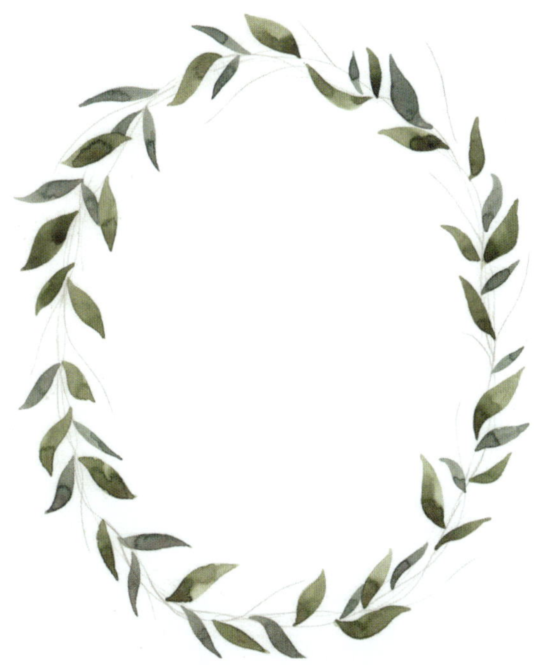

Mix Viridian Green with Cadmium Red to make a dark green. Use a medium round brush to paint more medium leaves, placing them evenly around the wreath.

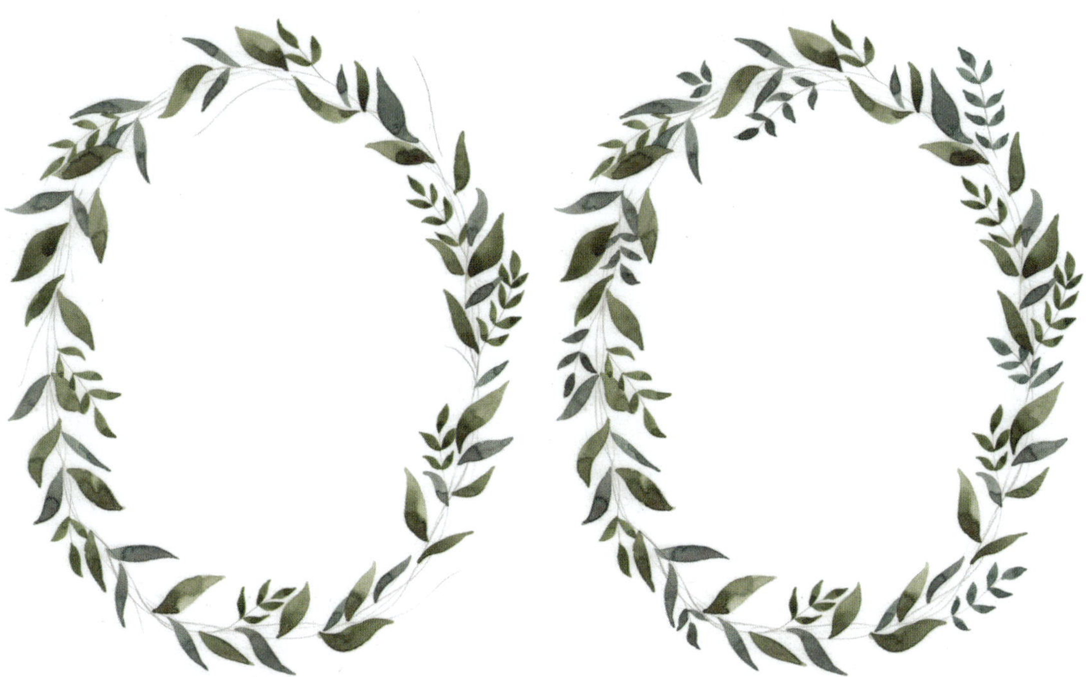

Add more Sap Green and Sepia to your first paint mix, and use your small brush to paint small leaves on some of the stems extending into and out of the wreath.

Mix more Sap Green and Cadmium Red, and use your small brush to paint small leaves on the remaining vines.

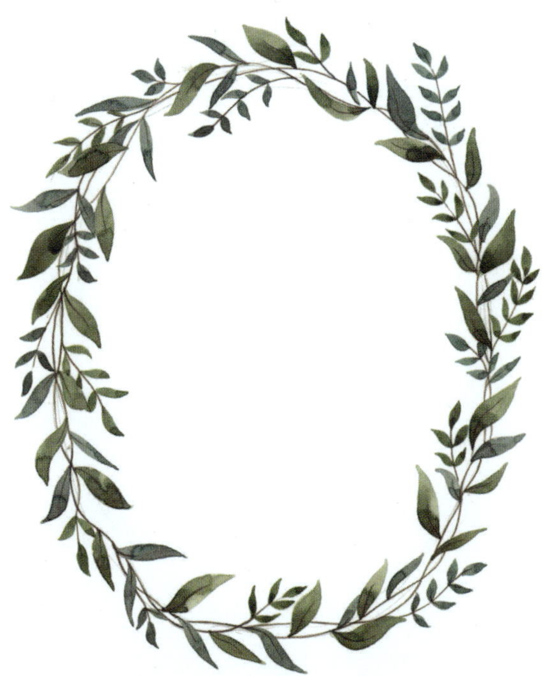

Use Sepia and your small brush to carefully paint the intertwining branches and stems of the wreath. To get nice, thin lines, make sure the paint isn't too wet. Very carefully paint the veins in the centers of some of the larger leaves. When completely dry, carefully remove any excess pencil lines using your eraser.

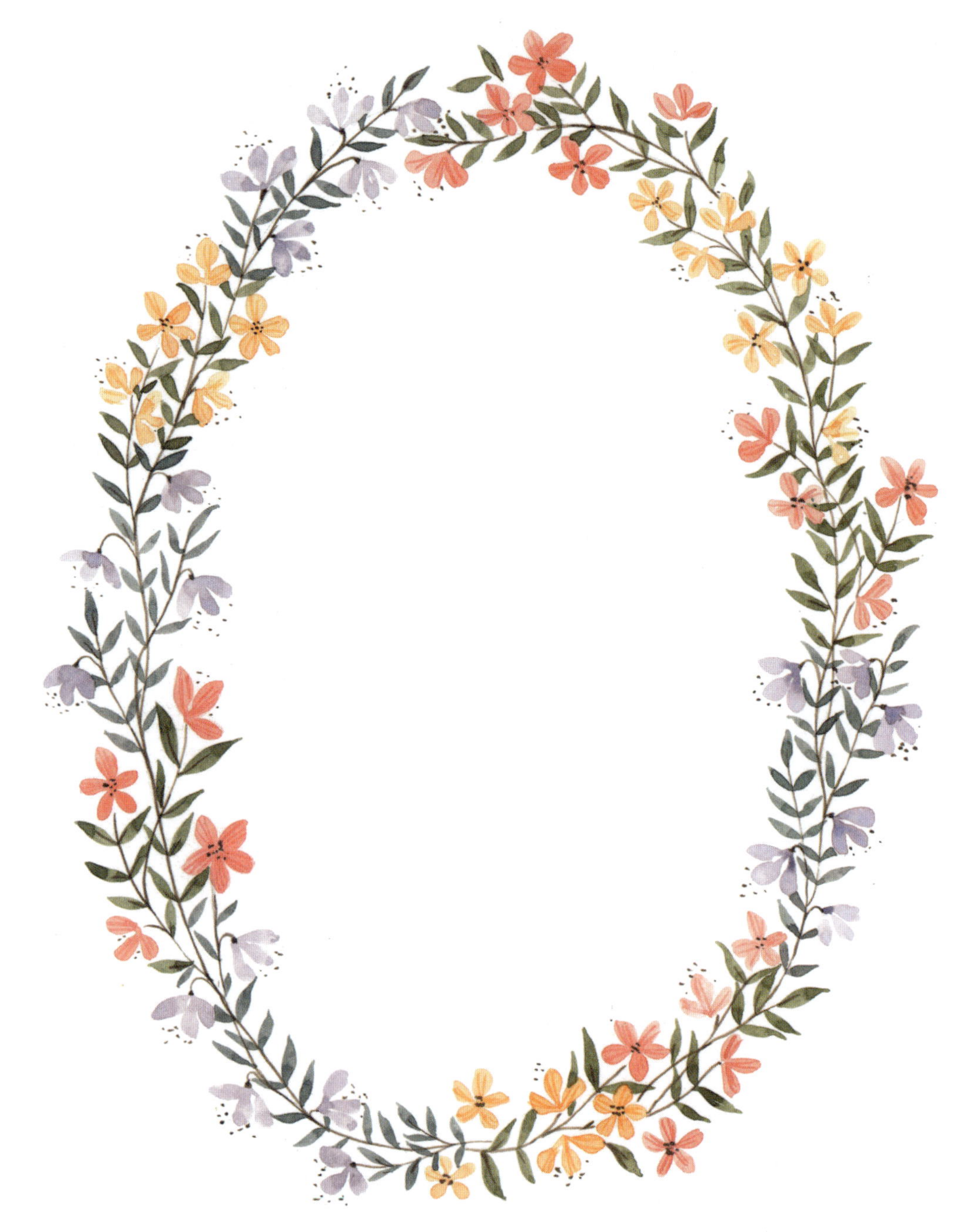

Floral Wreath

This is a beautiful decorative wreath. It's a bit more complex than the simple wreath made of leaves we painted earlier in the chapter, but it's not too complicated when you take it step by step. You can always play around with different color combinations, but it's best to keep things simple and don't use more than three colors for the flowers.

Materials Hot press watercolor paper • Pencil • Eraser • Medium round brush • Small round brush
Colors Used Cadmium Red ● Alizarin Crimson ● Cadmium Yellow ● Ultramarine ● Sepia ●
Sap Green ● Viridian Green ●

Lightly sketch an oval using your pencil, then add intertwining stems all the way around. They should start at the bottom and meet at the top of the oval.

Mix Cadmium Red with a bit of Alizarin Crimson and lots of water to make a pink. Use your small round brush to paint simple flowers around the wreath. Paint a variety of five-petal flowers pointing toward the viewer and three-petal flowers pointing to the side. Paint each petal in the shape of a teardrop, and try to keep the petals separate so they don't merge into one blob.

Use Sepia and your small round brush to very carefully paint the intertwining stems. Paint thin stems to connect the flowers to the stems, and paint some offshoots to which you can add leaves later. Make the stems connecting to the blue flowers slightly curved over.

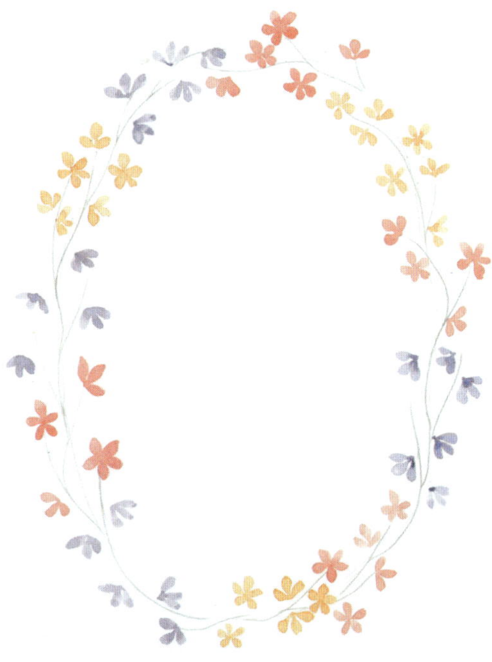

Mix Cadmium Red and Cadmium Yellow with lots of water to make a light orange. Using the same technique as before and your small round brush, paint more flowers around the wreath.

Mix Ultramarine with a little Alizarin Crimson and lots of water to make a bluish purple. Paint three-petaled flowers using your small round brush. Paint each petal in a teardrop shape.

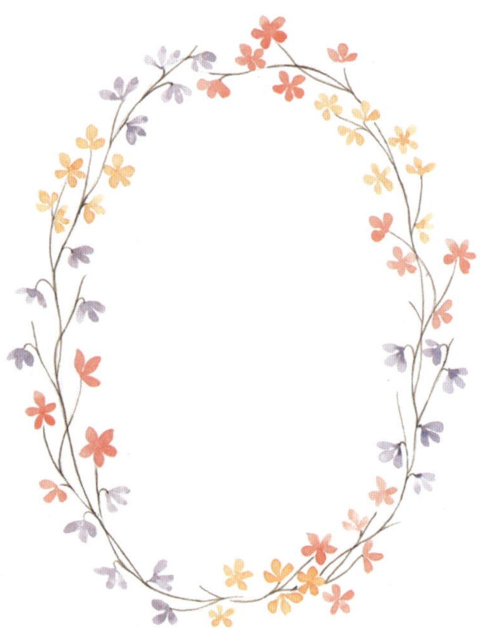

Mix Cadmium Red and Alizarin Crimson, and use your small brush to very carefully paint thin lines on the pink flowers. Mix Cadmium Red and Cadmium Yellow, and use your small brush to very carefully paint thin lines on the orange flowers. When completely dry, use Sepia and your small brush to paint dots in the centers of the flowers and around the edges of the petals of flowers pointing to the side. Use Sepia and your small brush to add veins to a few of the leaves.

Mix Sap Green with a little bit of Sepia to paint small leaves around the pink and orange flowers using your small round brush.

Mix Viridian Green and Alizarin Crimson to make a muted green to paint small leaves around the blue flowers.

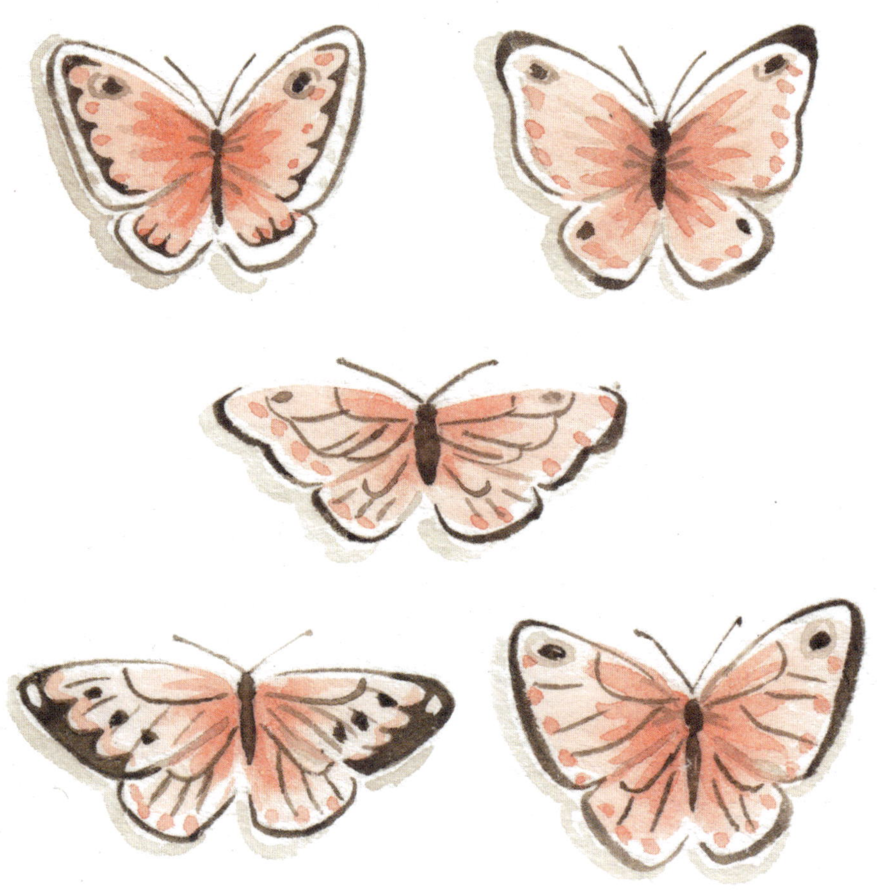

Simple Butterflies

This super simple piece makes a lovely repeat pattern. Once you have the hang of painting these beautiful butterflies, you can try them in different colors or add more to create a larger pattern.

Materials Hot press watercolor paper • Pencil • Eraser • Large sable brush • Medium round brush Small round brush • Tissue or cloth for blotting brush
Colors Used Cadmium Red ● Sepia ●

Using your pencil, very lightly sketch the outline of five butterflies, including their bodies and antennae.

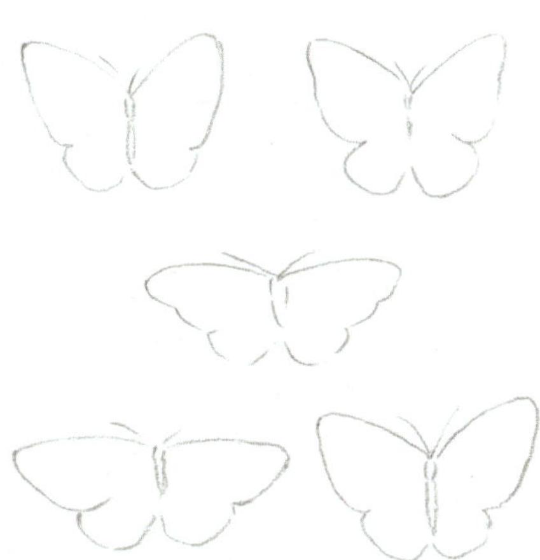

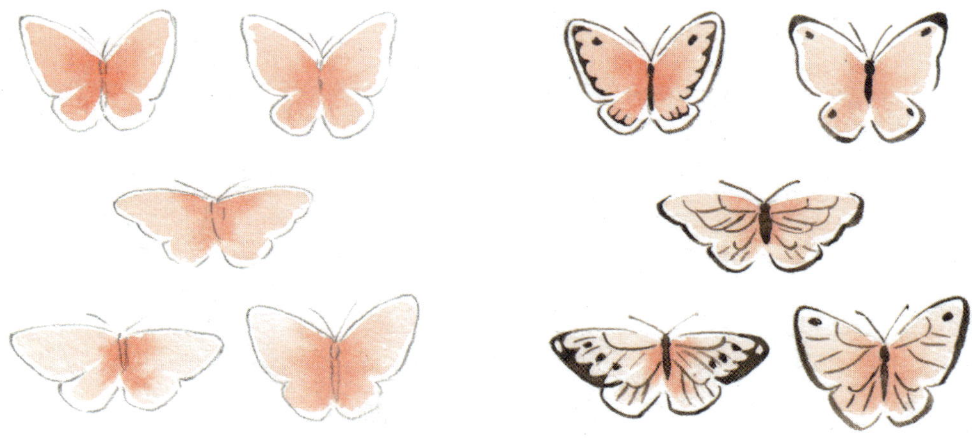

Make a very watery mixture of Cadmium Red. Create another mixture of Cadmium Red with less water. Use the lighter mixture of Cadmium Red and your medium brush to paint the first butterfly, painting just inside of the pencil lines. While that is still wet, add some of the darker Cadmium Red mix to the center. Repeat the process for the rest of the butterflies.

When that is completely dry, use Sepia and your small brush to carefully add details to the butterflies. Paint the butterflies' bodies, antennae, and markings, and outline the outside of the wings. To make certain the lines are nice and crisp and there isn't too much paint on your brush, blot your brush with tissue or cloth before getting started.

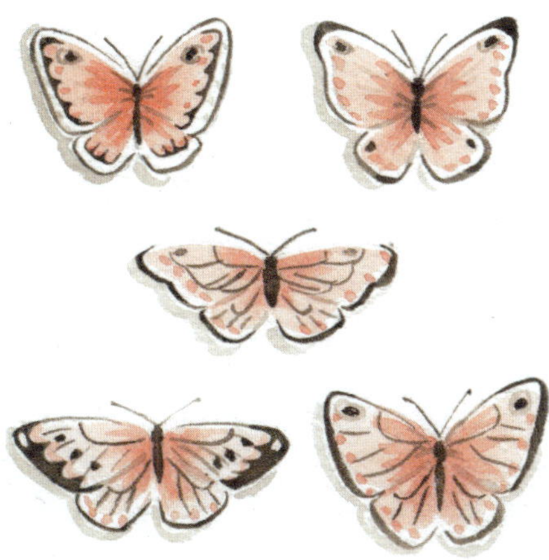

When that is completely dry, carefully remove the pencil lines with your eraser. Use a watery mixture of Cadmium Red and a medium brush to add markings to the butterflies. Add some little dashes around the outside of the wings and detail to the area where the wings meet the body.

Use your small brush and a very watery mixture of Sepia to add a little shadow around the wings and a few little details to the butterflies. Add a ring around the spots on their wings and a little shadow to show where the two wings overlap.

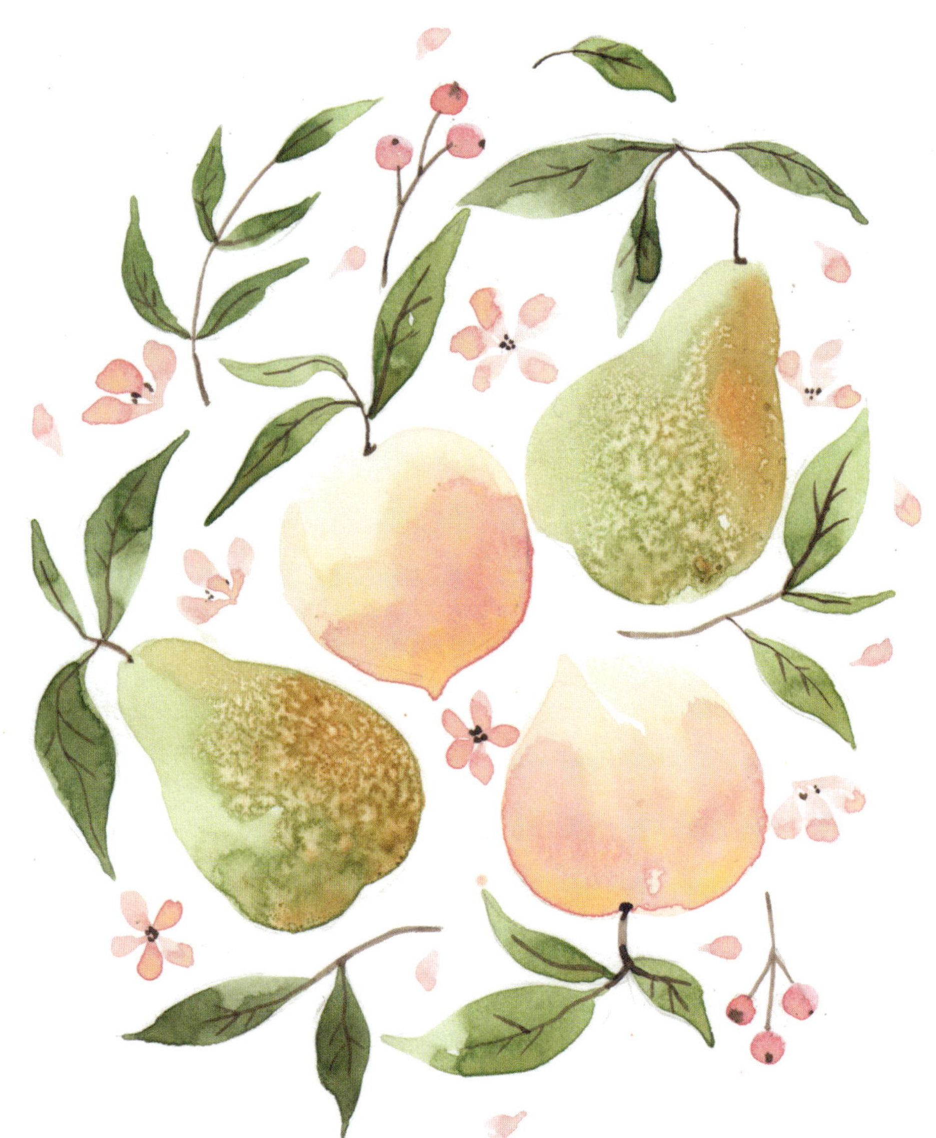

Summer Fruit

This is a decorative piece inspired by peaches and pears. We use a combination of wet-on-wet techniques and expressive brushstrokes to paint this piece. We also use a little sea salt, which creates a fun effect. You can alter this piece by trying different fruits.

Materials Hot press watercolor paper • Pencil • Eraser • Large sable brush • Medium round brush Small round brush • Sea salt

Colors Used Lemon Yellow ● Permanent Rose ● Sap Green ● Yellow Ochre ● Cadmium Red ● Sepia ●

Lightly sketch two pears and two peaches in pencil. Add foliage and berries around them to create a loose oval. Don't worry about things being perfect; the more imperfect the fruit and leaves are, the more natural they will look.

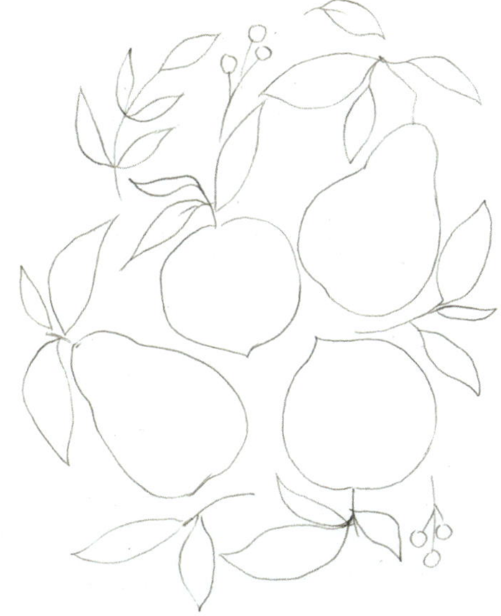

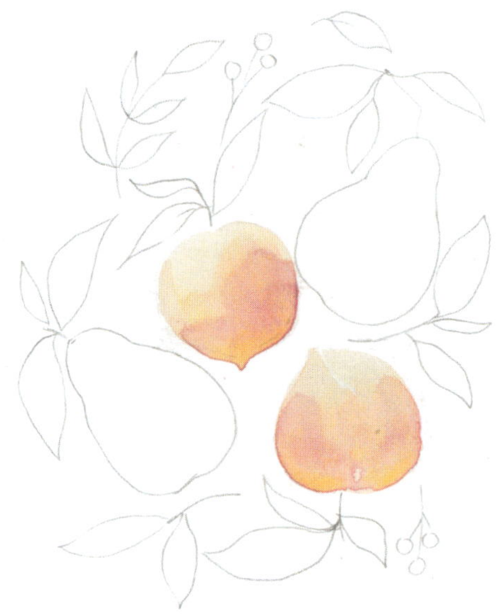

Create a mix of Lemon Yellow with a little bit of Permanent Rose to create a pale yellowy orange. Create another mix of Lemon Yellow with slightly more Permanent Rose to create a peachy pink. Loosely paint the two peaches using your large sable brush and the yellow-orange color first. While it's still wet, add some of the peachy-pink color.

TIP If you paint slightly inside the pencil lines, it's easier to remove them afterward.

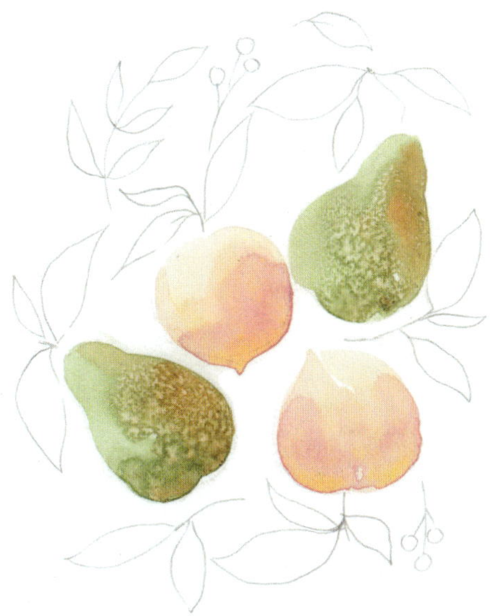

Mix Sap Green and Yellow Ochre and lots of water. Paint the two pears using your large sable brush. While they are still wet, add more Yellow Ochre using your large brush.

Quickly, while the paint is still wet, sprinkle sea salt over the wet pears. The salt absorbs some of the water, which gives the pears a freckled appearance.

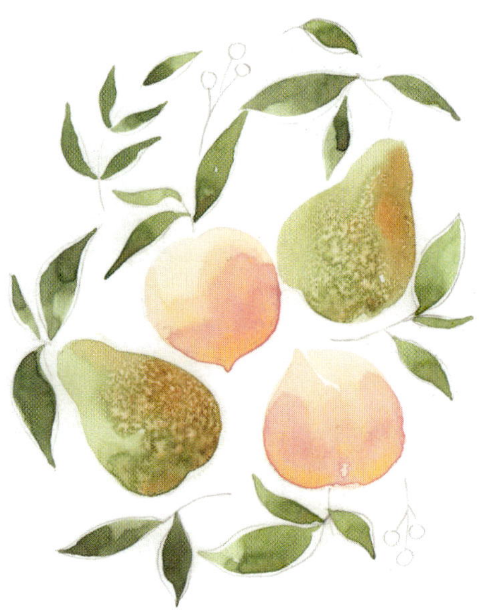

Mix Sap Green with Cadmium Red to make a slightly muted green. Using your medium round brush, paint the leaves on the pears and some of the loose sprigs of leaves. Vary the pressure of your brushstroke so it's fuller in the middle of the leaf and tapered at the end. Depending on the size of the leaf, you might need to make a couple of brushstrokes to create the shape you want. Don't worry if your leaves are a little bit wobbly; they will look more natural than perfect leaves.

Mix Sap Green with Yellow Ochre. Use the same process and your medium round brush to paint the peach leaves and the remaining leaves in the design.

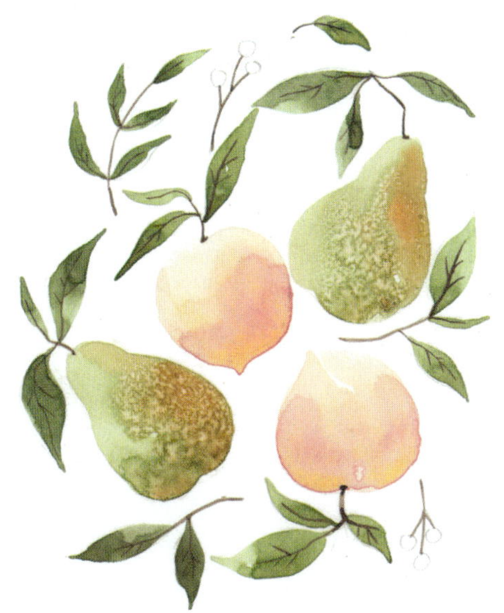

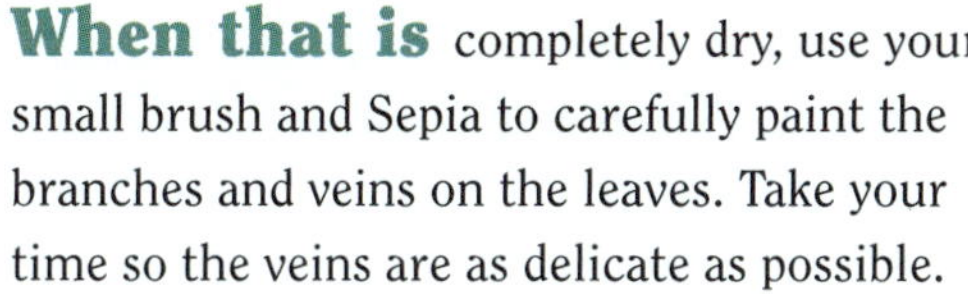

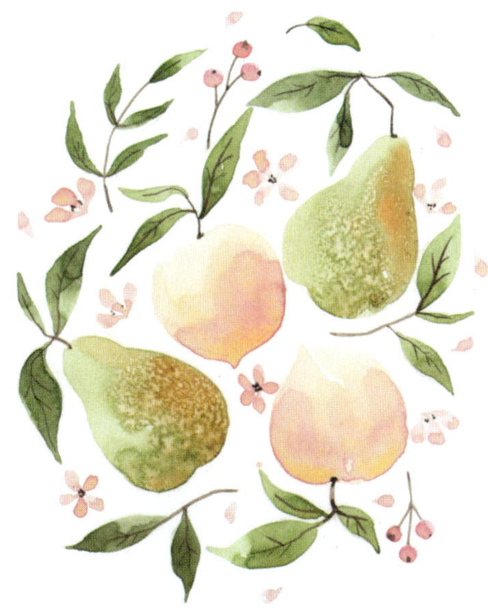

When that is completely dry, use your small brush and Sepia to carefully paint the branches and veins on the leaves. Take your time so the veins are as delicate as possible.

Mix Permanent Rose with a little bit of Lemon Yellow and lots of water to create a pinkish peach. Paint blossoms dotted around the design where there are white spaces. Paint each petal one at a time using your medium round brush. Start with a thin line, then apply more pressure to create a round petal. Create a mixture of flowers pointing toward the viewer with five petals, flowers pointing to the side with three petals, and individual petals. Add more Permanent Rose to the mixture, and paint the berries using your small brush. When the berries and flowers are completely dry, use your small brush to add tiny dots of Sepia to the centers of the flowers and the tops of the berries.

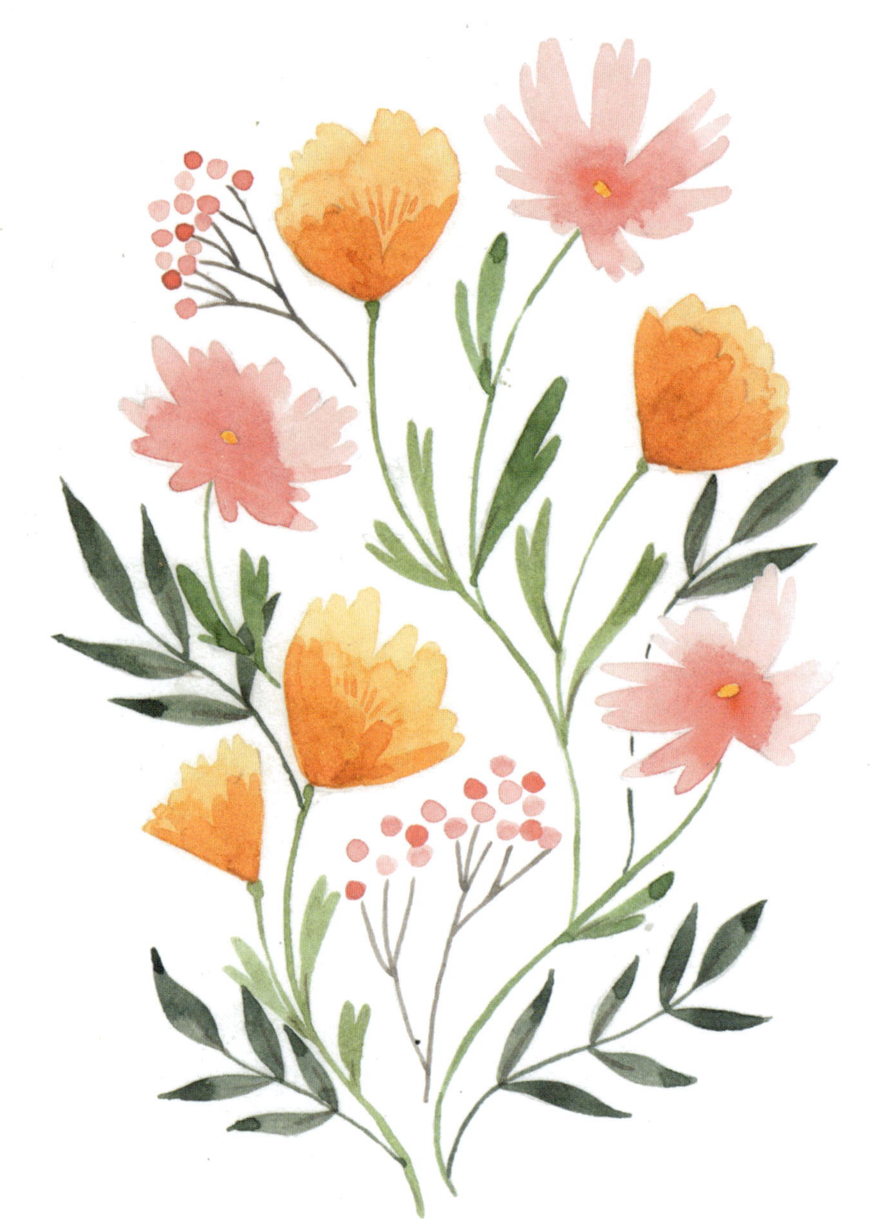

Wildflowers

This piece was inspired by vintage illustrations of wildflowers and the beautiful orange California poppy. Although it takes its inspiration from nature, the arrangement of flowers is whimsical and decorative.

Materials Hot press watercolor paper • Pencil • Eraser • Large sable brush • Medium round brush Small round brush
Colors Used Cadmium Yellow ⬤ Cadmium Red ⬤ Alizarin Crimson ⬤ Sap Green ⬤ Yellow Ochre ⬤ Sepia ⬤ Ultramarine ⬤

Sketch the flowers using my sketch as a reference. Make sure the composition feels balanced.

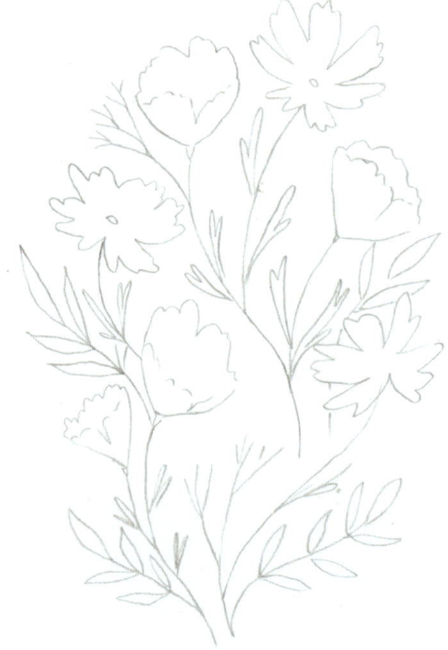

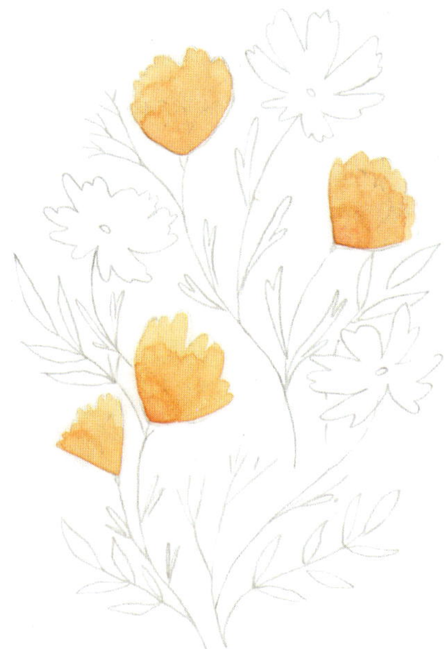

Next mix Cadmium Yellow with a little bit of Cadmium Red and lots of water to make a light orange. Use your medium brush to paint the California poppies, allowing more color to pool at the bottom.

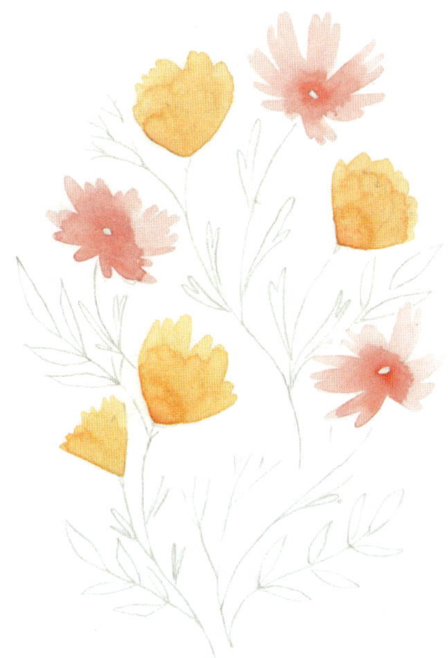

Mix Cadmium Red and Alizarin Crimson; add more water to one side of the paint mix to make a light pink. Use the light pink and your medium brush to paint the other flowers one at a time, leaving the centers unpainted. While the paint is still wet, add some of the darker pink mix to the flowers around the center.

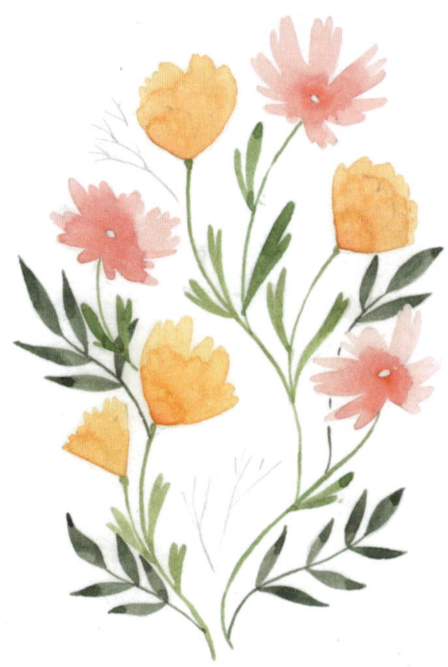

Mix Sap Green and Yellow Ochre, and use your small brush to paint the stems and leaves of the poppies. For the leaves, apply more pressure at the widest part of the leaf and taper toward the stem.

Mix Sap Green and Sepia and lots of water. Use your small brush to paint the leaves and stems of the other flowers using the same technique.

Mix Sap Green, Sepia, Ultramarine, and lots of water to make a dark green, and paint the remaining leaves with your small brush. Allow more color to pool in the tips of the leaves to add variation.

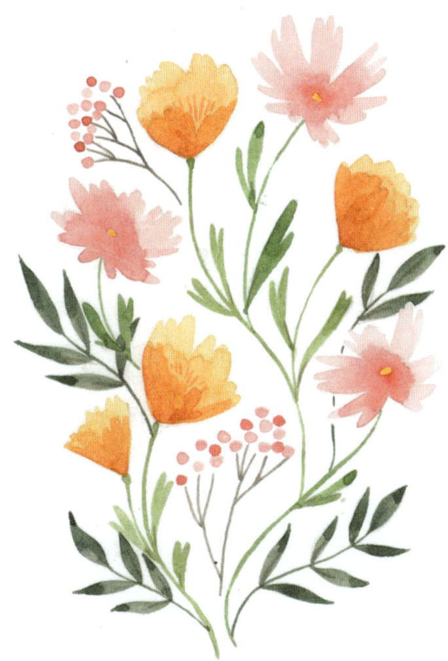

Mix Cadmium Yellow with Cadmium Red to make an orange, and paint the outer petals of the poppy with your medium brush. Use your small brush and the orange mix to paint thin lines in the center of the flower.

Paint the centers of the pink flowers with Cadmium Yellow using your small brush.

Make a watery mixture of Sepia, and use your small brush to paint the stems of the berries and thin lines on some of the leaves. Mix Cadmium Red with Alizarin Crimson, and use your small brush to paint the berries, varying the amount of water to vary the color.

Final Thoughts

It probably seems like an overstatement to say learning to paint with watercolors is life changing, but for so many people, it is. Not only does it give you a chance to rediscover your creativity, but it is a rewarding hobby that brings calm and tranquillity. It also changes the way you see the world around you. Once you've learned to draw and paint, you'll begin to notice the beauty in the everyday. You'll spot pleasing color combinations, beautiful patterns, unusual textures, the delicate interplay of light and shadow. For a painter, even a stroll around the neighborhood can be full of inspiration. Hopefully, by using this book, you will learn many skills, but the one I really hope you learn is the skill to see the world as a painter and find inspiration in everyday life.

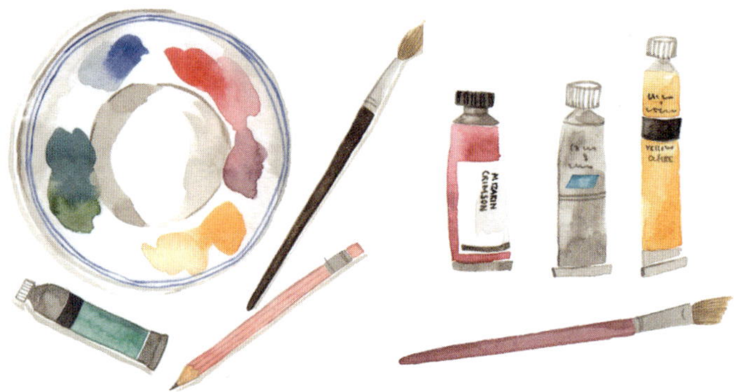

Acknowledgments

Thank you so much to the readers of my first book,
The Joy of Watercolor, who very much inspired this book. Seeing your paintings online and hearing your stories of what learning to paint has meant to you has been a huge inspiration.

Thank you to my editor, Jess, for being so enthusiastic about this project and so wonderful to work with. Thank you to the book's designer, Amanda, for always being brilliant to work with and for always making my books look beautiful. As always, a huge thank you to my agent, Leslie, thank you for always believing in me and making sure I always have something exciting and fulfilling to be working on. Thank you for helping me to share my passion for painting with the world.

A huge thank you to my husband for supporting me whilst I wrote this book heavily pregnant and with a very young baby. Thank you for taking Herbie on some extra long walks so I could get my work finished! Thank you for all your love and support throughout a crazy year.

Index

About the Author

Emma Block is a successful freelance illustrator who uses watercolors in a fresh and modern way and isn't afraid to break the rules. Her watercolor and gouache paintings have brought an enthusiastic following on Instagram (@emmablockillustration) and she has become a reliable source of online watercolor advice. Emma is the author of *The Joy of Watercolor, Get Started with Gouache*, and the *Slow Travel Journal*. She has taught hundreds of students to paint with watercolors and gouache in London and across the UK.

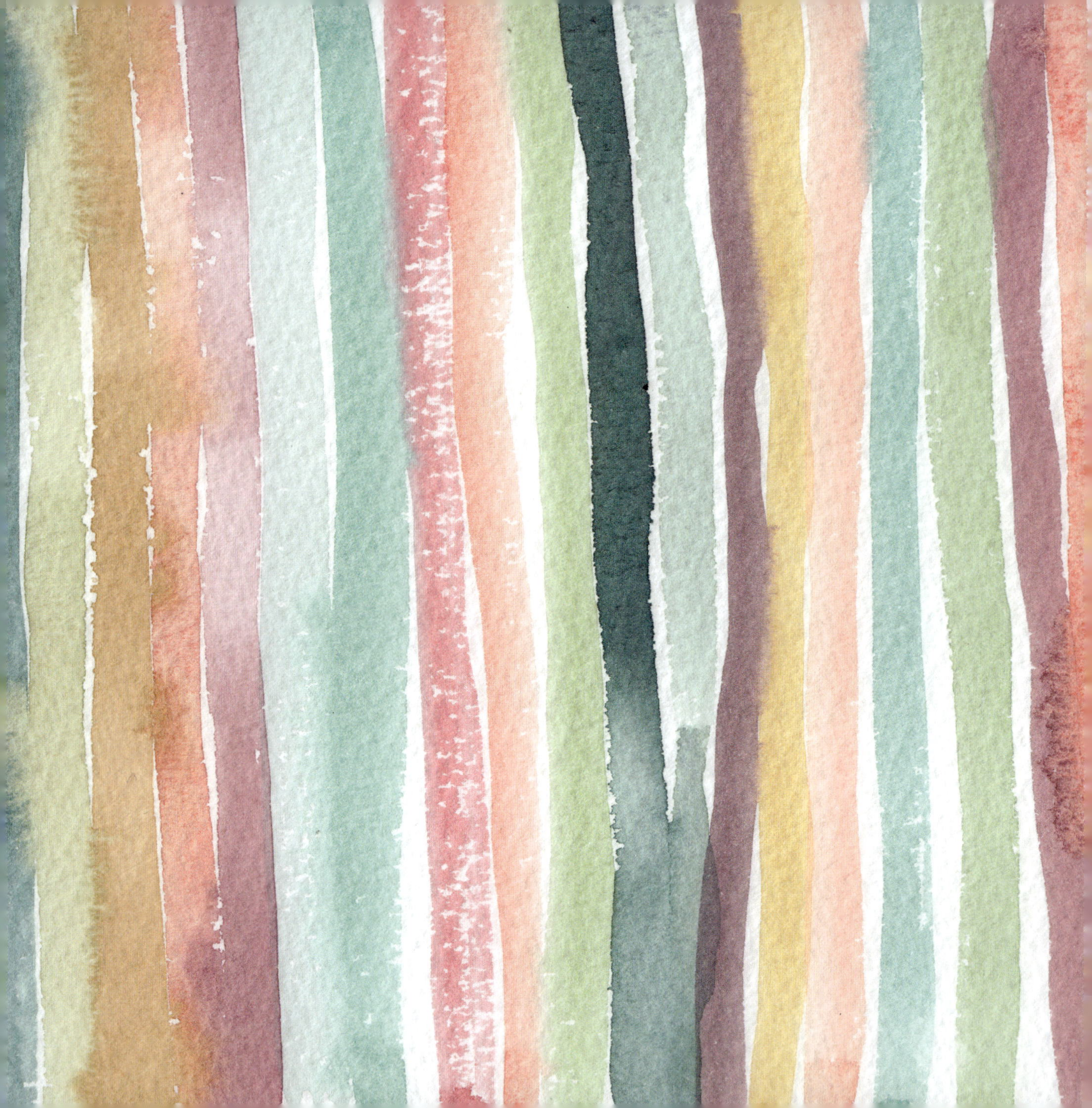